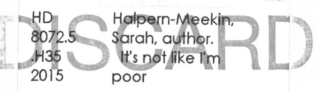

It's Not Like I'm Poor

HOW WORKING FAMILIES MAKE ENDS
MEET IN A POST-WELFARE WORLD

Sarah Halpern-Meekin,
Kathryn Edin, Laura Tach,
and Jennifer Sykes

UNIVERSITY OF CALIFORNIA PRESS

University of California Press, one of the most distinguished university presses in the United States, enriches lives around the world by advancing scholarship in the humanities, social sciences, and natural sciences. Its activities are supported by the UC Press Foundation and by philanthropic contributions from individuals and institutions. For more information, visit www.ucpress.edu.

University of California Press
Oakland, California

Library of Congress Cataloging-in-Publication Data

Halpern-Meekin, Sarah, author.
    It's not like I'm poor: how working families make ends meet in a post-welfare world/Sarah Halpern-Meekin, Kathryn Edin, Laura Tach, and Jennifer Sykes.
    pages   cm
    Includes bibliographical references and index.
    ISBN 978-0-520-27534-8 (cloth:alk.paper)
    ISBN 978-0-520-27535-5 (pbk.: alk. paper)
    ISBN 978-0-520-95922-4 (e-book)
    1. Working poor—United States—History—20th century.   2. Public welfare—United States—History—20th century.   3. Tax credits—United States.   I. Edin, Kathryn, 1962– author.   II. Tach, Laura, author.   III. Sykes, Jennifer, author.   IV. Title.
    HD8072.5.H35   2015
    332.0240086'9420973—dc23   2014016886

Manufactured in the United States of America

23   22   21   20   19   18   17   16   15
10   9   8   7   6   5   4   3   2   1

In keeping with a commitment to support environmentally responsible and sustainable printing practices, UC Press has printed this book on Natures Natural, a fiber that contains 30% post-consumer waste and meets the minimum requirements of ANSI/NISO Z39.48–1992 (R 1997) (*Permanence of Paper*).

To the Malcolm Wiener Center for Social Policy at the Harvard Kennedy School and the Multidisciplinary Program in Inequality and Social Policy at Harvard University for bringing us all together in the first place

Contents

List of Illustrations and Tables   ix

Acknowledgments   xi

Introduction   1

1. Family Budgets: Staying in the Black, Slipping into the Red   23

2. Tax Time   59

3. The New Regime through the Lens of the Old   100

4. Beyond Living Paycheck to Paycheck   126

5. *"Debt*—I Am Hoping to Eliminate That Word!"   152

6. Capitalizing on the Promise of the EITC   182

Appendix A: Introduction to Boston and the Research Project   217

Appendix B: Qualitative Interview Guide   224

Notes   235

Bibliography   261

Index   283

Illustrations and Tables

FIGURES

1.	Structure of the 2011 EITC benefit	7
2.	Number of families using government assistance programs	39
3.	Number of government assistance programs per family	40
4.	Categories to which tax refund is allocated	64
5.	Number of AFDC/TANF and EITC recipients in Massachusetts	109
6.	Number of families on AFDC/TANF in the United States	110
7.	Changes in TANF, SNAP, and unemployment in the United States	111

MAP

1.	Location of recruitment sites and respondents	12

TABLES

1. Respondents' and Spouses' Occupations over the Prior
    Twelve Months   32

2. Respondents' Annual Household Earnings, by Marital Status   35

3. Respondents' Average Monthly and Annual Incomes,
    by Marital Status   36

4. Respondents' Average Monthly Household Expenses   41

5. Proportion of Respondents with Assets and Average
    Asset Values   131

6. Respondents' Asset Holdings by Asset Category   143

7. Type of Debt and Median Debt Amount   159

A.1. Stratified Sample of Respondents   223

Acknowledgments

This book owes its existence to Kathryn Edin, Jeffrey Kling, and Ruby Mendenhall's project "Investing in Enduring Resources with the EITC: Barriers and Pathways to Social Mobility," which was generously funded by the Ford Foundation (Kilolo Kijakazi, program officer). Several others were essential to the "Investing in Enduring Resources with the EITC" study. Peter Tufano and the research group at H&R Block, Roxanne Reddington-Wilde of Action for Boston Community Development (ABCD), Boston's Association of Community Organizations for Reform Now (ACORN), the East Boston Area Planning Action Council (APAC), and Susan Crowley made critical connections in securing data collection sites. Jennifer Sykes, the project director, and Gretchen Wright, the project coordinator, managed details and logistics. The Population Studies Center at the University of Pennsylvania provided an institutional home for the study. We offer special thanks to Herbert Smith and Irma Elo for their support. Our thanks go to David Ellwood for his visionary leadership in supporting the Inequality and Social Policy program and to Pamela Metz for deploying her extraordinary skills on its behalf. Interviews in Boston were conducted by April Baskin, Susan Crowley, Kathryn Edin, Sarah Halpern-Meekin, Vanessa Lopes, Eva Rosen, Sara Sternberg-Greene, Jennifer

Sykes, Laura Tach, and Holly Wood. Assistance in preparing the data came from Gretchen Wright, a team of transcriptionists at Penn, and Jordan Parekh; Kristin Turney conducted related analyses of Consumer Expenditure Survey data.

Our work on the book benefited greatly from the suggestions and ideas of those around us. David T. Ellwood, Wendell Primus, and Janet Holtzblatt shared their insights into the policy story behind the modern EITC. H. Luke Shaefer was our go-to person for the best research on other means-tested programs. Christopher Jencks offered sage advice. Special thanks to those who commented on the book prospectus and/or manuscript: Lisa Adams, Paula England, Jeffrey Kling, Lawrence Mead, Stacey Oliker, Sharon Parrott, LaDonna Pavetti, Nils Ringe, Eldar Shafir, Margaret Sherraden, Michael Sherraden, Timothy Smeeding, and John Wancheck. Finally, the book never would have seen the light of day without our editor, Naomi Schneider, and the editorial assistance of Barbara Kiviat, Jessica Matteson, Emily Parrott, Kathryn C. Reed, and Joanne Spitz. All the mistakes that remain are ours.

Finally, Sarah, Laura, and Jen would like to thank Kathy for including us on this journey. At the start, we were all in graduate school. Now, three graduations, five babies, and seven years later, we've finished the book!

Introduction

February means snow in Boston, and this year is no exception—nearly two feet of it last weekend and another three to six inches today. City workers in orange vests use snow blowers and shovels to dig out storm drains, while residents' shovels sit ready to clear the stoops and sidewalks once more.

Among East Boston's working poor, however, February means more than just snowfall. Indeed, despite the dreary weather, it is the most eagerly anticipated month of the year—some say that it's even better than Christmas. And it is this keen sense of anticipation that drives Toni Patturelli out of her modest triple-decker—three apartments stacked one on top of the other—on a day like today, and onto the #120 bus, which runs north from Maverick Station along Meridian Street to Central Square—the hub of the neighborhood's commercial activity.

Retracing the route Toni has taken each February for an entire decade, we note the hairdressers, barbershops, cell phone stores, mom-and-pop grocers, realty companies, nail salons, and ethnic restaurants jam-packed along Meridian Street and lining Central Square, all vying for the attention of any potential customer passing by. But among all these storefronts, one proprietor on Bennington Street is perhaps the most aggressive. Its vivid green signs have been mounted on wire standards, like political campaign posters, and planted in the snowdrifts in front of the door, announcing, "We're Open!" The windows are filled with more bright signs of welcome: "FREE SECOND LOOK REVIEW: WE FIND MONEY THAT OTHERS MISS"; "WALK-INS WELCOME"; "GET MONEY IN MINUTES."

There is clearly business worth fighting for here—we count six other businesses offering the same service within a two-block radius. Not surprisingly, some advertise only in Spanish—"RAPIDO" refunds—no doubt aware of the fact that Latinos have begun to outnumber the white population in this island neighborhood of roughly forty thousand residents. Beyond the glass door of the Bennington Avenue storefront are the offices of H&R Block, the well-known tax preparation service.[1] Its bright and cheery orange interior contrasts nicely with the brilliant green signage. A half-dozen Dr. Seuss books are arranged on the window seat in the waiting area, signaling a welcome to parents of young children. A smiling bilingual receptionist, a gregarious manager, and several professionally dressed tax specialists are on hand.

For much of the year, this H&R Block office escapes notice. But each February, when taxpayers who anticipate a refund file their taxes, it is among the busiest places in the neighborhood. Toni knows the drill and has made sure to bring everything that she needs: her government-issued ID, the W-2 form from the catering company where she works, and her kids' Social Security numbers. Just a few days from now, she'll return to collect a refund check that includes her family's earned income tax credit (EITC). This year, the amount will equal nearly four months of her wages. And what's more, she'll take pride in the fact that she "earned" the money. She'll call the check her "refund," but the EITC actually is not a refund at all—it's the fulfillment of an American promise: if you work, you should not be poor.

The belief that in America anyone can make it if he or she is willing to work hard pulses deeply in this neighborhood that has served as Boston's Ellis Island for two centuries, welcoming wave after wave of immigrants. Canadian shipbuilders were the first newcomers. Then there was a surge of Irish laborers in the 1850s and Scandinavians and eastern European Jews in the latter part of that century, followed by huge numbers of Italians in the years between the First and Second World Wars. Brazilians, El Salvadorans, Colombians, and other immigrants from Central and South America are the most recent arrivals.[2] This steady stream of immigrants makes East Boston one of the most racially and ethnically diverse neighborhoods in the city. As in Boston's North and West Ends, Italian families and their businesses once dominated the neighborhood; Santarpio's, East Boston's famed pizza purveyor since 1933, is so good it's a tourist destination. But nowadays such stalwarts are outnumbered by dozens of El Salvadorean, Colombian, Brazilian, Dominican, Venezuelan, Peruvian, and Mexican eateries. The owner of Jeveli's, a neighborhood standard for ninety years, tells us that the area used to be "completely Italian" and is now mostly "Spanish," but the neighborhood's economic character—largely working class and poor—remains fundamentally the same.

One hundred and fifty years ago, about the time that the immigrant Irish were first making their homes in East Boston, a Harvard-trained Unitarian minister named Horatio Alger began spinning tales of boys from humble origins who achieved prosperity through hard work. Among the best known was the 1867 twelve-part serial chronicling a homeless New York City shoeshine boy's rise to the middle class. The book version, *Ragged Dick*, was released the following year. It became wildly popular and remained in print for forty years. Alger's fame signaled the thoroughly American nature of his message: each character's life story is a fulfillment of the promise that America has held out to generation after generation of immigrants. Here, in America, no matter how lowly your origins, hard work will lead to prosperity.

It is an ideal articulated in the nation's founding documents, one that has seemed to bear constant repeating throughout America's history. Theodore Roosevelt firmly stood for the "square deal for the poor man"—the belief that everyone ought to have an equal chance, regardless of background. "The right to earn enough to provide adequate food and clothing and recreation" was a prominent feature of Franklin Delano Roosevelt's Second Bill of Rights. For Bill Clinton, the phrase "People who work shouldn't be poor" was a central theme of his presidential campaign and his presidency. Barack Obama affirmed Clinton's message, arguing that America must support "the basic bargain that built this country—the idea that if you work hard and meet your responsibilities, you can get ahead." Across the aisle, Wisconsin congressman Paul Ryan has declared, "If you work hard and play by rules, you can get ahead. That is what the American Idea is."

Living up to these pledges hasn't been easy for the nation, especially in recent decades. In the mid-1960s, unskilled men's wages reached an all-time high. But in the 1970s manufacturing faltered. A long-standing decline of unionization continued. Thus the wages of these men began to plummet, both from falling real wages and from a loss of work hours and jobs, signaling a fundamental shift in the economy that has now continued for decades.[3] In that decade, some industrial boomtowns that had fed the prosperity of millions of male laborers and their families, such as Detroit, became wastelands. Others, like Chicago, saw a sharp rise in the rate of concentrated poverty.[4] During those years, working-class women entered the labor market in droves, some seeking to supplement their husbands' earnings and to keep their households afloat.[5] Surging rates of divorce and unwed parenthood meant that more and more of these women were heading their own households. To support their kids, they had to compete for a dwindling number of living-wage jobs. All of these changes made it more difficult for those without a college degree to get ahead.

The nation floundered as it tried to address the problems of the working poor. Then came the EITC, a strategy that emerged more by accident than by design. The template for the approach was forged in the debate over Richard Nixon's proposed 1972 Family Assistance Plan, which proposed a guaranteed minimum income that would have replaced welfare.[6] That plan failed, in large part because lawmakers like Senator Russell Long rejected any policy that offered benefits to people without jobs—any such plan was deemed "antiwork." Instead, Long championed a "prowork" policy—a tiny refundable tax credit with a wonkish name that offered tax relief to low-wage workers with children by refunding Social Security payroll taxes. The plan was called the earned income tax credit (EITC).

The nation's first refundable tax credit was popular on both sides of the political aisle; President Reagan proclaimed it "the best anti-poverty, the best pro-family, the best job creation measure to come out of Congress." Dramatic changes in the early 1990s would transform the program from tax relief for the working poor to a major antipoverty program.[7] But the program would still be deemed "prowork" by most. Indeed, it would be designed so that, for low-wage workers like Toni, the more you worked, the more you got from the program, up to a point.[8]

Throughout the 1970s and '80s, this modest tax credit, offering just a few hundred dollars to eligible households each year, did little to lift workers out of poverty. Policy makers saw it as a way to abate poor households' tax burdens, nothing more. In 1990, though, the logic of what the credit should do began to change, at least among academics and policy analysts: Why just use it to ease tax obligations? Why not use the credit to substantially boost the incomes of the working poor?

When he joined Clinton's presidential campaign as an adviser, Harvard economist David Ellwood took the idea of using the EITC to give a pay raise to the working poor with him. Under Ellwood's plan, the maximum amount a household could claim would rise dramatically, from several hundred to several thousand dollars each year. Like its modest predecessor, the new EITC would give eligible families the full amount they qualified for as a cash transfer from the government once tax liabilities had been satisfied. Though the program's name would remain the same, the innovation was to treat the EITC not just as tax relief but as a way to truly "make work pay," a central theme of the Clinton campaign.

The proposal was like political gold. Republicans favored expanding tax credits over other plans, such as raising the minimum wage, in part because it could be targeted to groups they most wanted to help: only working parents of children would receive significant subsidies, not teenagers working at after-school jobs. The implementation of the tax credit was astonishingly easy, as it required no special means test and only the same documentation that every working American had to submit at tax time—W-2 forms, plus the Social Security numbers of household members. No government workers needed to be hired and trained—families could fill out the forms themselves, or the friendly folks at H&R Block would do the filing for a fee. The credit wouldn't even call for any new bureaucracy—the IRS could administer the program, since it was already in the business of cutting refund checks. Now it just cut more of them, for larger amounts. And, its architects reasoned, by burying the plan in the obscurity of the tax code, they could protect the EITC from subsequent political threats. Under the Clinton administration, the maximum annual EITC for a family with two children increased from $953 in 1990 to $3,556 by 1996 and was indexed for inflation.[9] This dramatic increase in support for the working poor represented a historic transformation in the nation's safety net, but the story of welfare policy in the 1990s instead was dominated by the debates surrounding "welfare reform." These legislative efforts ultimately changed the nation's main cash welfare program, Aid to Families with Dependent Children (AFDC), from an entitlement to a time-limited benefit with work requirements and stringent sanctions, called Temporary Assistance for Needy Families (TANF).

On the ground, though, word got around among single mothers (the group most likely to qualify for the credit) that, no matter how low paying the job, if you worked, you could get a big refund check when you filed your taxes. For women with limited skills, the payoff for low-wage work shot up just as the ease of staying on the welfare rolls declined. And single mothers responded. Unprecedented numbers of them went to work, and many analysts claim that the new EITC was one of the main reasons why.[10] Meanwhile, the number of adults on welfare (TANF and its predecessor, AFDC) fell from roughly 4.5 million in 1993 and 1994 to about 1.8 million by the end of the 1990s. By the time we met Toni Patturelli in 2007, only about 1.1 million adults remained on the welfare rolls—fewer than at any time since the 1960s.[11] Indeed, the proportion of Americans receiving cash assistance has now fallen to about 1.4 percent; even among the poor, only 10 percent get TANF.[12]

In many ways, cash welfare is no longer the way that we support low-income families in the United States. Working or not, poor families with children have access to in-kind benefits such as food stamps, now called SNAP (Supplemental Nutrition Assistance Program), and Medicaid. But the EITC has become central to a new work-based approach to addressing the needs of the poor.

THE SAFETY NET REIMAGINED

It would be wrong to call the EITC the new welfare—it is unlike welfare in nearly every way one could imagine. For one thing, there is the entirely novel way that the benefits are structured: for a low-wage worker like Toni, EITC benefits actually rise if she works more. For example, in 2011, the credit increased until annual earnings reached roughly $13,000 for a typical EITC-eligible household (a single parent with two children); it leveled

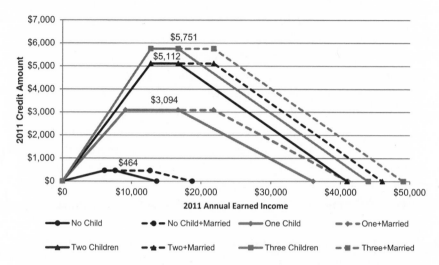

Figure 1. Structure of the 2011 EITC benefit. Source: Authors' tabulations from the EIC table of the 2011 IRS 1040 instruction booklet.

off until earnings exceeded about $17,000; and then it slowly phased out, cutting off at about $42,000 (see figure 1). In terms of the share of households served, the reach of the EITC today is roughly five times that of the old welfare system, even when the welfare rolls reached their peak of roughly five million households in 1993 and 1994. This is due to a very gradual falloff in benefits that extends EITC eligibility to households well up the income ladder. Thus, though targeted to low-earner households with children, the EITC serves such a large percentage of American households (about one in five) that it looks more like a universal program than a program for the poor, at least from the point of view of those at the bottom.

Those who might have relied on welfare prior to the 1996 welfare reform are only one subset of the EITC's beneficiaries. But contrasting this new work-based safety net against the old welfare entitlement—a safety net based on need and not predicated on work effort—brings the contours of the new system into bold relief.

Welfare recipients are often perceived as getting money for doing nothing.[13] However, decades of on-the-ground studies of welfare recipients have shown that the program has extracted at least a psychic price.[14] In describing their experiences to researchers, welfare recipients themselves have clearly articulated this cost. On the eve of welfare reform, one recipient summed up her experiences: "They treat you like an animal just because you need a little help getting back on your feet. I don't know anyone who likes getting welfare because of the [garbage] you have to deal with at the welfare office." Another, who had just left welfare for a low-wage job, explained: "Since I have gone off welfare I have vowed to never go to any government agency for help again. You know that saying, 'I'm from the government and I'm here to help'? That's the scariest thing that anyone can ever say to you [because of how they treat you]."[15] One recipient described a central reason she found being on welfare so difficult: "[Caseworkers] talk to you like you're an imbecile. They talk down to you like you're a second-class citizen."[16]

Indeed, such experiences were not unique to American welfare recipients near the end of the twentieth century. T. H. Marshall observed that the British Poor Laws, established in the 1600s and in existence until the 1940s, "treated the claims of the poor, not as an integral part of the rights of the citizen, but as an alternative to them—as claims which could be met only if the claimants ceased to be citizens in any true sense of the word." To get relief, Marshall wrote, the needy had to "cross the road that separated the community of citizens from the outcast company of the destitute."[17] Under the British Poor Laws of the time, this was often literally the case. The poor were usually required to enter an institution—a workhouse or poorhouse—to claim relief. As the examples above show, while America's welfare system was a far cry from the Poor Laws, in twentieth-century America welfare recipients were still made to feel like outcasts from mainstream society, stripped of the social rights of citizenship—socially marginalized and stereotyped as deviant.[18]

Even FDR, John F. Kennedy, and Lyndon Johnson, the very architects of the modern US welfare state, excoriated the "dependency" associated with cash assistance. Presidents Nixon, Ford, Carter, and Reagan all tried to alter the welfare system dramatically. When Bill Clinton first made his bid for the White House, he ran on the promise that he would "put an end to welfare as we know it." No nationally popular politician made it a point to defend welfare.

The most in-depth portrait of the day-to-day lives of the welfare poor under the old system came from research conducted by Kathryn Edin and

Laura Lein, who interviewed hundreds of low-income single mothers in cities across America just before welfare reform. Repeated in-depth conversations with each mother provided a rich sense of welfare-reliant single mothers' daily lives and a detailed accounting of their monthly expenses and income. Edin and Lein's research demonstrated that welfare didn't provide households with nearly enough cash to pay their bills—rent alone could easily equal, if not exceed, the value of their check. The rest of the story was thick with irony. Often charged with being freeloaders who did nothing but sit around watching TV, most were actually supplementing their welfare checks by working.[19] But if they were to make ends meet, their labor had to remain hidden from view—if their welfare caseworkers were to learn of their employment, their much-needed benefits would get cut. In short, single mothers collecting cash welfare were forced to become "cheats" in order to take care of their children.[20] The covert nature of their economic lives added to the sense of shame they felt about collecting handouts from the government. As one welfare recipient Edin and Lein interviewed flatly stated: "They make you feel like dirt in the street."[21]

Edin and Lein concluded that the reason many recipients stayed on welfare for so much of their adult lives was simple: on-the-books work "cost" more than welfare. Unless she was unusually lucky, an unskilled single mother couldn't easily afford to leave welfare for an aboveboard job. Wages usually exceeded cash welfare, even in states with the most generous benefit levels. But work also entailed additional expenses for transportation, child care, clothing, and the like. These costs more than swamped the benefits of working. Plus, while welfare provided a stable source of income, a working parent never knew when she might be laid off from her job or see her hours cut. These mothers often felt that they were damned by society if they didn't work on the books but damned by harsh financial realities if they did.[22]

During the 1960s and '70s the cash welfare rolls had expanded dramatically. Partly in response, in the 1980s and into the 1990s, most states ceased adjusting their benefit levels for inflation. Thus the average welfare check lost about half of its value in real terms. New work requirements were also added. With these adjustments, politicians and policy makers expected the number of recipients to drop. Yet during those years millions of single mothers remained on welfare. By 1990, there were fourteen million people—nearly five million parents and their dependent children—still collecting cash welfare. Edin and Lein argued that the answer to the puzzle of why so many single mothers were choosing welfare over employment was simple: single mothers with little education stayed on welfare because they couldn't afford to leave—the math just didn't add up. David Ellwood, the welfare expert and Harvard economist who became an adviser to the Clinton campaign, had also deduced this logic. He concluded that what America needed was not just a bigger "stick" to punish the poor for not working but a more appealing "carrot" to reward work.

AMERICA'S NEW SAFETY NET

Just about a mile from the East Boston H&R Block's busy storefront is a particularly gloomy reminder of the old welfare system: a dark brick building straight out of a Dickens novel, once the neighborhood's welfare office. A century of grime grips the aged exterior. Small, filthy windows are covered with wire mesh. A massive flagpole, bereft of its flag, is mounted just above the second-story windows, and, above the utilitarian metal and glass doors, in bold capital letters, are the words "OVERSEERS OF THE PUBLIC WELFARE." The building is almost a throwback to the way things were—the edifice connotes stigma and shame—but it is also a symbol of welfare's demise. The structure has lain vacant for years.

The difference between that dark structure and the bright, welcoming interior of the local H&R Block, located just blocks away, is deeply symbolic. The decidedly upbeat vibe at the tax preparation office represents a dramatically different vision of what helping poor and near-poor Americans can look like. Claimants under the old system often complained about abysmal treatment at the welfare office and caseworkers who, according to recipients, treated the money as if it were their own;[23] at H&R Block, Toni is a customer, offered service with a smile. The slogan that parents like Toni remember best from their visit? "You've got people"—the company ad that signifies solidarity with their customers.

Here is the most revolutionary aspect of America's new safety net: no longer must the needy trade their feelings of citizenship and social inclusion to receive assistance. The move from a need-based entitlement—

welfare—to the new work-based safety net does exactly the opposite: it brings the needy who work back into the mainstream (so long as they can find jobs). The EITC not only lifts the incomes of millions of poor households above the poverty line, but, as we show, it motivates people to work and affirms the value of employment. The "refund" that arrives at tax time offers the working poor a chance to clear the ledger of back bills and debt. But it does more than that: it gives them an opportunity to invest in a better future—to set aside money for a rainy day, buy a used car to get to a better job in the suburbs, or pay a semester's tuition at a community college. Maybe they could even manage to save for a down payment on a home, or perhaps treat the kids to something special. In this way, the once-a-year windfall allows poor, hardworking families to dream. This is nothing short of a radical change.

To understand what life is like for those on the front lines of this new system, we set out to learn about the financial lives of the people who have experienced it. With large sandwich boards in hand ("Earn $10 for 2 minutes of your time!"), we traveled to a half-dozen Boston neighborhoods, meeting low-wage workers as they filed their taxes—at H&R Block offices or with the assistance of a volunteer at a community nonprofit—or as they dropped their preschoolers off at a local Head Start center (see map 1). We spent hundreds of hours—mornings, afternoons, evenings, and weekends—at these sites from February through April in 2007. We asked everyone we met whether they had claimed the Earned Income Tax Credit. Nearly all who did were eager to answer our short questionnaire about the size of their refund and how they planned to spend it; we were able to survey 332 people in all. From those we surveyed, we identified families for the in-depth portion of the study. After ensuring that we would have even numbers of blacks, whites, and Latinos and (within each racial and ethnic group) one-third married and two-thirds unmarried parents, we chose our in-depth sample at random.[24] In the months that followed we spent time with those families who agreed to participate in the in-depth study—115 of the 120 originally chosen—in their homes, gathering detailed information about incomes and expenses, so we could understand how they managed their finances day to day and month to month.[25]

Our study offers insight into how a racially and ethnically diverse group of lower-income working families think about their financial futures and

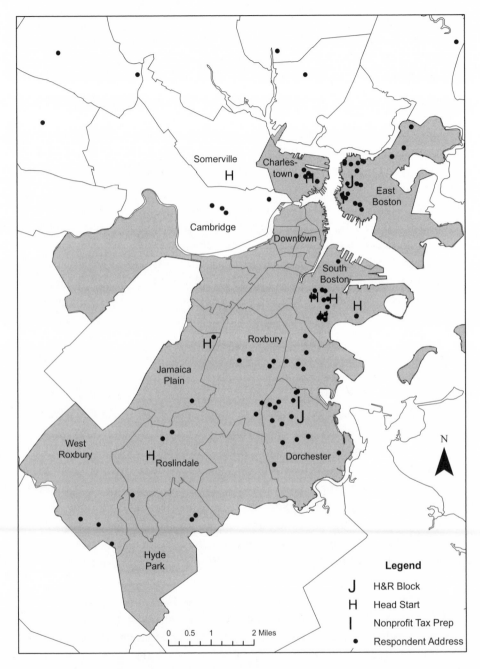

Map 1. Location of recruitment sites and respondents.

Legend

J — H&R Block
H — Head Start
I — Nonprofit Tax Prep
• — Respondent Address

forge hopes of achieving the American Dream.[26] Boston, the setting for our study, is rich in such diversity. Despite its deserved reputation as a magnet for waves of Irish and Italian immigrants, today its residents are of many national origins and include immigrants from around the world. Half of the city's residents are white, one-quarter are black, and approximately one in six are Hispanic.[27] Its neighborhoods are also economically diverse. Boston's cost of living presents challenges for many residents, particularly those with limited incomes. Even those who aren't below the federal poverty line often find that financial security is out of reach. At this writing, the median home price in Boston is $419,500, compared to $192,400 for the country as a whole. Not surprisingly, therefore, there are more renters than home owners in Boston. Renters here occupy nearly two-thirds of housing units; in the United States as a whole, the proportion is one in three.[28] On the other hand, public health insurance (MassHealth) and various housing subsidy programs are more readily available here than elsewhere, which helps to compensate for the steep living costs.

The 115 families who participated in the in-depth study had key features in common: they all worked, were able to claim the EITC, received a substantial refund (at least $1,000), and lived in the Boston metropolitan area.[29] All households contained children; indeed, at least one child had to count as a "qualifying child" under the EITC guidelines (age, relationship, and residency tests). One baby, Kwame Marshall, was only nineteen days old on the day we spoke with his mother, Laeticia, already a parent to Kwame's sister, two-year-old Namari. Other households included "children" in their late teens and early twenties, like Sharon Ingram's twenty-one-year-old daughter Deja, who, along with Sharon's fifteen-year-old son Tyrell, counted as a "qualifying child" because she was living under her mother's roof and was still in school.

The study included parents in their early twenties and grandparents in their sixties with custody of their grandchildren; families ranged from single mothers to parents who lived together but weren't married to married and stepfamily households.[30] A small number of families earned less than $10,000 a year, while a few reported incomes in the $30,000 range; most fell in between. There was considerable variety in educational levels and occupational titles. We met high school dropouts, those with vocational degrees, and a few college graduates. These families were headed by home health aides, convenience store clerks, and hospital bookkeepers, among a host of other job titles. Housing situations also varied. Our study included home owners, renters, and those fortunate enough to have a rent subsidy in a housing market that can place market-rate apartments out of reach. Although we were often introduced to spouses, live-in partners, children, and other family members when we visited each home, we typically talked with the adult who was primarily responsible for managing the family finances (although, on occasion, both members of a couple would sit down with us).[31] In this book we describe stories and relate perspectives from sixty of these families by name (52 percent of respondents); their experiences are offered as illustrations of others like them in our study.[32] We worked to represent the most common themes we heard across families, while also giving the reader a sense of the range of responses in our data.

THE FINANCIAL LIVES OF THE WORKING POOR

To understand how families are faring in the era of the new safety net, we first have to know how they make ends meet in the months they don't have that big refund check from the government to draw on. While February, March, and April are typically good months—the time period when they generally spend down their tax credits—May through January are often not. Thus this book begins with the dollars and cents: How much money does each family take in over the course of the year from all sources combined? What are the family's basic bills and other expenses? In a typical month, are they living in the black or in the red? And, if the latter, how do they cope with the shortfall?

In chapter 1, we introduce Ashlee Reed, a twenty-nine-year-old white college graduate who lives with her three children and her boyfriend, Adrian, in South Boston. Ashlee, who has a stable job as a preschool teacher, pursued a college education to ensure she'd struggle less than her mother, a high school dropout, had to. Ashlee has a cable TV package and an Internet subscription. Yet her income places her at the government's official poverty line—approximately $27,000 for a household of five (the poverty rate for a family of four—which is how Ashlee's family unit would officially be classified, since Adrian wouldn't be counted as part of the family because they are unmarried—is just under $24,000). Some might say that, on the basis of what households like Ashlee's consume, they aren't really impoverished. Yet a close look at Ashlee's budget reveals that she's often unable to pay even her basic bills—food, shelter, and clothing— much less that cable/Internet bundle. For households like Ashlee's, a variety of government programs, but especially the EITC, are the keys to economic survival. Ashlee views these programs not as handouts but as a hand up. Yet the help that working parents like Ashlee try to wrest from the "system" is often slow in coming, if it comes at all. The main complaint these working parents lodge, however, is that unlike the EITC, many of the other programs seem to "punish" those who work and play by the rules; most programs reduce benefits for each dollar you earn. Indeed, in some programs, just one dollar more in earnings can push households off a cliff—suddenly, they're no longer eligible for the benefits at all.[33]

The finances of families in our study place them firmly on the lower, but not the lowest, rungs of America's economic ladder. Half were in the bottom 20 percent of the nation's income distribution (around $20,000 or less in annual income), and the other half were between 20 and 30 percent—still well below the national median income. That the EITC reaches well into that second fifth of the income distribution is due to the program's design—it offers the most generous benefits to those able to work full time, all year, at a minimum-wage job. Plus, EITC benefits phase out only gradually as workers earn more.[34]

While other forms of relief for the poor sharply restrict people's discretion over how they can spend the money—SNAP, for example, allows the purchase only of specific food items—families can spend their tax refund however they want. Do parents blow it on frivolous purchases? Do they get swindled by special tax-time deals offered by the local used car salesmen and rent-to-own furniture stores that often punctuate the commercial strips in low- and moderate-income neighborhoods? Or, as some policy makers have hoped, do families take advantage of the "forced savings" feature of the program—the refund's large lump sum—to build assets and try to get ahead?

Debra McKinley, a twenty-eight-year-old white waitress and mother of two young girls, opens chapter 2 by describing the keen sense of anticipation that she experiences each year at tax time. After she has scrambled to pay the bills all year and taken on debt when wages fall short, her tax refund offers significant financial relief. In February, when her refund comes in, she and Sonny, her fiancé, can finally catch up on bills and get the car in working order again. But it is what she does with the rest of the money that brings a smile to her face: providing a dream birthday for her older daughter—the kind she herself never had. Tax time has become the highlight of the year for lower-income families like Debra's. The stories of the families we studied offer us a glimpse of the meaning of this special, and often large, windfall that comes each tax season beyond the mere dollars and cents. Because of its peculiar and highly innovative features, the EITC not only offers the opportunity to splurge on that rare treat for a child, it inspires families to aspire to something more. It is viewed as the engine for upward mobility that few could hope for without that magical lump sum. And in keeping with that special meaning ascribed to the refund, nearly four in ten refund dollars are invested—used for purposes households associate with upward mobility—or saved.

In chapter 3 we meet Johanna and Mack Clark, a white married couple in their twenties who are parents to a four-year-old daughter and a seven-year-old son. Currently Johanna works as a medical assistant and goes to college part time in pursuit of a nursing degree while Mack, who was injured at work, stays home with the kids. Their first son came along before they were really ready, they say—both had dropped out of high school, and only Johanna had earned her GED. To turn things around, the pair moved in with Mack's mother, and Johanna signed up for welfare, just for a few months, while she earned certification as a medical assistant. After that, she found a way to combine schooling with employment.

Johanna and Mack have never forgotten their brief time on welfare, but the lengths they go to in order to try and "explain away" this spell—it was due to forces beyond their control (an unplanned pregnancy), and it was only temporary—reveal the deep stigma that they, like most other Americans, attach to welfare. Both excoriate welfare recipients, whom they describe as "lazy" people content to "sit on their asses" despite the fact that they were once beneficiaries of the program themselves.

Americans have always shown a strong distaste for any form of cash assistance without significant strings—such as work requirements—attached. David Ellwood, one of the modern EITC's chief architects, got a strong taste of the vitriol with which Americans viewed the welfare poor when he tried to defend the system in the mid-1980s. His efforts were met with sharp condemnation—even by the welfare poor themselves. Because of this, he concluded that welfare had to be replaced, not merely reformed. It was simply too inconsistent with American values. Soon, a wholly new system of providing assistance to the needy—focused almost solely on the working poor, a group everyone agreed was deserving—would replace the old.

Remarkably, welfare state scholars have virtually ignored tax credits' potential to confer a sense of inclusion and social citizenship. Previous research has shown that other social welfare programs can have an impact that extends well beyond their dollar value. The old cash welfare system stripped people of their dignity and sense of social inclusion, but we find that the new safety net—reserved for workers—does not seem to do the same. Something about the EITC makes it different from getting welfare or benefits like SNAP, Medicaid, and subsidized housing that many may also rely on from time to time.[35] What is it about tax credits, we asked, that seems to generate pride?

The genius of the EITC, in part, is that it is folded into one's total tax refund, rather than being a separate check from the government. Because of this, no one is quite sure whether it is merely a refund of withheld earnings or a transfer of government funds. Most of our households know that they get back more than they paid in, but at the same time they insist that they "earned" it. No one we spoke to believed it was even remotely like welfare. In addition, families claim the EITC in exactly the same manner as other taxpayers claim tax refunds due to overwithholding—by filling out the forms online or, more commonly, by paying a fee for H&R Block or one if its competitors to do it for them. The refund check comes once a year as a windfall, so beneficiaries see the money as "special." Perhaps because of that designation, a portion of the money is almost always earmarked for special purchases, rather than merely viewed as funds to meet their usual obligations. Finally, it is large enough to inspire what social psychologists call "future-oriented behavior." Accordingly, only about one refund dollar in ten is "blown"—usually on modest treats for the kids—while nearly 40 percent is either saved (at least initially) or devoted to purchases that families equate with getting ahead—a used car, durable goods, tuition, or even, occasionally, a home purchase or upgrade. Debt payoff, often for the purpose of cleaning up one's credit in order to get ahead, is also common.

In chapter 4, we introduce Jacinta Estrada, a twenty-six-year-old Hispanic hospital payroll coordinator and mother of four—one preschooler and three children in elementary school—who dreams of one day owning her own home. She claims it is the EITC that has inspired her to dream. But her attempts to save are two steps forward, one step back. A year or so earlier she was out of work for several months; that ate into the savings. More recently, her live-in boyfriend was socializing with friends on his grandmother's front porch when a car screamed by spraying bullets. Wounds in his arms have left this mechanic unable to work, another drain on their savings account. Nonetheless, Jacinta's zeal is undiminished—she is determined that in the not-too-distant future she'll have enough saved to make a down payment on a home.

An astonishing number of the families in this study hold dreams like Jacinta's. Few have substantial savings, even fewer have retirement accounts, and untarnished credit is rare. Yet they do have a vital asset—that windfall at tax time. When that check from the IRS comes, many of the families we spoke with show keen motivation to retire their debt and repair their credit, invest in what they see as mobility-enhancing assets, and save for big future goals such as college for the kids or a home of their own. In short, dreams for a better life are inspired, and bolstered, by the expectation of a big tax refund. Even if their dreams for this year's lump sum are ruptured by debt and other pressing needs, the working poor continue to hold tight to the promise of next year's refund.

Maureen Ellis, the thirty-one-year-old white divorcée whom we feature in chapter 5, tries to balance her job as a waitress, her classes at the local community college, and parenting two small children. Maureen makes enough to cover her basic expenses, but debt is dragging her down. She tells a familiar story: frivolous spending in her late teens and early twenties—treating her credit cards as if they were ready cash—set her up with seemingly insurmountable debt. She tries to be more careful now, but when she faces an expense she hadn't expected, it is her credit card she turns to more often than her family or friends, and this drags her even further into debt.

It is surprises on the expense side of her budget ledger that are driving Maureen's growing debt. But for other households we studied, debt also results from sharp, and often unexpected, drops in income. If you get laid off or lose hours, how do you stay afloat? What do you do when the car breaks down? First, you try a financial juggling act—this month you'll make your student loan payment on time, but next month you'll skip it because the car insurance is due. When that fails, the credit card is often the go-to safety net.

A recurring cycle of debt, some long term but much of it accumulated throughout the course of the year, is a common feature of our families' financial lives. Debt is the force that often wreaks havoc with the year's carefully laid plans for how the refund will be saved and invested. Dreams must be deferred for the following year, or the year after that.

Debt doesn't fit with the bright financial future for which so many of our families are striving. Those with the strongest aspirations for upward mobility—especially those who aspire to own homes—are often those with the most disciplined spending habits. For such household heads, debt payoff and credit repair are the first step toward their longer-term goals and are a top priority at tax time. In sum, the EITC seems to inspire future-oriented goals. And to some extent, it also seems to prompt the financially responsible behavior—thrift and debt payoff—that could lead to their fulfillment. But tight budgets and financial shocks can drive up debt during the rest of the year.

DIGNITY AND DREAMS

It's Not Like I'm Poor will illustrate—vividly—that the EITC is like nothing we've ever tried before.[36] By providing a pay raise to low-income workers, it helps keep that age-old American promise: if you work, you shouldn't be poor. It supports all of the things that Americans value—work, saving, paying debts, asset building, and the desire to get ahead. It confers dignity by confirming claimants' identities as workers, rather than marking them as dependents waiting for a government handout. Beyond offering a chance to balance the books, it gives families some financial wiggle room to dream and to make plans for the future. Meanwhile, at tax time, families feel that they can spend just a little extra to provide for their children's "wants" and not just their needs—that's why some say it's better than Christmas. And the householders we studied—who see themselves as playing by society's rules—often insist that as workers they should be able to afford a few indulgences once in a while. As one parent we interviewed explained, "It's not like I'm poor!"

Through the EITC and the other refundable credits that have followed in its path, America has brought at least a portion of the poor into mainstream society in a way that has seldom been done before by an antipoverty policy. No welfare bureaucrats are controlling their lives. The working poor can exercise autonomy and spend that gloriously large lump sum however they please. When they arrive at that H&R Block office to collect their refund check, their status as beneficiaries of a cash assistance program is invisible. They are there because they filed their taxes just like every other hardworking American. Some evidence suggests that an enhanced sense of social inclusion might lead to other forms of prosocial behavior, such as political and civic engagement.[37]

Traditional means-tested benefits like cash welfare, which seldom covers families' food, shelter, clothing, and other necessities, and SNAP, which covers only a portion of families' food needs, are not designed to prevent families from experiencing scarcity.[38] In contrast, the families we studied enjoy a considerable surplus in the months following receipt of the tax refund. Experiments conducted by Sendhil Mullainathan, Eldar Shafir, and their colleagues suggest that alleviating scarcity may make working-poor parents and their children not only happier and less stressed but smarter and more attentive too—and thus better able to make the sound decisions that may make them less likely to remain poor.[39]

Beyond these economic, social, and psychological benefits, a spate of recent research has shown that the EITC has positive impacts on mothers' health—including improvements in mental health and self-reported health status and decreases in inflammation, blood pressure, and smoking; children's health—including more prenatal care and higher birth weights; and children's educational success—as measured by test scores, college enrollment, and college graduation.[40] The EITC's ability to improve so many dimensions of recipients' lives speaks to the program's power.

But at the same time, a close look into the lives of the new safety net's beneficiaries reveals that we are still a long way from solving the problems of the working poor. These families have never been better off, both economically and socially. But the financial ups and downs they experience have probably never been so great, nor their debt loads so high.

In short, the new safety net has its dark side. The welfare system that ended when Toni was in her twenties had one crucial, often overlooked, advantage: it provided a stable floor of cash that households like Toni's could count on each month. True, by the early 1990s the real value of a welfare check had fallen so dramatically that it covered only three-fifths of the typical poor household's monthly expenses. Edin and Lein likened the other two-fifths of the income that recipients had to garner through various strategies to a continually unraveling patchwork quilt—one strategy or another was always coming apart. Thus the financial ups and downs of the welfare poor were considerable. But the women that Edin and Lein spoke with still felt that they could rely on that foundation that welfare provided—the benefit check was the cornerstone around which they built their monthly budget. Today, most poor families have no such financial floor, save whatever in-kind benefits they manage to qualify for; while impoverished families may receive Medicaid coverage and SNAP benefits, these don't help put a roof over your head, keep the heat and the lights on, or put clothes on your kids' backs.

Then there are those who are left out of the new work-based safety net, the millions of poor Americans whose stories are outside the scope of this book because they aren't working or don't have qualifying dependents. This includes the 1.46 million households with children who, in any given month, have fallen completely through the cracks, living with virtually no income from work or welfare, on little more than in-kind benefits—if that. The EITC may rescue over three million children from poverty each year, but in any given month about the same number of children are living in households with incomes of less than $2 per person per day—a common metric used by the World Bank to measure Third World poverty.[41]

Some critics point to the irony that while the government will subsidize your wages if you take care of other people's kids, they won't pay you to take care of your own.[42] This perspective would argue that there is no better evidence of the collapse of the idea that caregiving ought to be assigned value in our society than the transition from the old safety net to the new. Another critique is that it is employers paying low wages, and not their employees, who benefit most from the EITC.[43] The availability of the EITC may put less pressure on employers to pay higher wages or, by drawing more workers into the labor force, may depress wages.

In many ways, the new work-based safety net has redrawn, and perhaps made more pronounced, the line between the "deserving" and the "undeserving" poor, where one's work behavior and parental status are very nearly the sole measures of deservedness among able-bodied, nonelderly adults. Of course, many cross this line repeatedly as jobs, and the "deservingness" they bring with them, are found and lost. Fundamentally, the work-based safety net is predicated on the availability of work. The shortcomings of such a safety net were thrown into sharp relief during the recent Great Recession, which prefigured what economists predict will be long-term instability in employment among the least skilled Americans. In contrast to programs like SNAP, TANF, and unemployment insurance, the EITC may not ease families' struggles very much during financial downturns. Families who lose jobs also lose access to the EITC.[44] There is a basic incompatibility between a volatile economy and an antipoverty policy that conditions benefits on work behavior.

It is time to assess the costs and benefits of the new work-based safety net. In the final chapter of this book, we suggest some ways to ease the work-based safety net's downsides and augment its strengths. We might celebrate the remarkable success of this fundamental change to the American welfare state that rewards workers and reinforces national values. But we must also find a way to minimize its flaws and to care for those who can't meet its demands, all the while doing more to make good on the promise that, here in America, parents who are willing to work hard will be able to provide a minimally decent life for their children in the short term and will have the chance to get ahead over time.

1 Family Budgets

What does it really mean to have a social safety net organized around the principle that, if you work you shouldn't be poor? The American poverty line is neither an absolute measure of what it takes to survive—an estimate of what a basic "market basket" of necessities costs—nor a relative measure, like poverty thresholds in Europe that identify households falling below some percentage of the median income; the figure in the European Union is 60 percent. Instead, it is based on 1950s surveys of the cost of a minimally nutritious diet on an "emergency" or short-term basis (which assumed that a family consumed powdered milk and no fresh vegetables), multiplied by three (at that time, the average family spent a third of its income on food). Since the poverty threshold was set in the 1960s based on these calculations, the dollar amount has simply been adjusted for inflation.[1]

Because of the poverty line's odd origins, no one is quite sure what "poor" really means in America, and, perhaps for that reason, hardly anyone likes the official measure. Some on the political right, for example, charge that the threshold is way too high—Robert Rector of the Heritage Foundation argues that it overestimates poverty because few poor Americans truly go without food, most have air conditioners and cable, half have personal computers, and a third even have fancy TVs. "For most people, the word 'poverty' suggests near destitution: an inability to provide nutritious food, clothing, and reasonable shelter for one's family. However, only a small number of the 46.2 million persons classified as 'poor' by the Census Bureau fit that definition," he writes.[2] This is not mere punditry: surveys show that the poor do report possessions that many Americans—especially those of a previous generation—would deem luxuries. Because of this, some economists have called for a new poverty measure based on consumption, not income, arguing that it does the best job of identifying the neediest Americans.[3]

In contrast, those on the political left often complain that the poverty line is much too low—little more than a back-of-the envelope, midcentury calculation based on national patterns of consumption that no longer hold; Americans now spend only about a sixth of their income on food, for example, but more on child care and medical costs than they once did. At this writing, the poverty line for a family of four is just under $24,000 in income, or about $2,000 a month. Critics in this camp ask, is there any place in America where a family of four can actually make ends meet on that amount? Columbia University's National Center for Children in Poverty estimates that, on average, a family would need an income of about *twice* the poverty level to truly get by.[4] Ordinary Americans seem to side with the Columbia University researchers. In 2007, Gallup pollsters asked Americans from across the country: "What is the smallest amount of yearly income a family of four would need to get along in your local community?" The median response was $45,000, with a mean above $50,000.[5]

The EITC was designed to bring a minimum-wage worker and his or her family above the official poverty line. The controversy over the poverty line raises the question of whether this is a worthy goal. Some might argue that, if the working poor have Internet and cable TV, supplementing their incomes with a cash transfer from the government is not an appropriate policy objective. Others might contend that, if the working poor are willing to play by the rules—stay employed—it is unjust, even immoral, not to ensure that they have the wherewithal to provide their children with a minimally decent life, as Americans define it. Indeed, for those meeting this fundamental requirement of the American social contract, just getting by may not be enough; those in this camp might argue that society should ensure that they have the real possibility to reach for more.

Accordingly, this chapter is devoted to examining the finances of working-poor and near-poor households who claim the EITC. At present, one minimum-wage job will provide an income of $14,500 a year, provided the work is full time and full year. The EITC and other tax credits fill the gap between that figure and the poverty threshold. Here we ask which of the two views of the poverty line is correct. Are people below the threshold truly struggling, or are they blowing money on big-screen TVs and cable packages? We'll find that the answer isn't one or the other, but both.

Our logic in addressing this question at the start of the book is simple: if we want to understand the real impact of the EITC, and whether it is worth the cost to taxpayers, getting a detailed look at household budgets is a critical first step. But, as we've indicated, the ultimate question this chapter raises is much larger: What bundle of goods and services is "enough" for those on the front lines of this revolutionary new approach to alleviating poverty, parents who are working but poor? Is it merely about financial need, or should our standard for what is enough be based on American notions of what workers "deserve"? In short, given the fact that these household heads all play by the rules—working, many full time and full year—do they need the EITC, and are they worthy of it?

We devote a later chapter (chapter 3) to comparing the new work-based safety net to the old welfare entitlement system that existed prior to the 1996 reforms, and to the time-limited welfare system that remains. Thus we will not engage in a full discussion of those differences here. Note, however, that the old system, which entitled a family to a certain level of resources based on their need, never came close to pulling families above the poverty line. Today, not one state in our nation offers enough in TANF benefits to raise a family much above even half of the official poverty threshold;[6] in fact, in the majority of states, TANF benefits are limited to less than a third of the poverty line, although TANF beneficiaries usually are also able to claim SNAP (formerly known as food stamps) and Medicaid. Nonetheless, the monthly TANF benefit for a family of three won't even pay the rent:[7] it is less than the cost of a modest two-bedroom apartment in any state, and, in twenty-six states it is not even half of that cost.[8] This shortfall is meaningful given the fact that nationally only a quarter of eligible families get any form of subsidized housing, and families with substantial assets are barred from the welfare rolls.[9]

Clearly, what remains of the traditional need-based safety net is not—and never was—truly about helping families meet all of their needs. Yet few politicians worry in public, and perhaps few even worry in private, that TANF benefits are too low. What standard of living, then, did Bill Clinton envision ensuring when he proposed a massive expansion of the EITC so that working Americans—at least those with kids—would not be poor? Was it bare-bones survival or something more—some notion of a "decent" standard of living that exceeded subsistence? The narratives we present in this chapter raise the question of what kind of reward American workers ought to get from their labor.

We first turn to Ashlee Reed, whose household financial situation is quite typical of that of other households in our study. Ashlee grew up in the South Boston housing projects watching her mother struggle financially while raising three kids on her own. A high school dropout, Ashlee's mom had to take whatever work she could find. Certification as a home health aide translated into long hours taking care of the elderly for little more than minimum wage. Perhaps as a result, she frequently lectured Ashlee and her siblings about the importance of education in the hopes that her children might rise above bottom-of-the-barrel jobs like hers and escape "Southie," the troubled neighborhood in which they lived. Ashlee bought into this message wholeheartedly; she excelled in high school and took out loans so that she could go to college. Four years later, she left with her bachelor of arts degree in hand, becoming the only college graduate in her family.

But life has fallen short of the comfortable living promised by her mother's stay-in-school mantra. Now, seven years after graduation, this twenty-nine-year-old white mother lives with her boyfriend, Adrian—who used to work as a cook in her college cafeteria—and their three young children on a run-down block that's just a stone's throw from the one that she was raised on. She is still saddled with $25,000 in educational debt, which she chips away at bit by bit. Because of the slack job market for teachers, she considered herself lucky when she landed a job at Head Start, earning $532 in gross wages per week, or $357 in take-home pay, during the forty-four-week school year.[10] But the job hasn't left her much better off than her mother.

We first meet this family of five in their small, two-bedroom apartment directly across from a convenience store on a busy street in Dorchester. This mostly black neighborhood borders South Boston, the largely white enclave to the east where Ashlee was raised. Inside the apartment, it is dark; the living room is crowded with outdated but carefully preserved furniture, and a washing machine sits prominently in the kitchen, taking up too much space. Though it's cramped here, order reigns; the only clutter visible is an overflowing pile of bills on the desk in the living room.

Ashlee has a housing choice voucher—a program known colloquially as Section 8, which limits her rent to roughly 30 percent of her income.[11] Without it, she would need to devote nearly all of her take-home pay to rent this modest apartment.[12] During the months that she is employed—all but eight weeks during the summer—her share of the rent is $575 (the government pays the rest). And, in this unit, the rent includes utilities, a lucky break. Years ago, Ashlee applied for a modification to her housing voucher, which would have entitled her to a three-bedroom apartment so that the three kids wouldn't have to all share a room, but she has heard nothing from the Boston Housing Authority about that request. She needs to be close to work—she purchased a car only recently—so Ashlee has ended up in Dorchester, a step down, not up, from Southie. She worries about raising her children here: the block is home to a bar that is open all day, and Ashlee says the street is full of "yelling and broken bottles."

Head Start teachers don't command high wages, but the job does offer some critical perks for this working mother of three. While she must leave her toddler with her boyfriend's mother while she works, she can bring her two older children with her. Though the two kids are not technically eligible for the program (she makes too much money to qualify), Head Start charges her only $300 per month for both children. Elsewhere, she might easily pay three or four times that amount.[13] Another perk is the schedule, which allows her to be home with the kids after school. She firmly believes that "no matter what, my kids have to come first." Despite the nice fit between her family responsibilities and her work schedule, running after a dozen or so preschoolers all day can be tiring, and, for the hard work involved in managing her classroom, she finds the compensation wanting. In an average month, her paychecks show gross earnings of $2,288, although she notes that payroll taxes, deductions for her share of her health care premium, and intentional overwithholding—a decision to "save" made when both she and Adrian were working—bring that amount down considerably.[14]

Employment entails a host of expenses—especially child care and transportation. A busy highway separates Ashlee from her job. Now that she has a car, she drives to work, piloting a dark blue Dodge Caravan older than her children's ages combined—five-year-old Warren, four-year-old Mallory, and three-year-old Johnny. She's proud that this "clunker" is paid off, but it isn't cheap to insure or maintain: in a typical month, she estimates that she pays $401 for transportation, between car insurance, gas, registration, and routine maintenance or the occasional parking ticket. That's nearly a third of her take-home pay.

Ashlee's financial struggles are particularly acute at the moment. Her boyfriend, thirty-three-year-old Adrian, can't pay anything toward the household expenses. After six years of steady work as a cook at her alma mater, he was laid off just before Christmas, along with all of his coworkers, when the college chose a rival food-service provider. By the time of our first in-depth conversation, Adrian's unemployment benefits have run out. And Ashlee is facing another financial hit: it's late June, and she has just been laid off from her job, as she is every summer. She, along with thousands of Head Start teachers across the country, applies for unemployment during the summer months, but unemployment insurance covers only a portion of her lost wages; in any case, the first check takes about four weeks to arrive.[15] While waiting for that check, Ashlee copes by using the only safety net that she has available—credit cards—to pay the bills.

For Ashlee and so many others working lower-wage jobs, there really is no *average* month. Instead, their financial lives are boom and bust. During the "bust," debt accrual is common. Most aspire to save, but the barriers to saving are high; unexpected financial upheavals quickly eat away at one's savings. During the forty-four weeks that Head Start is in session, Ashlee, Adrian, and the kids can count on at least one steady paycheck. But each summer Ashlee's income takes a nosedive. And she has no cheap source of child care available to make a summer job worth her while. Most years, Ashlee manages to limp along until February, tax refund time. In February, when her tax refund arrives, she can catch up on bills that may have been overdue for months, pay off some of her longer-term debt, and, in good years, save for the summer financial crunch.

FALLING BEHIND

We begin by considering Ashlee's financial situation in an "average" month, as if her income and expenses stayed steady throughout the year. In the typical month, Ashlee's expenses exceed her wages from her job. With monthly expenses totaling $2,856—this includes only minimum payments on the credit cards and on her student loans—and average take-home pay of under $1,600, the family is sliding into debt even during the months that she claims her full salary, as long as Adrian is unable to contribute.[16] The weighty load of Ashlee's credit card debt is testimony that she's relied on credit as a safety net in the past.

Ashlee lives as many lower-wage workers do, under a cloud of debt that grows rather than shrinks over time: currently, she owes five credit card companies a total of $4,080.[17] Each month, she tries to make at least the minimum payment on these cards plus a few dollars more, but, with interest rates of more than 20 percent (and one as high as 30 percent), her progress on paying down the balances is slow. Lately, she feels a sense of accomplishment in those months when she manages not to increase the amount she owes. On top of the credit cards, her student loan payment is $360 a month. She tries not to think about how long it will take to pay off the $25,000 that remains. Since Adrian has been unemployed, Ashlee has skipped these payments in order to provide for the family's basic needs.

BOOM TIME

Last February, Ashlee got a refund check from H&R Block totaling $4,704—more than three times the amount that she brings home in an average month. Ashlee keenly remembers the excitement she felt when she collected that check, walking it straight to the bank. By the time that the refund was in hand, she had spent months planning how she would spend it. She had fallen behind on her student loan during the prior summer and

had decided to put that particular debt at the top of the list. Ashlee typically prioritizes her student loan above her credit cards because, "once you
go so long without paying, they can default you." Defaulting on a federal
student loan triggers garnishment of one's tax refund, a risk she doesn't
feel prepared to take: "I didn't want to get there," she says.

After she had gotten up to date on that loan, the remaining $3,204
from the refund allowed Ashlee to pay down some of the principal on her
credit cards, which she had also accrued the prior summer, and to catch
up on the overdue cable and phone bills. Now, just as she faces another
layoff, the savings from her tax refund have nearly run dry. Thus, this year,
Ashlee made no progress toward her longer-term goal: "I try to save [a lot
of my refund]. My goal usually, even though I don't ever make it, is to have
enough money saved up for the summer for when I go onto unemployment, because . . . it takes like four weeks [to get my first unemployment
check]. That's four weeks without pay if I don't have anything saved up
from when I was working. So I usually have that goal, which is to at least
have enough to get me through that [month without any cash coming in]."
For Ashlee, having that cushion in savings would decrease her reliance on
credit cards and alleviate stress. Given the seasonal ups and downs in
Ashlee's financial situation, especially since Adrian lost his job, it is difficult to formulate, much less stick to, a budget.

All of the families we spoke with live on incomes considerably below the
American median.[18] All face the pressures of raising kids in a city with
high living costs while juggling work and family demands. Where do they
work and how much are they earning? How do they choose to allocate
their limited resources? When there is money left over after the bills are
paid, where is the surplus going? How important is the large infusion of
cash from the EITC?

Our goal in this chapter is to trace the flow of money in lower-wage
working households. As indicated above, we first present average monthly
expense and income figures calculated from detailed financial descriptions of expenditures over the prior year. However, as Ashlee Reed's story
shows, averages can be misleading. So we go beyond these figures to
describe the ups and downs families experience over the course of the
year. Few of our families enjoy predictable incomes and expenditures. Job

loss and fluctuations in hours are common, as are unexpected spikes in expenses. Uncertainty is not the exception; it is the rule.

We asked parents to recount their finances in great detail. We tried to account for every dollar that came in, every dollar they spent, and every outstanding IOU. Although it might seem inconceivable to some middle-class readers, many parents were able to provide us with this detailed accounting of their financial lives without much reference to documentation beyond an occasional glance at a credit card statement or utility bill. The strength of the financial recall of the poor puts the spotlight on one potential benefit of living under the constraints of a tight budget.[19] While social scientists have found that being impoverished can be mentally taxing—focusing so much on how to meet immediate needs can create a scarcity of attention for other tasks, like long-term financial planning— the flip side of this coin may be a facility with mental account keeping of the monthly cash flow that would floor many middle-class Americans.[20]

ORDINARY WORKING PEOPLE

Our families are among the more fortunate of America's lower-income households—they have worked enough during the past year to warrant sizable tax credit refunds from the government. These workers are employed in a variety of jobs that keep the local economy running. But these jobs often require few educational credentials and provide limited monetary rewards.

Some work in restaurants, prepping food in the kitchen or taking orders from sit-down customers. Others serve as receptionists and file clerks. Like Ashlee Reed, some take care of children, while others help the sick and disabled elderly in roles as home health aides, certified nurse's assistants, and medical technicians. In short, these are the ordinary working people who feed the rest of us, ring up our orders and hand over our change, sort our paperwork, watch our kids, care for our older relatives or us when we're sick, and provide many of the other services that are a daily backdrop to our lives.

Table 1 shows the range of jobs held by the parents we interviewed. Almost all work in some type of service occupation. About half hold jobs

Table 1 Respondents' and Spouses' Occupations over the Prior Twelve Months

Occupational Classification	N	Examples of Jobs
Office and administrative support	24	Auto shop receptionist, community college office worker
Education, training, library	23	Head Start staff, teacher's aide
Food preparation, serving	17	Dunkin' Donuts worker, pizza parlor cook
Sales	12	Convenience store clerk, Radio Shack salesperson
Building and grounds cleaning	11	School custodian, housekeeper, office cleaner
Health care support	11	Home health aide, medical assistant, nurse assistant
Transportation and material moving	9	Bus driver, elderly meal deliverer, truck driver
Health care practitioners, technicians	6	Nutritionist, medical coder, emergency medical technician
Construction and extraction	6	Painter, carpenter
Installation, maintenance, and repair	5	Cable TV installer, auto mechanic
Personal care and service	5	Hairdresser, child caregiver
Production	3	Baker, laundromat manager, curtain factory supervisor
Management	3	Assistant building manager, property manager
Business and financial operations	2	Seasonal worker at tax preparation business
Community and social service	2	Unemployment counselor
Total occupations[a]	139	

NOTE: Occupational classifications derived from Bureau of Labor Statistics occupational categories.

[a] Occupations total greater than the number of respondents (115) because some individuals hold more than one job, and for some married couples both partners have held employment in the past year.

in offices, restaurants, or child care centers. Most of the administrative workers are support staff, such as receptionists or clerical workers. Almost all of those in education work as preschool teachers, as public school teacher's assistants, or in day care centers.

Among these working-poor households we heard a recurring wish for *better* employment. All desire higher pay and benefits—vacation time, paid sick leave, and a retirement plan. More than that, they want stable hours, job security, some flexibility, full-time hours, and greater respect from employers and their clientele. Mostly, though, they just want steady jobs with a paycheck they can count on—and this was in 2007, before they felt the effects of the Great Recession. One in ten had experienced involuntary unemployment at some point during the prior year. Others, like Ashlee, had boyfriends, their children's fathers, or kin who lost jobs as well. With network support often vital to their financial survival, families felt the pinch of these job losses too.

The service workers we spoke with complained the most about the lack of predictability in their schedules. Rose Alvarez, an immigrant from El Salvador who is raising two teens with limited help from their father, tries hard to put in forty hours a week as a home health aide. Even when she has a full client load, she tries to pick up extra shifts when other aides call in sick. Yet clients come and go, so Rose's hours can change suddenly and dramatically. She explained, "Sometimes I work only five hours a day, so that's no good. But the reason is because when the people get more sick, they get put in a nursing home. Some of them, they go and pass away. . . . Sometimes I lost ten hours in one week." Rose tries to work as much as she can, but she ultimately has limited control over her schedule. Others have schedules that are more predictable, but the work is seasonal. Some have jobs that depend on favorable weather conditions or a strong economy, such as construction work and house painting. These jobs made financial planning a challenge.

It is an article of faith for most of these families that work will lead to upward mobility. With the arrival of tax season, workers can point to their refunds as evidence that it's worth sticking it out at their jobs. Most insist that their economic situations will improve someday, even if they are not sure how. Some simply believe that, if they stay at a given job long enough, they'll eventually get a raise or an increase in hours. Others predict steady movement up the job ladder—from a nurse's assistant to a medical technician to a registered nurse, for example—imagining they'll somehow manage to acquire the necessary certifications to claim the better-paying occupations they are aspiring to. Some have little hope for mobility in their current occupations but believe that they will manage to find a better job sooner or later. These low-wage employees have not given up on the American Dream.

THE BALANCE SHEET

We interviewed parents who claimed a relatively large earned income tax credit (EITC), which meant they had worked a considerable number of hours in the prior year. Ashlee Reed, whom we met at the beginning of this chapter, had earned approximately $27,500 annually in gross income, placing her above the mean in our sample—the families we studied earned roughly $22,000 on average. But nearly a quarter (24 percent) earned less than $15,000 annually.[21]

Table 2 shows income by marital status for parents in the study. Because the EITC has somewhat higher eligibility thresholds for married couples, the single parents we spoke with have lower incomes than the married couples do on average.[22] The typical married couple in our study reports about $29,000 in total income, while the unmarried parents have about $19,000. A few families report somewhat higher incomes than EITC eligibility thresholds should allow. Often these are cohabiters where one partner claims the kids and files as "head of household," just as the IRS forms direct (there is no separate filing status for cohabiters). When Ashlee and Adrian file their taxes, for example, Adrian claims one of their children while Ashlee claims the other two, each filing separately because they are unmarried. Others do not report all of their income to the IRS but were willing to disclose it to us. Income that goes unreported to the IRS is not common, and it isn't usually substantial.

As described in the introductory chapter, families' incomes routinely fall short of their expenses. To get by despite this shortfall in earned income, they rely on other sources of support—ex-partners who pay child support, kin and romantic partners who contribute, and government sup-

Table 2   Respondents' Annual Household Earnings, by Marital Status

Annual Earnings	Single (%)	Married (%)	All (%)
Less than $15,000	32	10	24
$15,001–$20,000	33	8	24
$20,001–$25,000	12	15	13
$25,001–$30,000	7	10	8
$30,001–$35,000	13	28	18
More than $35,000	3	30	12
Number of respondents	75	40	115

NOTE: *Marital status* refers to respondents' tax filing status with the IRS. Single respondents used the "head of household" filing status, and married respondents used the "married, filing jointly" filing status. Percentage totals do not equal 100 percent because of rounding.

port such as TANF or unemployment insurance. One in six (17 percent) of the households in our study receives child support through the formal system; these payments augment the average household income by an average of $230 for those who receive it. However, those receiving informal child support get even more: $360 on average each month. Some count on assistance from friends and family during lean months—one in five families (20 percent) get financial help from kin or romantic partners, gleaning $194 per month on average. Only a small number of families claimed anything in the past year from cash welfare, TANF, or other programs paying cash benefits, such as Supplemental Security Income (SSI). Many, however, claimed some benefits from SNAP. Taken together, TANF, SSI, and SNAP (when counted as cash) add an average of $271 monthly.[23] Table 3 summarizes the effect of these contributions and government benefits on the typical monthly budget.

As the next chapter will show, tax time is long anticipated and, for many, the only time during the year when income is sure to exceed expenses. Unlike the legions of upper- and middle-class families across America who dread filing their taxes (and who may wait until the April 15 deadline), lower-wage earners as a group tend to file as early as possible, at the end of January or early February when their W-2s come in the mail.

Table 3   Respondents' Average Monthly and Annual Incomes, by Marital Status

	Single	*Married*	*All*
Monthly Income			
Monthly Earned Income (EI)	$1,562	$2,496	$1,887
EI + Child Support (CS)	$1,608	$2,519	$1,925
EI + CS + Gov't Benefits (Gov)[a]	$1,879	$2,861	$2,221
EI + CS + Gov + Kinship Support[b]	$2,013	$3,021	$2,363
Annual Income			
Annual Earned Income (EI ×12)	$18,744	$29,952	$22,644
Tax Refund[c]	$4,545	$4,952	$4,686
Annual EI + Tax Refund	$23,289	$34,904	$27,330
N	75	40	115

NOTE: *Marital status* refers to respondents' tax filing status with the IRS. Single respondents used the "head of household" filing status, and married respondents used the "married, filing jointly" filing status. Incomes are in 2007 dollars.
[a]Government benefits include TANF, SNAP, SSI, utility assistance, and unemployment insurance. They do not include the value of housing subsidies.
[b]Kinship support includes contributions from adults inside or outside the household (other than romantic partners) and informal child support payments.
[c]Tax refund includes the refundable EITC, the refundable child tax credit, and refunds of paycheck withholding. It includes both federal and state tax refunds.

These working families say tax season feels like "hitting the lottery." It is no wonder. Their refund checks include the earned income tax credit, other federal tax credits, and any taxes overpaid throughout the year (either from their additional withholding or through employers' overestimation of owed taxes), minus any taxes owed. On average, this federal refund check from the US Treasury, taken together with their state refund check, which may contain additional state and local tax credits, boosts the family budget by $4,686 for parents in our study. It is difficult to overstate the importance of tax time in their financial lives. The average refund is equivalent to nearly three months of earnings.[24] Recall that the modern EITC was originally designed to allow a family of three with a minimum-wage, full-time, full-year job to escape poverty, and, for most of the families we spoke to, it does.[25] However, these workers also drew on the extensive in-kind safety net that bolsters needy families' resources: SNAP; the Special Supplemental

Nutrition Program for Women, Infants, and Children (WIC); housing assistance of various sorts; and public health insurance such as MassHealth.

In Massachusetts, SNAP is available to families with children who have incomes under 200 percent of the poverty line.[26] This means that a single parent with two children who has $2,767 or less in monthly income could receive some benefits from the program.[27] In 2006, our study's tax year, a family of three would have been eligible for a maximum $399 per month in food stamps if they had no earnings. Each dollar earned reduces the maximum benefit by 25 cents. Because eligibility for this program continues to be based on need, many of the households in our study qualified for a modest amount from SNAP.[28]

WIC helps pregnant and nursing women and children under five to obtain milk, eggs, baby formula, cereal, and other nutritious foods. The income limit for this program is 185 percent of the poverty line. This program offers in-kind benefits only, but the cash value of the monthly food package can total as much as $100 per month if two members of the household qualify.[29]

Housing subsidies generally come in one of two forms, public housing or housing choice ("Section 8") vouchers. These are not entitlements; they serve only a small fraction of those who are eligible. In many jurisdictions, wait lists for the voucher program are closed or are opened for only a brief period of time when vouchers become available. Qualified applicants are then generally chosen by lottery, though especially needy households, such as those that are homeless, sometimes receive priority. Families pay a portion of their income (generally 30 percent after certain deductions) for rent, and the federal government picks up the rest.[30] Housing choice vouchers can be used to rent market-rate units, providing the landlord is willing to participate in the program, the rent isn't too high, and the unit can pass the housing authority's inspection.[31]

When we launched our study, Massachusetts was the only state in the country with a health insurance requirement (paving the way for the subsequent federal overhaul of the health insurance system). MassHealth, instituted in 2007, is free of charge to children under 300 percent and adults under 133 percent of the poverty line. Other lower-income residents can buy MassHealth insurance at discounted rates.[32] Consequently, many in our study had access to relatively affordable health insurance.

Some families we spoke with reported that someone in their household had drawn income from SSI. This is a federal disability program that offers benefits to disabled adults and their minor children who do not have the work history to qualify for SSDI (Social Security Disability Insurance) or workers' compensation—or to children with disabilities serious enough to qualify them for SSI had they been adults.[33] State offices determine eligibility for disability payments, but the federal government pays for most of the benefits (approximately one-quarter of recipients nationwide—including those in Massachusetts—live in a state that offers an additional supplement). To be eligible, an adult must be deemed so physically or mentally impaired as to be unable to work for at least the next twelve months. Earnings below $300 a month are seen as one form of evidence of the inability to work, and there is also a $2,000 asset limit (for an individual). The federal benefit rate in 2006, the year just prior to our study, was $603 per month for an individual claimant.[34] For children to qualify, they must live in a low-income household and have "marked and severe functional limitations" expected to last for at least a year.[35]

Figure 2 shows the number of families in our study who report deriving income from each of these government programs.[36] In this sample of working families, with incomes ranging from well below to significantly above the poverty line, some were eligible for an array of government assistance programs above and beyond the EITC, but others were not, at least at the time of the study. While fifty-one families (44 percent) said they had used cash welfare (AFDC or TANF) at some point in the past, only nine families (8 percent) told us that they had received any cash welfare in the last year. In contrast, forty-five families (39 percent) had received SNAP, and a majority, seventy-three families (64 percent), got some form of housing assistance—a rate that is more than two times the national average among eligible households. In twenty-five families (22 percent), someone received SSI. Thirty-three households (29 percent) drew benefits from the WIC program. Eight families (7 percent) claimed unemployment insurance for a portion of the year. As indicated above, because our families lived in Massachusetts, in most—seventy-nine—households (69 percent) at least someone was covered by government-subsidized health insurance (usually MassHealth).

These working families are not dependents in the colloquial sense, but they are nonetheless recipients of substantial government assistance, even

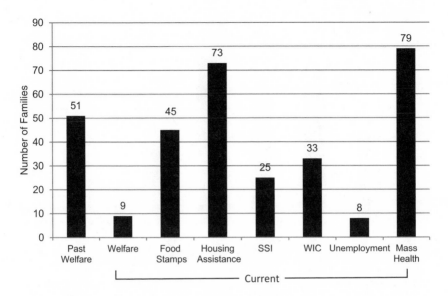

Figure 2. Number of families in sample using government assistance programs.
N = 115 families.

beyond the EITC. Figure 3 shows the number of programs families are currently claiming in addition to the EITC. Only sixteen of our families (14 percent) receive the EITC alone, while fifty-four families (47 percent) draw on three or more government support programs in addition to tax credits. Together, figures 2 and 3 show that the government safety net for the working poor extends well beyond the EITC, especially in the city of Boston, where housing costs are unusually high and housing subsidies are in greater supply than elsewhere.

THE EXPENSE SIDE OF THE LEDGER

Despite these various sources of government assistance, expenses exceed income in the typical month for the families in our study (see table 4). The average household spends roughly six in ten dollars (59 percent) of their earnings for just three items: housing, food, and transportation. Note that even *after* taking into account housing subsidies and SNAP benefits,

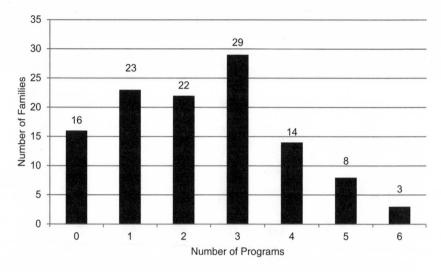

Figure 3. Number of government assistance programs currently used per family. N = 115 families. Count of government assistance programs excludes the EITC.

families typically spend nearly half (45 percent) of their wages just on housing and food.

Spending among the families in our sample is similar to that of other lower-income families nationwide. Our analysis of the Bureau of Labor Statistics' 2005 Consumer Expenditure Survey, when restricted to those respondents at or below 300 percent of the poverty line, showed that a household unit of three spent a monthly average of $381 on food at home (versus $398 for our sample), $90 on buying prepared food outside the home ($82 for our sample), $73 on clothing ($123 for our sample), $1,102 on housing expenses ($735 for our sample), $129 on medical costs ($68 in our sample), and $395 on transportation ($355 in our sample).[37] Thus the expenses among our sample of families are broadly representative of the allocations among disadvantaged families across the country.

Housing

As we've already noted, housing costs are higher than average in Boston and contribute heavily to the city's dubious distinction of being "one of the

Table 4 Respondents' Average Monthly Household Expenses

	Average, All Respondents	Average, Respondents with Cost	% Respondents with Cost	Average % of Monthly Budget
Housing costs				26%
Utilities	$139.97	$338.62	73.0%	
Rent or mortgage + utilities	$690.29	$708.78	97.4%	
Food costs				19%
Groceries	$420.26	$420.26	97.4%	
Eating out	$91.40	$104.59	84.3%	
Transportation				14%
Car expenses	$357.00	$743.52	62.6%	
Public transport/cabs	$31.11	$83.58	42.6%	
Medical expenses				3%
Insurance	$57.74	$188.97	28.7%	
Out-of-pocket medical costs	$13.83	$27.43	50.4%	
Other household expenses				19%
Phone (mobile and landline)	$102.18	$123.69	86.1%	
Child care	$89.29	$191.09	43.5%	
Children's school expenses	$43.52	$61.81	60.0%	
Children's clothing	$95.44	$105.67	73.0%	
Adult clothing	$55.51	$73.08	68.7%	
Adult hair care	$26.52	$44.20	54.8%	
Toiletries/cleaning supplies	$46.99	$54.30	39.1%	
Laundry	$28.95	$60.30	10.4%	
Furniture	$10.77	$69.98	13.9%	
Appliances	$6.13	$44.68	12.2%	
Nonessential purchases				13%
Entertainment	$76.06	$177.90	84.3%	
Cable TV	$41.64	$54.86	73.9%	
Internet	$22.09	$36.70	56.5%	
Cigarettes	$28.13	$87.60	30.4%	
Alcohol	$9.29	$34.93	25.2%	
Lottery tickets	$7.94	$30.11	35.7%	
Other	$158.52	$343.24	95.7%	
Debt payments				6%
Credit cards	$73.61	$175.66	38.3%	
Medical bills	$5.73	$37.04	14.8%	
Student loans	$16.05	$93.74	16.5%	
Other debt	$77.21	$267.67	13.0%	
Total monthly expenses	$2,683.19[a]			

NOTE: N = 115 families. *Debt payments* refers to the amount paid toward debts, not how much is owed. Expense values are in 2007 dollars.

[a]This total does not double count utilities, which appear twice in this column.

most expensive places to live in the U.S.," as noted in *Forbes*.[38] On average, our families earn $1,887 each month, while an average two-bedroom apartment in Greater Boston costs $1,345 per month, and a three-bedroom unit averages $1,609.[39] So, how do they manage? Very few— 27 percent—are paying the full cost of the housing that they occupy. While 64 percent get some form of subsidy, another 11 percent are doubled up, living with family or friends.[40] Housing expenses consume approximately one-quarter of the typical family budget; this is substantial, but it is a fraction of what the figure would be if all paid market rent. The reason so many Boston-area lower-income families have subsidies is that those without one are often priced out of Boston altogether. The Boston Housing Authority, which administers most subsidies, estimates that it provides a subsidy to approximately 10 percent of all city residents.[41]

In contrast to renters, the home owners among our families pay a premium for their stake in the American Dream. On average, they devote $2,101 per month toward their housing costs—including the mortgage, insurance, and taxes—considerably higher (by more than a thousand dollars) than renters who pay the full market price. Subsidized renters pay the least for their housing expenses, averaging under $400. Adding together housing and utilities, home owners pay about twice what unsubsidized renters pay and five times what those with subsidized housing must lay out each month.

Food

After housing costs, food takes the second-largest bite out of a typical family's budget—$512, or 19 percent on average (see table 4). Tamara Bishop—a thirty-three-year-old black single mother who works as an assistant preschool teacher, gets $70 from SNAP each month to help feed her four children—two teenage daughters and two sons still in grade school. But that benefit buys less than a week's worth of groceries, leaving her to cover the rest of the family's food purchases with cash: "You know, my kids, like they like to eat! I cook every day . . . and I don't even buy . . . things that they want, like snacks and stuff. I buy 'food food.' Sometime, like, especially the end of the month, it's like, like last month there was like nothing in the refrigerator; I mean nothing. I had to like borrow the money [from my mom]." Tamara usually spends $250 in cash on groceries each month in addition to SNAP.

Because the working poor and near-poor often live with financial uncertainty, it was not uncommon for us to hear stories of families buying in bulk at discount stores and filling pantries and deep freezers, especially at tax time. These stockpiles help to ensure that food won't run short when money gets tight. Brenda Hutchinson, a thirty-eight-year-old, married, white school lunch aide, explains that, when the tax refund check comes, she takes her two daughters—ages four and eleven—to BJ's Warehouse, a wholesale chain that sells groceries and other items in bulk. This year, they spent over $400 on meat, which she stores in her mother's stand-alone freezer. They also bought large quantities of pizza bagels and cases of soup. She tells us, "I just keep them like stocked up so you don't have to worry about running out of food, you know?" That families use their EITC money in this way reflects the reality that these parents often have too little income to make it through the month, even with SNAP.

Mariella Ambrosini, a white fifty-seven-year-old whose daughters, ages fifteen, twenty, and twenty-three, all live at home, has severe emphysema and relies on her husband's seasonal earnings as a construction foreman as well as her SSI check to get by. When visiting Mariella in her third-floor walkup in East Boston, we immediately notice that just inside the door is a large metal shelf overflowing with pasta, canned goods, chips, and cereal. She tells us, "My big expense is food, my refrigerator gotta be full all the time. Otherwise I get very depressed." For Mariella and many others, food represents security, and the state of Mariella's pantry serves as an important barometer of how she is faring financially.

Other Necessities

Transportation consumes $388 per month, or 14 percent of the typical family's monthly budget. About two-thirds of our families (63 percent) have cars and spend an average of $744 monthly on automobile-related expenses, including car loans, car insurance, gas, maintenance, excise fees, parking fees, and tickets (see table 4). In Boston, public transit is extensive, and more than four in ten families (43 percent) were entirely reliant on it when we spoke with them (including a few with cars that they could not afford to fix or insure). But buses and trains do not always run on time. And low-income neighborhoods in Boston are underserved by subway lines. Thus getting to work or to the store can mean navigating several bus routes, or riding a bus and then the subway.[42] Using public transportation saves money but costs time—time parents can sometimes ill afford while juggling child care or multiple jobs.

Although our families live in Massachusetts and have access to MassHealth, they still report some medical expenses: $72, or 3 percent of total monthly income on average. As noted above, by virtue of their incomes, many qualify for free or subsidized health care coverage under MassHealth. For the 29 percent who pay something toward their health care, the expense is relatively small—$189 on average—probably because so many receive at least a partial subsidy.

In their study of spending practices of low-income single mothers, Edin and Lein found that, when money ran short at the end of the month, the phone bill was one obligation that families let slide—telephone service cost their households only about $30 on average in the mid-1990s, when they conducted their research.[43] What is considered a household "necessity" clearly changes over time; now, a decade and a half later, phone costs have spiraled—averaging $102 among our families. Most (86 percent) have either a cell phone or a landline, and many (71 percent) have both. The cell phone bill is often a high priority because many are locked into one- or two-year contracts with their providers and can be assessed a hefty fee for late payments. Some have pay-as-you-go plans; while this option is relatively expensive for anyone who uses his or her phone very often, they pose no risk of broken contracts and potential late fees.

Child care and educational expenses consume $133 of the typical family's monthly budget. The fifty families with child care expenses (44 percent) pay only $191 each month on average, far below the market rate, because many have managed to secure subsidies. Yet for some, even the assistance they qualify for does not feel like enough. When administrative assistant Corine Samuels, forty-nine, black, and separated from her husband, took in her four-year-old granddaughter, Tamika, she did not anticipate the bite of her share of the child care bill: "They told me when I had custody of my granddaughter that . . . I wouldn't have to pay for child care; this year they told me I gotta pay child care. I have to pay $27.50 a week

for her to go to child care. [The caseworker] told me, 'Oh, that ain't nothing!' It's . . . nothing if I had it. When you don't have it, it's something! If
you don't have it, [even] $5 is a lot."

Clothing constituted $151 of the typical family's monthly budget. When
it comes to shopping for themselves, many parents rely on discount stores
such as Target, T.J.Maxx, and Marshalls, but usually only when they absolutely need to shop for something—an outfit for a job interview, a uniform
for work, or sneakers when the old pair has holes. Occasionally, though,
parents will treat themselves to an inexpensive item of clothing that they
don't strictly need. Twenty-six-year-old Rita Ramirez, a Hispanic hairdresser and mother of two children, ages one and nine, whose boyfriend
lives out of state, says, given how hard she works, she believes that she's
earned the right to a few new $7 T-shirts or a $15 pair of flip-flops.

While adults can put off buying clothes for years, growing children
often require new clothes—with chilly Boston winters and humid summers, most children require some new items each spring and fall. Usually,
our parents scour the city for sales, supplement with hand-me-downs, and
solicit their relatives for clothing as Christmas and birthday gifts.

Another $158 each month goes to hair care, toiletries, and cleaning
supplies. This includes trips to the laundromat; families who don't have
washing machines at home spend $60 each month on average to wash
and dry their clothes. Buying or renting furniture or appliances isn't
uncommon; 14 percent of families made a furniture purchase or paid rent
on their furniture in the last year, while another 12 percent are making
payments on household appliances, such as washers, dryers, refrigerators,
or air conditioners.

Nonessential Spending

Though expenses generally exceed incomes, families still devote 13 percent
of their budgets to nonessentials (see table 4)—the rare personal indul-
gence, a drink at happy hour with coworkers, or a treat for the kids, usually
no more than a family trip to the arcade. For the most part, this spending
is done without apology—after all, they emphasize, for all their struggles,
they are *working* families, and being a worker gives one the right to
spend on a few special extras every now and then. In keeping with this

philosophy, more than eight in ten (84 percent) say they spend something on entertainment, mostly for DVDs, the occasional excursion to a family reunion, or a trip to the movie theater. In addition, half pay for Internet service; these parents typically justify the $37 average monthly cost by explaining that their children need the Internet for homework (although many may also use it for entertainment or to keep in touch with friends and family). Nearly three-quarters of all households have a cable television subscription, a quarter spend something on alcohol in a typical month, nearly a third buy cigarettes, and more than a third play the lottery. Almost all spend on other nonessentials as well: tithing to a church, purchasing pet food, buying gifts, or helping out needy family members or friends.

Debt Payments

Debt plays a pivotal role in the financial lives of these families, and we devote chapter 5 to this subject. For the purpose of creating an average monthly snapshot of their budgets, we asked parents to talk in depth about which debts they pay regularly, which are more hit or miss, and which are ignored altogether. The typical household pays $173 monthly toward outstanding debt, or 6 percent of monthly expenditures (see table 4). Note that this does not include rent or regular monthly payments on big-ticket items like furniture, appliances, or cars, which are categorized separately as household expenses. The 38 percent of families who make credit card payments dedicate an average of $176 per month to these bills; just under a third of families are paying on other kinds of debt, usually medical bills or student loans.

FINANCIAL UPS AND DOWNS

Averages mask important ebbs and flows in income and expenses. A few families with whom we spoke have a stable pattern of income and expenditure despite their lower earnings. Most, however, live financially precarious lives, without a substantial private safety net (like savings or access to significant financial assistance from kin), and are therefore sensitive to financial *shocks*—sudden shifts in income or expenses.

Many say they have almost come to expect that something will derail them financially at some point during the year. Jerry Morales lives with his wife, Tessa, their three children, ages five, seven, and fourteen, and his mother in a housing project in South Boston. This white thirty-two-year-old works two jobs—full time during the week in the mailroom at a community college and on the weekend as a truck driver for a bakery, a 2:00 A.M. shift delivering doughnuts. Sometimes he gets discouraged by how surprise expenses seem to crop up with such frequency. "My dream basically is to get a house and be settled financially, everything. That's all I ever wanted. No matter how much we try, there's always something that just kicks us in the butt." Jerry's wife, Tessa, recalls the year when they faced a fourfold financial nightmare. First, she lost her waitressing job. Then "My mom passed away. I just had [my youngest daughter]. Jerry got sick [and couldn't work]. So, it was a stressed year."

A car repair, a family member in need, or even something as small as a parking ticket can be the jolt that "kicks us in the butt" when a household is living paycheck to paycheck. Family income may likewise dip abruptly because of lost hours at work or a layoff. Some life events, like illness or pregnancy, increase expenses while decreasing one's ability to earn. In the face of a financial shock, families go without, borrow, skip bills, or turn to their credit cards. A generous tax credit in February can halt the downward spiral or—for those who save some of the refund—prevent a subsequent one.

STRUGGLES WITH GOVERNMENT SUPPORT

By their own definition, these families have fulfilled their part of the American social contract: they work and take care of their children to the best of their ability. As chapter 3 will show, they disdain those who are dependent on welfare.[44] Because they view themselves as upstanding citizens and taxpayers who contribute into the system, they believe that they are worthy of a little help from the government—a hand up—when times are tough. This doesn't mean that the help they believe that they deserve is always forthcoming. Despite the plethora of programs one might, in theory, be able to draw on, in their view assistance is often wanting or slow in coming.

Some complain about eligibility and benefits that are based on gross, rather than net, income. Tanya Salazar, a twenty-eight-year-old married black mother of three who range in age from five months to twelve years, works at a clothing factory. She complains, "This apartment['s rent] is based on my income. It's based on my gross, not my net. How can you base my living expenses on money I'm not going to see? Yeah, you know that's why they took my Section 8 away, because gross I was getting like $1,000 [every two weeks]. After taxes I was only getting seven-something. And then, when you just added up my expenses alone, yeah, I had change left over, but once you took the [Section 8] certificate, I'm paying $1,400 [in] rent. It just doesn't add up."

Talisha Watson, a black twenty-five-year-old who lives with her boyfriend, Daven, and her elementary school–aged daughter, Jasmine, recently lost her job as a medical coder. She shares a similar story.

> I have one kid, and they [the welfare department] feel I was making enough money. I didn't feel like I was making enough money. I said, "Okay, you count gross pay. That is a lot. But let's talk about after taxes. . . ." I am paying health insurance . . . and then you have dental. . . . You have your 401k. . . . And God forbid if I work overtime. . . . The taxman get that back. I don't see that money. You know, so it's like . . . I should be able to splurge on something. . . . I work for this, but nooooo!

Talisha decries programs that take, rather than give, as earnings rise, and is even angrier about programs where eligibility abruptly ends once income exceeds a certain level. She echoes what is a key source of frustration for many: doing what's right—trying to better oneself through earnings—earns you a slap if not a shove out the door from "the system." Work ought to be rewarded, not punished, they insist. Ironically, the EITC also declines as earnings rise once families reach the phaseout range in benefits, but the way the total tax refund check is calculated is fairly mysterious to most. Further, the "refund" is adjusted for the ebbs and flows in earnings only once a year. Thus the declines in SNAP or one's housing subsidy are experienced as a "punishment" for working, while any eventual reduction in tax credits is not.

Nonetheless, the most common complaint is that most programs are built around the assumption of a steady income rather than on the ups and downs that are endemic to the financial lives of the working poor. Marissa Lopez is a thirty-one-year-old Hispanic single mother of three, ages five, eleven, and thirteen. She is relatively well educated—she has completed some college course work and is certified as a medical assistant, so her wages are higher than those of most. The catch is that she has not been able to get a full-time job in her field. Instead she's worked for a temp agency for the past seven years, filling in at various hospitals and doctors' offices. It's hard to predict how long any given assignment will last or how many hours she'll get. And there are sometimes weeks, even months, between assignments. "Sometimes I'm able to get forty hours a week. Other times I'm lucky if I get eight hours a week," she explains. SNAP has added to, rather than eased, the ups and downs in income, because the benefits are based on the prior month's earnings. Worse still, each time she is deemed ineligible because of an unusually flush paycheck, she must apply again during the next lean month and then wait for her case to be approved, an often lengthy process. In her words: "My income is not always stable. So one month I could be eligible for food stamps and the next month I'm *not* eligible for food stamps." Marissa must be diligent in updating her caseworker, since failure to report a new job, or any substantial increase in hours or wages, can result in steep sanctions. In some states offenders are barred from future receipt of SNAP benefits.[45]

Bitterness over "unfair treatment" can flow from these experiences. Luanna Fields, a white woman who smiles as she declines to tell us her age, is an education coordinator who is currently working on her master's degree at a local university. She lives with her husband, Colin, the grocery store manager she married a year ago, and her teenage son, Dustin, in a single-family home on a quiet, dead-end street in Malden, a lower-middle-class inner suburb north of Boston. Luanna and Colin have a rent-to-own agreement with their landlord.

The Fields ask us to arrive at eight o'clock on a Saturday morning so that Luanna can keep her promise to take an elderly friend shopping at 10:30 A.M. We move to the kitchen, which is spick-and-span, noting the nautical theme—the lighthouse knickknacks mingling with Colin's collection of wine bottle holders. We sit in the breakfast nook, which looks out over the neighbor's backyard, where Luanna shares strong opinions about the help she gets—and doesn't get—from the government. "I think that people like us that are the middle class [can't get anything from the government]. If you're really rich and you have all this kind of money, then you—I think that they make out somehow better [than us]. And then the lower class, it seems like even though they're all struggling, they get, you know, all those [benefits]. But the middle class, it just seems like we get stomped on. . . . Either you make it or you don't, you know. Trial and error." Until she married her husband, Luanna earned just enough to escape poverty, yet she views herself as part of the middle class—a group that she feels is left out, "stomped on," by the system.

Similarly, thirty-six-year-old Juana Vega, a married Hispanic mother to eleven-year-old Milo, works as a disability specialist at a local preschool and conveys her deep sense of frustration that, because they are doing the right thing (going to work, attempting to support themselves), her family is getting less than those who are less deserving:

> Because we're like a working family, we're like in the middle of everything. Like people who, like my sister-in-law, they're poor by the eyes of the government, they get all this money—welfare—and they get fuel assistance and they get food stamps. And they don't work because it's easy that way. Why go to work and make [money on your own]—she's getting her gas paid. I'm not. I can't get my gas paid because I'm working, you know? And sometimes I feel like, all these people getting all this money without—by lying and doing *nothing*, and the people like me that live check by check. . . . I work so hard, I pay so much in taxes, and maybe it'd be easy if I lie [down] too and just— you know what? I'm gonna live on welfare, I stay home, watch TV all day and I get paid [by welfare], you know? This is a working family; let's give it a relief!

Juana's claims are far from accurate—welfare benefits get a family to only half of the poverty line even in an unusually generous state like Massachusetts, and they are subject to strict time limits and participation requirements (which don't allow one to "stay home, watch TV all day"). And, other than the sales tax imposed on certain purchases, Juana gets back more in her tax refund than she pays in. In fact, the EITC and other tax credits that families like Juana's receive are at least as generous as welfare is to those with no outside income. But this is beside the point. Poor or near-poor workers like Juana often see themselves as the beleaguered "middle class," stuck between those who are eligible for what they imagine are big handouts and those who can truly afford to go without such assistance.

SUPPORT FROM FAMILY AND FRIENDS

People often turn to their families and friends for help when times get tough, as is true among those in our study. Since anthropologist Carol Stack's seminal 1974 ethnographic work *All Our Kin*, which showed how crucial kin were in poor families' daily struggles for economic survival, the accepted wisdom is that family and friends play a key role in lower-income people's lives, buffering them from financial hardship.[46] But statistics actually show it is the more advantaged who draw the most resources from their networks. They are more likely than the poor to have friends and family with substantial assistance to offer.[47] This does not mean that the kin support that lower-income families do draw on is unimportant. While it is true that such support seldom compensates for the large gap in resources between the poor and the better off—and almost never offers the leg up that families need to buy cars, make down payments on homes, or save for college or retirement—kin support is often vital for routine survival.

Kin don't usually offer a once-in-a-blue-moon handout when times get particularly tough. Many of our families are involved in ongoing recipro-cal and one-way exchanges with family and friends. Being embedded in such a social network, however, comes with the risk that someone else's financial woes can quickly become one's own.[48] Given the financial situa-tions of the households we studied, they are only rarely the most well off in their networks; many are on the receiving end the majority of the time, garnering small loans of a few dollars here and there and, quite frequently, toys, clothes, meals, and special extras for their children. The $20 bor-rowed here and there to keep the lights on or the extra bag of groceries that appears at the doorstep can't usually make up for a significant short-fall of income, but it can ease stress for households with budgets that come up short. It is important to reiterate, however, that help from family and friends is generally neither asked for nor offered to cover outstanding debts. This ultimately limits the value of kin, who may help to prevent a family from falling further into material hardship but don't—or perhaps can't—aid families when they're trying to dig out from under pressing financial obligations. Debt limits families' abilities to build assets, especially purchasing a home, or to get good credit terms on other big-ticket items like cars, or even to rent an apartment in a more desirable neighborhood, because of the impact on credit scores.

Dominique Henderson is a twenty-three-year-old, single, black mother of a preschool-aged daughter and works as a teacher's aide at a local school; she relies on a variety of people who offer her financial help from time to time. When she needed to buy living room furniture, a friend was willing to put the purchases on her credit card with the promise that Dominique would pay her back at tax time. Dominique also wants to save for a home. She's opened a bank account with her brother where she can deposit savings toward this long-term goal; keeping the account in her brother's name makes withdrawing the money for other purposes more difficult—and this is the point. Her sister lets Dominique use her bus pass that the sister only rarely puts to use (she has a car) to help her save money on transportation; Dominique says she can also borrow that car, or her brother's car, when she needs to. When she missed the deadline for financial aid at community college, Dominique's brother and sister each stepped up with $600 so that she could enroll that semester. When she attempted to reimburse them at tax time, they refused the money. Then her brother bought her a used car and paid the insurance on it for several months. "My brother—anything! He will do it for me." In a sense, Dominique's family and friends are her bank—extending loans and acting as creditors—but they don't charge interest and more readily forgive debts.

Dominique's kin are particularly helpful when it comes to providing for her three-year-old daughter, Tatiana. When Tatiana's swimming lessons went from $30 to $50 per eight-week session, Dominique told her daughter that she would have to quit, but Dominique's brother and sister offered to pay for the lessons. They knew how much their niece loved to swim. Dominique's cousin bought Tatiana a bed, and her brother got a mattress for it; to complete Tatiana's bedroom, Dominique's cousin bought the girl a TV. Her sister also buys clothing for Tatiana using her employee discount at the Gap. Dominique values her family's contributions, noting, "I get lucky."

The benefits that many of our families gain from their networks are not just financial—there are psychological benefits as well. When emergency medical technician LaWanda James, a twenty-three-year-old black single mother with a seven-year-old son, gets stressed from falling behind on bills, she finds solace in the knowledge that she can turn to her sister if she needs to: "My sister has always told me, 'Don't stress! As long as I have, you have.' So I have to say I've been blessed in that, since that I never really want or need for anything. And when it does get to that point, [my sister is] yelling at me like, 'Why didn't you ask me sooner? Here.'" Similarly, when we ask Debra McKinley, an engaged, twenty-eight-year-old white waitress and mother of two little girls, to estimate how much she owes her half sister, from whom she borrows most frequently, she laughs and exclaims, "My life! I couldn't put a dollar amount, you know. And the thing is, she doesn't put a dollar amount to it."

Although Dominique gets a great deal from her network, she also gives quite a lot. If she has money and someone asks for it, she'll always share if she can, even if she knows she's going to need it later on. "Do you know how much money like I have out that I still didn't get back?" she asks rhetorically before estimating that she's loaned out nearly $6,800 that hasn't been repaid. Eight hundred went to a close friend whom she trusts, so she thinks she will eventually get that money back, but she doesn't trust the other friends or her ex-boyfriend—additional recipients of her generosity—to act so responsibly. Her willingness to loan is an essential part of her ability to stay afloat; she loans out money when she can because she knows that if she were to need help, those who were able to would reciprocate. Because family members are generous with loans and gifts, she's more likely to have the income to spare when friends ask her for a loan. In many ways, her generous kin are a boon to her wider network of friends.

Shari Barfield, a married, black, thirty-six-year-old realtor, and mother of three—ages one, five, and twelve—gets cash only here and there from her kin, but she gleans a lot of in-kind support. Her mother watches her youngest child, so she doesn't need to pay for child care. When her daughter was born, her family sent loads of clothes and other baby items. Her sons also benefit from grandparents who "spoil them" with gifts every time they visit. Shari and her husband, in turn, help her brother out financially every now and then when he needs it—they don't expect him to reciprocate. Her husband also gives his ex-wife cash over and above his child support when his children need money for a school field trip or some other unexpected expense. The Barfields' finances, like those of so many, are not independent from those of their family and friends. Rather, they are intertwined, to greater and lesser extents, with money, clothes, toys, and food being passed around from those who can afford to help to those who need a hand.[49] Most of our families are receivers but also givers, sometimes simultaneously.

Not all, however, are so lucky to have family or friends to rely on. Carmen Sanchez, a forty-year-old preschool teacher and mother of four, who emigrated to the United States from Honduras, struggles to get any support from her children's father, from whom she's separated; their children range in age from three to seventeen. Every few weeks he'll give her $20—that is, unless she really pushes him. "I said, 'Look, I cannot be just doing the whole thing by myself. One week I will go [to the grocery store] and the other week you will go.' And he said, 'I don't have the money.' But, then, last week he gave me $100 because I said to him, 'Do you want me to look for another man that can feed my children?' He gave me the $100. I was surprised. I was really surprised. I went and paid my cell phone." In addition to struggles with her ex, Carmen and her mother battle over finances. Her mother lives on the second floor of Carmen's apartment and is supposed to be paying her $700 a month in rent. But it's been almost a year since the woman has paid at all. Recently, her mother promised she'd start paying $50 a week toward the rent; several weeks have passed since this offer was made, but Carmen has yet to see any cash. Rather than serving as a resource, Carmen's mother increases her financial burden.

Carmen's story hints at a darker side of personal ties. They not only smooth consumption in tough times but can be the *cause* of tough times: for example, a grandmother's finances can be thrown into disarray when she must suddenly assume responsibility for her grandchildren because her daughter is about to lose custody of her children to the state.[50] Unlike a bank, which is required to disburse money you've deposited, or a government entitlement that must support those meeting its criteria, support from family, friends, and exes can be unreliable and may be subject to their changing emotions and financial circumstances. Furthermore, as we alluded to above, these are often reciprocal relationships. One must be prepared to give as well as to receive. For families like those in our study, who already struggle to make ends meet, giving over even a small portion of their meager resources can be a major hit to an already-strained budget.

Looking at average earnings and spending patterns allows us to get a sense of how much a typical family—such as Ashlee Reed's—earns and spends over the course of a year. But we've also tried to give some sense of the variation that these monthly averages obscure. Many of our families are living near the financial edge. Because of low earnings and frequent financial surprises, only 11 percent are in good financial shape—they have minimal debts and substantial assets such as personal savings to provide a cushion should a bump in the financial road come along. Though all of the families in our study include at least one worker, earned income does not typically stretch to fully meet monthly expenses. Thus putting away a little each month in anticipation of a rainy day is difficult; families' financial planning more often includes figuring out which bill they can most easily neglect, not what they will do with their surplus funds.

Although most families we spoke to engage in some discretionary spending—a child's birthday present or a weekly lottery ticket—their budgets reveal a good deal of thrift as well. Despite their complaints that the "rules" of various government programs often exclude them or penalize them for working—this is an especially common claim among those with fluctuating work hours, like Marissa Lopez—these families are also the focus of a new, work-based safety net—the EITC—which allows them to claim cash assistance on top of their wages, and not in lieu of earnings, as was the case with the welfare system. And most get at least some in-kind assistance—SNAP, government-subsidized health insurance, a housing subsidy—as well. Many draw considerable aid from their networks, but network support is unevenly distributed and can sometimes be more of a hindrance than a help.

Are families spending and saving beyond what they can afford with their monthly earnings *because* they know the tax refund check is coming? We do see some evidence for this, particularly with heating bills, which parents can put off paying as most jurisdictions prohibit utility companies from discontinuing service because of nonpayment during the winter months. The February refund check happens to be perfectly timed to satisfy these obligations just before the restriction on shutoffs ends in March. Parents also sometimes say they buy Christmas presents on credit in anticipation of the tax refund. However, such behavior is not widespread. This may be because many are unsure of how much they will receive in their tax refund check from year to year—an issue we discuss in the next chapter. Further, financial shocks are so common that families often make spending decisions in response to events beyond their control (a job loss, new brake pads for the car, or a plumber's bill for a clogged pipe). Thus advanced planning of any kind is difficult.

Research on the psychology behind financial decision making has explored whether people make impulsive decisions, rather than well-thought-out plans, because of a lack of willpower, limited cognitive control, or limited attention due to other demands on one's "bandwidth" (how much of our mental capacity is available to us at any given time). Researchers consistently find that those who are operating under strain are less likely to make optimal decisions.[51] Like the dieter who, after avoiding the office candy bowl all day, breaks down at the end of the night and reaches in the freezer for a pint of ice cream, someone operating under tight financial conditions—trying to carefully monitor each dollar coming in and going out—may be more likely to make a rash spending decision that conflicts with her long-term financial goals. The key insight from this research is that a lack of willpower to avoid impulse buys or to align one's behavior to one's long-term financial goals is not characteristic of low-income individuals per se; rather the *condition* of scarcity takes up valuable bandwidth, in turn hampering optimal spending behavior.

Are the families in our study "overspending," even for the basics? Could they secure housing, food, and transportation more cheaply? The question of how much is "enough" is relative, at least in a rich nation like ours. Thus the closest we can come to answering this question is by comparing the expenses among our households to what other lower-income households in the United States spend to meet basic needs. As discussed above, parents in our sample are not engaging in profligate spending relative to their economically constrained peers across the country. While many could potentially trim some of their spending on the basics, not to mention the "extras" they sometimes consume, economic psychology helps us to understand why they fail to do so: making sound economic decisions that are consistent with long-term financial goals requires bandwidth that may be in short supply.

In future chapters, however, we'll argue that the "scarcity" perspective is not sufficient to explain much of the behavior we observe. Rather, spending and saving decisions are guided by the meaning households attach to the EITC. Further, as we will show, what outsiders may deem "frivolous" spending is often deeply meaningful to these parents—and arguably their children—and may have value that can exceed its monetary cost.

Let's revisit the question we opened this chapter with: Do families like the Reeds really need the additional resources the EITC offers? Ashlee Reed takes home about $1,600 in a typical month, but her bills exceed $2,800. Her finances are wildly out of balance right now because Adrian has no job and has run out of unemployment insurance. But, even when he's working, the money doesn't stretch far enough in the summers, when Ashlee goes for two months without a regular paycheck. Currently, shelter, food, transportation, and child care alone exceed her take-home pay.

Still, Ashlee does spend on some "extras," like cable TV and an occasional six-pack of beer. Some might argue that she should be saving that money to guard against circumstances like those in which she now finds herself. Ashlee would probably contend that she is a worker and thus deserves to splurge a little now and then.

At the outset of this chapter, we outlined two views of poverty. On the one hand, many point to the fact that the poverty line falls far short of what most Americans view as the minimum amount necessary to live on. But on the other, the American poor now consume more than ever before. In light of our data, both views of American poverty are correct. Using the lens of consumption, the Ashlee Reeds of the world are consuming more than the generation that came before, even though they hover around the official poverty line. But when we consider expenses relative to income—even for basic necessities like shelter, food, child care, and transportation—many working-poor households are living in the red at least some, and perhaps much, of the time. Since they work, they believe they shouldn't have to live as if they were impoverished. They believe that they earn the freedom from scrimping from time to time. And, as long as they are playing by the rules and working, they also deserve—at least in their own minds—a hand up from the government when income doesn't stretch to meet expenses.

2 Tax Time

"Thank God for tax season!" Debra McKinley exclaims, as she reflects back on the hardships of the past few months. Debra, a twenty-eight-year-old white mother of two, and her fiancé, Sonny, who is eight years older, have been behind on their bills all year. Sonny works seasonally as a carpenter, and until recently Debra worked on and off at a restaurant owned by her sister. But there is a familiar refrain to the balance sheet: even in a good month Debra and Sonny bring home barely enough to cover their expenses. This past month, Sonny earned nearly $3,000—a top-yielding month—but half of that went to pay the rent for their three-bedroom apartment in a Dorchester triple-decker. Of what remained, Debra spent $600 on groceries, $280 on electric and gas, $360 on insurance and fuel for the '95 Saturn, just over $100 for the cell phone bills, and another $120 for the cable television, home phone, and Internet bundle from Comcast. After those bills were paid, only $30 or so remained. Things were better before Debra had to quit her job because of her advancing pregnancy. But since then it's been tough; in the last few months, the couple has paid nothing on the thousands of dollars in outstanding credit card debt that Debra holds, or toward the medical bills resulting from Sonny's trips to the emergency room—he is a severe diabetic.

Debra and Sonny have known each other since childhood, but they started dating only after Debra's relationship with her children's father ended three years ago. They have been planning to get married for a while—Debra already wears a wedding ring, and they consider themselves husband and wife—but they decided to postpone the wedding after they learned that Debra was pregnant. She wants to fit in to the wedding dress that she had already purchased for the occasion prior to the pregnancy. Debra gets about $200 a month in child support for nine-year-old Lacey and four-year-old Holli, but they don't see their father that often. Sonny treats Debra's children as if they were his own.

Debra had a rough childhood. She and her sisters were removed from their home when she was eight because of her parents' drug addiction. They were placed in foster care and were subsequently abused by their foster parents. A woman Debra calls "Nana," the mother of a half sister on her father's side, agreed to take the girls after they ran away from the foster home. Nana was caring but could barely provide the basics. Debra is determined to give her children a better childhood than she herself had.

Each year in February, along with millions of other low-wage workers across the United States, Debra and Sonny each file their taxes at H&R Block. This past year, Debra got a refund of $2,150 because she qualified for the earned income tax credit (EITC). Debra claimed Holli as a dependent on her tax return; Sonny claimed Debra's daughter Lacey and got a substantial refund as well.[1] Debra knows little about the details of the tax code other than that the EITC is for "people who don't make too much money" and that your refund grows larger when you have more children. She feels that she "earned" that refund because she "works hard." Yet she doesn't feel that the money is only hers. She explains, "That's not my money. I have children. That is *their* money. I wouldn't get that if I didn't have them." Because she views the refund as the kids' money, and because she strives to give her girls the childhood she never had, Debra makes sure to spend at least some of the refund on Lacey and Holli.

This year, Debra used $700 of her refund check to repair her car, which needed a new transmission. She also paid off $200 in parking tickets that had accrued while the car was broken down on the side of the street; they hadn't had the money to have it towed, much less repaired. She bought a $200 bunk bed to create space in the girls' room for the baby on the way and spent an additional $300 "stocking up for the house" at Walmart, buying toilet paper, laundry detergent, soap, and other household goods in bulk.

But it was what she did with the rest—about $450—that brings a smile to Debra's face. She gave Lacey the kind of birthday that she herself could have only dreamed of as a girl. Debra had promised her daughter, who struggled in school, that if she passed the fourth grade she would treat her to "the best seafood restaurant in America" for her birthday. The girl, who loved seafood, kept her end of the bargain, and one might expect that when Lacey's birthday came the family of four would head to one of Boston's legendary seafood restaurants. But the best seafood restaurant in America is not in Boston. It is not even in Massachusetts. Indeed, Debra and Lacey's dream dinner was at the Red Lobster restaurant chain, which couldn't be found in Massachusetts. The closest location is in Connecticut.

Thus the family of four, together with another carload of relatives, embarked on a weekend excursion to Connecticut. The junket entailed an overnight stay in a hotel—a treat the family had only rarely experienced. Debra struggles to remember the exact price of that Red Lobster meal, but there is one price she clearly remembers: "The only price I know is my nine-year-old spent $68 on her meal and ate every bit of it. . . . I know that she had a good birthday. . . . I didn't have good birthdays [as a child]. Because of that . . . I try my hardest to give [my girls] anything that I've ever wanted and could not have."

Debra clearly enjoys the opportunity to give her kids something special, a chance afforded by her tax refund, because "they deserve it, my kids are wonderful." The months following tax time are the one time of the year when she can offer her children not just what they need but also some of what they *want*. She staunchly reserves some of her tax refund to dote on her girls, something that she can't often do during the rest of the year. Because of their trip to Connecticut, Debra spent more than double the proportion of her refund on her daughter's birthday than the average household spent on such treats. But the memory of Lacey's delight in that overflowing plate of seafood—the thrill of being able to give her child an experience that she herself had never had—was worth every penny to Debra. Next year, when she's had the baby and is working again, she hopes to use the refund to take the family on their first-ever weeklong vacation—

she even fantasizes about Disney World. But she isn't sure how the refund might be affected by the changes in her circumstances. She has had to spend months out of work because of the difficult pregnancy. Plus, she's getting married, and she's about to have her third child. All of these factors will affect the tax credits she is eligible to receive. She hopes that her tax refund will grow. "Hopefully it will double!" she exclaims.

The EITC is now the largest antipoverty program for families with children in the United States: this tax credit alone could be as large as $5,372 for a family with two children in 2013.[2] The EITC and the other major refundable tax credit, the child tax credit (CTC), push more families above the official poverty line than either SNAP or housing subsidies, if counted as income. Because of these programs almost 9.5 million adults and nearly 5 million children—3.1 million of these children from the EITC alone—made it above the poverty line.[3] In 2011, the child poverty rate was more than four percentage points lower when counting the EITC.[4] In contrast, TANF alone does not get any household it serves even close to the poverty line.[5]

In 2011, tax filers could receive the credit as long as their adjusted gross income did not exceed $40,964 for a head of household with two qualifying children ($46,044 for married couples).[6] The maximum credit was $5,751 (with three or more qualifying children). The amount of the credit increased with earned income for those making less than about $13,000 (with two or more qualifying children); it leveled off between roughly $13,000 and $17,000; and then it gradually phased out for those with higher earnings.[7] Each year, the EITC is adjusted to account for inflation. The credit is administered through the IRS and comes with the federal tax refund.[8]

The total tax refund—which can include refundable federal tax credits like the EITC and the child tax credit, state tax credits, and the return of funds overwithheld from paychecks during the year—can constitute a very large portion of a family's total annual income. A single mother of two earning $7.25 per hour at a full-time job could qualify for a federal EITC of $5,036 in 2011. This amounts to about one-third of her annual income. She could also claim $1,725 from the child tax credit. Among those we spoke with, the average refund for the 2006 tax year (collected in 2007)

was $4,686, the equivalent of three months' earnings.[9] The EITC, there-
fore, provides a substantial pay raise for parents who are working but poor.

Tax time has become the highlight of the year for many of modest
means, often likened to Christmas, winning the lottery, or even an act of
divine intervention. Because of often excruciatingly tight monthly budgets, the arrival of the refund brings a palpable sense of relief. Finally, an
economically strapped family can catch up on those outstanding debts
rather than dodge the bill collectors. Nine in ten of our households have
some sort of debt, and 60 percent have credit card debt. As figure 4 shows,
fully a quarter of all refund dollars are devoted to debt payoff; those who
put anything toward debt typically reduce their debt load by half.[10] To buy
relief from the financial pressures that are likely to come in the months
ahead, families also take the opportunity to stockpile, buying basics such
as toilet paper in bulk—enough for several weeks, if not months. They
stock up on food—filling the pantry and the stand-alone freezer to overflowing. And why not pay ahead on the car insurance or even the rent?
Stockpiling, paying ahead, and enjoying the simple pleasure of being able
to meet one's obligations in full for a few months—all of which we have
included under the label "Current Consumption"—amount to nearly a
fourth (24 percent) of families' allocations of their refunds.[11]

The EITC offers its beneficiaries complete freedom over how to disburse this large sum. Some might view this as a license for irresponsible
consumer behavior. "Treats" do consume 11 percent of all refund dollars.[12]
Usually, it's a prized extra for a child or the purchase of a priceless
experience—like a meal at Red Lobster. Dreams of a Disney World vacation, while commonly held, were not realized by any of our households via
the refund.

While Debra's long-term aims haven't yet stretched much beyond
Disney, she is unusual in this regard. Most parents we spoke with tie the
EITC to strong aspirations for upward mobility. Accordingly, 17 percent of
refund dollars are saved, while 21 percent are devoted to expenditures that
our families explicitly link to getting ahead: furthering their educations,
doing home repairs, and especially purchasing or repairing a car and
investing in other durable goods that may save time or money or enhance
well-being (e.g., a stand-alone freezer, a kitchen table, or a bed).[13] Though
it may seem odd to include durable goods in "getting ahead," these items

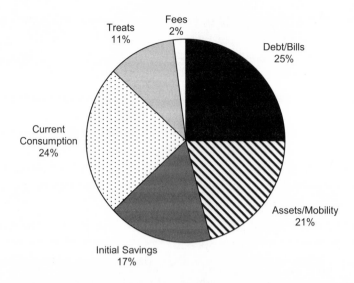

Figure 4. Categories to which tax refund is allocated by percentage.
N = 115 families. "Assets/Mobility" includes purchasing or
increasing the value of one's home, meeting educational expenses,
starting or increasing the productivity of one's business, purchasing
or repairing a car, and obtaining durable home goods like furniture
and appliances. "Debt/Bills" includes any payment on a bill that is
late or past due and any credit card payment. "Current
Consumption" is categorized as regular monthly expenses, including
all on-time bill payments or paying ahead on a bill; groceries,
toiletries, and household staple items; adult and child clothing; car
expenses like gas or routine maintenance; public transit; personal
grooming; and routine child expenses, including diapers,
medications, school supplies, and allowances. Expenditures
categorized as "Treats" include eating out; entertainment; gifts
purchased for others; vacations; toys, games, and gifts for one's
children; alcohol and cigarettes; and lottery tickets. "Fees" includes
tax preparation costs, overdraft fees, and check-cashing fees.

often save time and money, offer an immediate boost to a family's quality
of life, and give households a sense that they are upwardly mobile. The
remainder of the credit—just over $200 or 2 percent of the refund—goes
for tax preparation and rapid refund fees. The tax preparation industry
makes a substantial profit on EITC claimants each year.[14]

Is the refund money wasted or wisely spent? The answer is in the eye of the beholder, but our own view is that these economically strapped households show remarkable discipline in how they dispense the money. They splurge a little but also demonstrate what many might see as responsible behavior (paying off debt, buying in bulk, and paying ahead). They also make investments in the future (saving and spending for mobility purposes). While we ought to consider what motivates families to splurge somewhat given their scarce resources, it is also reasonable to ask what accounts for the surprising restraint these households show.

Princeton sociologist Viviana Zelizer has famously argued that "multiple monies matter as powerful, visible symbols of particular types of social relations and meanings. But they are more than that; they directly affect social practices. People not only think or feel differently about their various monies, but they spend them, save them, or give them for different purposes and to different people."[15] Similarly, behavioral economists have explored how dramatically people's financial thinking is altered by the mode in which they receive money.[16] Zelizer adds a deeper dimension to this work, arguing that, beyond the method of disbursement, money has a "social meaning" that is determined by broader cultural forces. For example, she points to the fact that people spend money differently depending on whether it is defined as a gift, an entitlement, or compensation.[17]

Following Zelizer, we argue that the meaning households attach to the EITC is key to understanding how they spend (or save) it. A starting point is to explore the language that families use to describe the credit. Most refer to the tax credits that they receive as a "refund," even though some know that they get more back than they paid in. As we've shown, many say that it's like "hitting the lottery" or "better than Christmas," reflecting the fact that, though they generally hope to receive a refund, it's still viewed as a bonus and its exact size is seldom known in advance.

Parents also refer to the EITC as "found money," "treat money," "the kids' money," or "family money," indicating its special standing vis-à-vis earnings and other income sources. Many refer to the refund as "savings," highlighting the fact that they've often mentally earmarked the refund for specific things that require a substantial lump sum—typically a car purchase, furniture, appliances, or even a down payment on a home or saving for the children's college tuition. In short, the refund is described in ways that seem to set it apart from earnings or other sources of income, including mean-tested welfare programs such as TANF, SNAP, or housing subsidies. No one in our study refers to tax credits as a handout.

FINANCIAL RELIEF

The theme of financial relief is paramount in our families' narratives about the EITC, emerging spontaneously in nearly three-quarters of our interviews (71 percent). There is a huge relief associated with being able to make it back into the black with a large lump sum. This is not surprising: wages cover only about two-thirds (68 percent) of our families' monthly expenditures on average. SNAP, cash contributions from relatives and friends, child support, and especially the EITC and other tax credits have to make up the rest. Significant debt payoff usually only occurs at tax time, in part because families seem to feel special relief in paying off a debt all at once.

Carla Daniels is a black, recently divorced fifty-three-year-old who has two stepchildren she claimed as dependents. When she filed her taxes, "All I was thinking about was survival. All I was thinking about was 'What do I need to do to save this family from eviction?' And we were eligible for the earned income tax credit. I said, 'Thank you, God!' To be honest, I was so thankful that we were eligible because I knew that that was going to keep us out of eviction court."

Lizann Moretti, a forty-two-year-old white mother of two teenage boys, lost her job several years ago and, despite considerable effort, hasn't been able to find another, so the family relies solely on her husband's wages from installing insulation. She tells us, "I paid five years' worth of [back property] taxes [with the refund]. It was almost—it was close to $4,000. . . . Yes! Do you know how I *felt* after I paid 'em? I was like *Oh my God!* It felt so good. 'Cause [I said to myself], 'Oh my God, if I wait any longer . . . we're not going to own the house anymore. They're going to [take it from us].' I felt like, 'Oh my God, the more I wait, we're going to have a serious problem.'"

Sandra Ruiz, a Hispanic home health aide and mother of two, used the refund to pay $2,000 toward overdue utility bills. When we ask her, "What would have happened without the refund?" she replies, "Uf! I'd have to go live down [under] the bridge."

THE STRUCTURE AND MEANING OF THE EITC

The ways in which families think about the EITC seem inextricably tied to specific features of the credit. First, there is a unique aspect of the credit that makes it especially "prowork": up to a threshold, the more you earn, the more you get from the EITC. Second, it is delivered in a lump sum, and families view it as generous. In contrast, the welfare recipients that Edin and Lein interviewed in the early 1990s viewed their welfare checks, which came every month, as paltry, even though the annual benefit back then was about as large as our families' annual refund is today. Third, recipients know that receipt is tied to their work efforts. Thus, though many recognize that their refund amount includes overwithholding, they believe that they earned their refund check and view the credit as a just reward for work. Finally, what determines one's total refund is complex (overwithholding, various federal and state tax credits, deductions of various kinds, and so on), so families are uncertain about how large their refund will be each year. This uncertainly prompts parents to view the large sum as a windfall, special money that should not be allocated like earnings—just for bills—but reserved for special purposes, especially upward mobility.

A Just Reward for Work

In interview after interview, parents told us that they had "earned" their refund. The "I-earned-it" theme is strong, though many know that they're getting back more than they paid in taxes. It is the EITC's link to employment—the conditional nature of the cash transfer—and the fact that it explicitly excludes those who are allegedly "sitting on their asses"—the characterization our families often use to describe welfare recipients—that is probably responsible for the fact that it is not perceived as a government handout. In fact, it is seen as the antithesis of a handout; it's a well-deserved hand up.

But the EITC is more innovative than most cash transfers. Unlike other programs, which cut benefits for each dollar of earnings, the EITC is structured so that the more you earn the more you get—to a point. After that, the EITC offers gradually diminishing benefits as earnings rise. Thus the EITC is seen as a program that actually rewards those who play by the rules and work full time, full year.

In short, the specific and unique way that the credit is structured bolsters recipients' identities as workers, not dependents. Because of this, this cash transfer can be claimed with pride—as "earned." In turn, families often link claims that the credit is "deserved"—a just reward for work—with specific kinds of allocations, including modest amounts for splurges or "treats," like a trip to Red Lobster.

As indicated earlier, about one dollar in ten is typically allocated for treats. As we've shown, to some degree, the priority given to treats is evident in routine financial behavior, not just at tax time. Even when disbursing scarce earnings during those months of the year when they don't have tax refund dollars to draw on, families justify small splurges—especially for their kids. And they do so while referencing their status as workers, which they feel buys them the right to treat their children, or even themselves, now and then. Living as if you are not poor, at least in small ways, seems to be vital to these parents' identity. Thus the claim "It's not like I'm poor" supports parents' explanations of their out-of-the ordinary expenditures—like a name-brand pair of tennis shoes—that are not, strictly speaking, necessary. Invoking the right to splurge is especially evident at tax time, when many justify devoting several hundred dollars of the refund to the purchase of special items and experiences with the declaration "I'm a worker. I earned it."

This sentiment is shared by Claire Haynes, a twenty-five-year-old white single mother with three daughters, aged seven, five, and three. Claire received welfare for part of the past year, getting by on about $400 a month in cash assistance and another $300 in SNAP. She got off welfare when she landed a job as a home health aide for an elderly woman who lived in a distant suburb—this job qualified her for the EITC. But she eventually left that job because of the long commute. Now she works part time as a waitress at a small, family-owned restaurant in South Boston and usually brings home about $200 a week in tips (she is paid no salary), though she doesn't report this income to the IRS. She shares responsibility for the bills with her boyfriend, Randy, the father of her two youngest girls. Because finances are so tight during the year, Claire tells us that, in a typical month, "the kids get what they need, but it's not what they want. It's what they need, but they may not like it."

This year, Randy claimed their two daughters as dependents, while Claire claimed her oldest daughter. With her $2,500 tax refund, and Randy's similarly sized windfall, Claire was able to satisfy not only her children's needs but some of their wants as well. She purchased the Dora the Explorer child-sized wooden table and chairs so many children covet. Her youngest girl delights in eating her dinner there. She also took all three girls to Target and allowed them pick out whatever outfit they chose—a truly rare treat. "It might have been a couple of dollars more expensive, or it might have been even double the price [I would have usually paid], but the point was they got what they needed and at the same time they felt like a million bucks. Because they actually got what they *wanted*." Even though events like this modest shopping spree often constitute only a small portion of the total refund, many parents like Claire cherish the opportunity to make these spending decisions above all others.

The Lump Sum: A Springboard for Mobility

The method by which the EITC is delivered—in a lump sum, and usually via a for-profit tax preparer like H&R Block—also sends strong messages about its meaning. A substantial majority of EITC claimants nationwide— about two-thirds—turn to professional tax preparers for assistance in filing their taxes each year. Among our households, there is no stigma to walking through those doors. The largest of these firms is the behemoth H&R Block, which charges, on average, $192 for the most basic return, plus fees for each additional "schedule" (such as the one for the EITC).[18] At H&R Block, one is a client, a taxpayer. And it is perhaps for this reason that parents' narratives about the EITC are so dominated by hopes and plans for upward mobility. These workers believe that they have the right not only to claim financial relief and consume a little more at tax time but to live the American Dream as well—the majority aspire to save for college for their kids or to save for a home, envisioning using their refund to do so.

Households often explicitly build their aspirations for upward mobility around the promise the refund offers, rather than on their regular income or further investments in their own human capital. And these aspirations are reflected, at least to some degree, in their behavior: as noted above, the average family devotes nearly four refund dollars in ten (38 percent) to what they associate with upward mobility—17 percent to savings and 21 percent to the purchase or repair of a car, durable goods (sometimes furniture, but especially appliances), and, more rarely, educational expenses, college savings, and home purchases and repairs. Perhaps far more important than the spending and saving decisions that we observe, though, are the mobility aspirations that the EITC seems to inspire, especially for college savings and home ownership, a subject that we will return to in chapter 4. The large lump sum that arrives at tax time provides families with an opportunity to dream of doing things that they say they would never be able accomplish otherwise.

Though moms and dads may fantasize about taking the kids to Disney World, on a more practical level, they often earmark the refund for vital purchases of durable goods—a new refrigerator, for example (Boston landlords are not required by law to provide refrigerators), or a time- and money-saving washer or dryer. Buying or repairing used cars is a popular use of the refund. Retailers have clearly caught on to the fact that it is at tax time—and, often, *only* at tax time—that these assets can be accrued. Walmart offers "online refund specials," and you can now get your taxes filed right in the store for a truly one-stop-shopping experience. DFW furniture offers special tax-refund sales. *Dealer Marketing Magazine* advises "how to get customers to spend their tax refund at your auto dealership" in an article entitled "Tax Season Is Here."[19] Every year, in late winter, tax refunds pump billions of dollars into businesses in low- to moderate-income communities and into the hands of large retailers, such as Walmart, Target, and Sears.

The lump-sum nature of the refund gives parents the rare chance to "think big" and to spend and save accordingly. Because the year's payout is reserved until February, rather than being disbursed little by little each month, families believe that the EITC allows them to "save." Debra tells us that what economists call the "forced-savings" feature of the credit is vital—it's the only way to protect her resources from the demands imposed by frequent financial shocks.

If [I had to save that money] every week, and I had to take $100 or $200 [out of each paycheck] to add up for a trip at the end of the year, it's like something comes up and I know I have the vacation money and I'll touch it. Or, "We're $100 behind on this, we'll take it from that [savings]." And, realistically, when you do it that way, is it all going to be there at the end of the year? No. . . . I love the lump sum because something always happens. You always need your tax return.

Debra's sentiments about savings—that it is nearly impossible to save on one's own, without the help of the EITC—are widely shared among those we spoke with. Touching that money would just be too tempting, or too necessary, to resist if it were paid out a little at a time.[20]

However, the forced saving that the disbursement method creates is not without cost. These working-poor households, whose wages cover only two-thirds of their expenses, could presumably use the money throughout the year. As described in chapter 1, most experience financial strain while waiting to receive their full refund at tax time. And many rack up debt in the meantime, accumulating interest and late fees as unpaid bills pile up, a theme we'll consider in more depth in chapter 5. These families also suffer from the stress of pinching pennies to pay the rent and juggling the light and gas bills to put food on the table.

Given that most of our parents believe that their refund is "earned," one might presume that they could see forgoing the refund until the end of the tax year as equivalent to providing the federal government with a no-interest loan. At the time of our study, households in fact had the option to receive a portion of their estimated EITC in "advance"—in monthly increments in their paychecks. Nationwide, the number of filers who selected the advance EITC was so low that the government has since discontinued that option. And no family in our study complained that the government was improperly withholding the money. Many, in fact, explicitly said that they would rather have the windfall than receive the same amount spread out over twelve months. This is not only due to the desire to have a surplus with which to splurge a little and purchase big-ticket items but also a reflection of their determination to save—a strongly held value among many we spoke with, but one that they have found difficult to live up to. Since the government holds on to one's refund until tax time, it creates an ironclad "commitment mechanism"—to borrow a term from economics—that allows households on the economic margin to protect a portion of their resources from other pressing financial demands. This is valued immensely, in part because it allows households to rise above the grind of mere survival and look to the future.

The lump sum is also popular because low-wage workers are strongly averse to a particular form of financial risk: owing the IRS money at the end of the year. Not only is it frightening to have the IRS as your creditor—it can take actions against a family that few other entities can, including property liens and wage garnishment—but, until the debt is paid, future tax refunds, including refundable tax credits, are seized. The IRS can garnish claimants' refunds for unpaid federal student loans, child support, and back taxes. In short, its power to deny is as strong as its ability to bestow.

COMPLEXITY AND UNCERTAINTY

The lump sum nature of the refund and the fact that, up to a point, the more you work the more you earn (with only a gradual reduction in benefits once a household reaches the phaseout range of earnings) are both vital features of the credit. A third important feature is that the rules governing it are complex. And it comes as part of a larger tax refund that has several constituent parts. Thus, while families believe it is likely they will get a refund, few are familiar enough with the tax code to accurately predict how much they will receive. Uncertainty with regard to the amount of the refund is not the exception; it is the rule. H&R Block does have a tax-refund calculator on its website, but only one of our parents (out of 115) availed herself of this resource, methodically reentering her information with each fluctuation in income.[21]

Though the paperwork clients receive from H&R Block after tax filing delineates how much of the refund comes from various sources, households rarely take note of this information (for those who chose to share their tax-return paperwork with us, we nearly always had to show them where this information appeared on their forms) or make any distinction between the two parts of their refund: the money that is returned to them because too much was withheld from their paychecks during the year—

their own money being returned to them—and money that comes from refundable credits such as the EITC, which is extra money above and beyond their own earnings. As we noted above, this combining of funds also may bolster the sense that the refund is earned and not a handout.

To understand the role that uncertainty over the amount of the refund can play in how households allocate their refund, we turn to the story of Brenda Hutchinson, a thirty-eight-year-old white mother of two girls— Shannon, eleven, and Molly, four—who files her taxes each year with her husband, Ted, at H&R Block. Ted works in the Boston Public School system as a custodian. Brenda hasn't worked since Molly was born, but she was just hired part time as a school lunch monitor and will start her new job in the fall. The family lives in a South Boston triple-decker on a narrow street that has seen better days; the sagging front porches on the block are littered with old furniture, and the houses are in need of a fresh coat of paint. Despite this, the neighbors are friendly, calling greetings to each other from across the street. Brenda's brother owns the house that she lives in and gives Brenda and Ted a discount on rent. Brenda's mother, who broke her hip after falling down the stairs, is now living with them so that Brenda can care for her.

When Brenda and Ted make the trip to H&R Block each year to file their taxes, they try to get the same "professional" they had the prior year so that not too many people "know your business." When they arrive at their local franchise, in East Boston, their preparer pulls up their paperwork from the previous year, collects their W-2 forms, and updates their wage and dependent information in the system. Then comes the moment they've been waiting for—the verdict on how large their federal and state refunds will be. Each year, they hope and pray for a big refund, but they try not to expect it. Brenda is the family optimist and attempts to gauge her expectations on the basis of past experience. But all she knows is that when she and Ted were both working full time and had only one child they got only a small refund—about $1,200. The first time they got a big check—$5,000—was after their second child was born and Brenda had left her job to stay home—she says that day "was like hitting the lottery!"

That first year they claimed a refund, they filed their own taxes, but the next, they went to H&R Block because they "needed the money *that day*" in order to capitalize on a used-car deal. Brenda knew full well that H&R

Block would charge her several hundred dollars in exchange for a tax refund anticipation loan, on top of the regular preparation fee, but in her view "it was worth it because we got five thousand back and we wanted the car." The $400 or so in fees seemed like a drop in the bucket compared to what she was getting back from the IRS. Each year since, they've also used H&R Block, though they haven't always gotten the rapid refund, an H&R Block product that provided same-day refunds for a hefty fee.[22] Since they qualified for that first big refund check, this couple has received between $4,000 and $5,000 back each year. Brenda feels some degree of confidence that they will get about that amount next year. Ted, however, is "always negative"—he routinely predicts that "we're only gonna get two thousand."

If the rules governing the refund aren't well understood, it is for good reason. As we have indicated, what lands in families' pockets around tax time is determined by a complex set of calculations that depends on filing status, number of qualifying children, earned income from employment, and other factors. Many of those in our study have a general sense that the EITC is a cash transfer that you receive if you work and you are the parent primarily responsible for at least one child, but they often confuse the EITC with the child tax credit—the credit of up to $1,000 that they receive on top of the EITC for each child. When we ask Brenda what she knows about the earned income tax credit, she says, "I just know it's extra money that we get. . . . If our income's at a certain level, we get it . . . and the kids have to be under a certain age, from what I understand. I think it's under sixteen or something, thirteen or sixteen. . . . You get so much per credit per child." Brenda's winding description reflects her vague (and, in some respects, incorrect) understanding of what matters in determining the size of the tax credit: there is an income limit and children are involved.

In sum, because the rules are complicated, and the refund varies with the number of children, marital status, dependent status, and who claims which children—not to mention fluctuations in income—it is hard to rely on past experience to make an educated guess as to how big the refund will be. Widespread uncertainty surrounding the exact amount both heightens families' feelings of anticipation and lends the sense that the credit is a surprise—a windfall—even for households who receive it year after year. "Winning the lottery" is an analogy many families use when describing the EITC, and not just in reference to their first big check. Similarly, as we've said, it is often described as a gift or even a blessing. There is often immense gratitude, along with relief, when the refund check arrives.

Even optimists like Brenda, but especially pessimists like Ted, routinely tell us that they can't—and shouldn't—"count on" the EITC. Here, the uncertainty that fuels the sense that the refund is a "miracle" reveals its ugly side: the economic straits and financial ups and downs of many families create concerns that tax time could bring a nasty surprise, a bill rather than a refund. Most families have at least an inkling of this risk, presumably because various forms of garnishment are so common in low-income communities. Noncustodial fathers' wages are routinely garnished for child support, for example, and their tax refunds can be garnished too if child support is owed. In addition, it is not uncommon for EITC recipients to receive benefits one year but not the next.[23] For this reason, the families we spoke with are generally averse to the idea of "counting on" a large refund, even though many dream about, and plan for, what they will do with the refund all year long.

This is not mere risk aversion, though; there is a sense that "knowing" in advance will "ruin" an experience that is deemed "better than Christmas." This feeling is so pervasive that TurboTax even uses this phrase as a slogan to advertise its products. As noted above, some parents said they prayed for a big check and praised God if the outcome was positive. To quote Carla Daniels, "We were eligible for earned income [tax] credit, [and] I said thank you God!" In sum, a large refund that arrives in the face of uncertainty is perceived as a special, even divine, event. So, along with strong notions of what is owed to workers, we argue that uncertainty is also part of why these economically strapped households are able to allocate nearly half of the refund (49 percent) for things other than debt payoff and the items we include in the "current consumption" category (11 percent for treats and 38 percent for mobility purposes). Though the anticipation of a refund of some kind may entice households to modestly elevate their "normal" consumption patterns in the months leading up to February because they anticipate a windfall from the IRS, uncertainty seems to dampen the temptation to overconsume during this period. It follows that greater certainty—a simpler tax code or a more transparent process of delivery—might actually decrease the amount that families were able to set aside for such purposes.

"YOU'VE GOT PEOPLE" AT H&R BLOCK

A large number of working Americans file their taxes through for-profit tax preparation companies like H&R Block. While welfare claimants must stand in line at the welfare office, which exists to serve the economically needy, most recipients of the EITC claim their benefits by doing business with a firm whose mission is to serve those in the mainstream. The H&R Block office in Dorchester's Fields Corner is located in a strip mall fronted by a huge concrete parking lot, with a McDonalds on its left and a discount grocery store on its right. The neighborhood is predominantly black, with a mix of Afro-Caribbean and African American residents as well as a small Vietnamese community. Although traditionally a hot spot of violent crime, Fields Corner has undergone a renaissance in recent years, with many new eateries. There are Irish pubs, Vietnamese restaurants, and soul food takeout, as well as a farmers' market. New pharmacies and banks are buying up renovated commercial spaces along "Dot Ave," the local slang for the main business thoroughfare, Dorchester Avenue. The H&R Block is steps from a recently renovated subway station connecting Fields Corner to downtown Boston and is across the street from a large, well-kept park that affords opportunities for recreation, including a playground and a baseball diamond.

Moving through the glass door that marks the entry to the H&R Block, one passes below a brightly lit green placard featuring the company logo and flashy posters with a multiracial rainbow of smiling professionals proclaiming, "You've got people!" and "You deserve Peace of Mind!" These slogans are a repeat of what we observed at the East Boston franchise that serves Toni Paturelli's family. Cassandra Jackson, who has come to file her taxes here, is a twenty-three-year-old black single mother of a twenty-month-old who lives just a mile up Dot Ave and works as a receptionist at the Dana-Farber Cancer Institute. At H&R Block, a smiling receptionist greets her, takes down her name, and gives her a worksheet to complete before she meets with a "tax specialist." She is also given a flier, which provides a set of guidelines and a list of required documentation. The open office space is full of blue cubicles with low walls, where about a dozen employees dressed in business casual sit in clear view. Customers sit in blue plastic chairs opposite the preparers' sleek metal desks. The tax specialists busily click away at their computers, intent on issuing the verdict on how large each customer's refund, or obligation, will be. After registering at the front desk, Cassandra takes a seat in the waiting area, a series of metal chairs in a semicircle located on the left side of the office, to fill out the required forms. A mix of others—singles, couples, and a few families with children—also wait there.

After about twenty minutes, Joe, a middle-aged black man dressed in a blue button-down shirt, striped tie, and khakis, enters the waiting area and calls Cassandra's name. She walks over and Joe shakes her hand, asking her how she is doing. He walks her over to his cubicle and offers her a seat. Joe tells her that he has just finished serving a customer who owns a small insurance business in Dorchester, and now he readies himself to prepare Cassandra's taxes. He guides her through a series of prompts on his computer screen, asking for information about dependent children and inputting employment information from the collection of W-2s she has brought with her. Eventually, Joe looks up from his screen and announces the grand total of her refund: $5,900! He prints out a copy of her tax forms, tucking it into a large white envelope with the H&R Block logo, and hands it to Cassandra. He tells her that she has the option to receive her refund that very day on an H&R Block debit card, evocatively named the Emerald Card, for an additional fee. Or, if she has a bank account, the refund will arrive via direct deposit in just a few days' time. A third option is to receive it the slow way—to wait two weeks for a paper check to arrive in her mailbox; this option incurs no extra cost beyond the fee that H&R Block will deduct for preparing her taxes. She opts for the Emerald Card because of the urgent need to replace her current car, which was badly damaged in an accident several months back and is not worth the cost of the repairs. Cassandra reckons that the expense associated with the instant refund is worth it; after all, she needs that car to get around.

PROFESSIONALISM AND PROTECTION

At H&R Block and its competitors, lower-income families like Cassandra's file their returns and receive their refunds along with millions of other taxpayers; here, they are customers who pay for services rendered. This strengthens their identities as workers. Families often note, and appreciate, the professionalism of for-profit tax preparers. But they also want the protection offered by such businesses: many fear filing taxes on their own, since making a mistake could lead to a penalty or an audit. The majority believe that, because of the complexity of the process and the heavy hand of the IRS, it is downright dangerous to prepare your taxes yourself. As we noted earlier, H&R Block charges a fee for each additional schedule it prepares as part of a tax return, and the "EIC" schedule is one of those that incurs such a fee—therefore, it is in the company's interest to have its tax preparers ensure that customers file for it if eligible. Perhaps this is one reason the take-up rate for the EITC among taxpayers with dependent children is so high—roughly 83 percent. For all of these reasons, the cost of tax preparation is often perceived as "well worth it." Angeline Troncoso is a white mother of four children, who range in age from five to fourteen. Her husband works in maintenance for a local welders' union. She used to do their taxes herself, but, as her family grew and their expenses increased, "it just got more complicated. I was afraid I was making mistakes." Mainly, Angeline was concerned that if she filled out the forms herself, the refund might not be as high as it should be—she wanted to make sure that she claimed all of the deductions and credits for which she was eligible. H&R Block is by her side, helping to ensure that she does.

H&R Block's annual advertising campaigns—which promise the maximum possible refund, the reassurance of audit protection, and rapid receipt of the refund (all for a fee)—motivate thousands of Boston's low-wage workers to make the annual trip to the Fields Corner H&R Block office, one of the city's busiest. H&R Block's advertising slogan reassures customers that they are not alone in the event of an audit, proclaiming "You've got people!" For $29, filers can purchase audit protection, called the "Peace of Mind" plan, which ensures that H&R Block will work with the IRS on the taxpayer's behalf and serve as his or her representative in an audit proceeding.

These advertising campaigns are apparently so persuasive that families spontaneously draw upon them when they explain why they choose to go to H&R Block rather than prepare their taxes themselves. When we asked Tiffany Grier, a twenty-two-year-old white single mother of two preschoolers who works as a video store clerk and lives in Boston public housing with her mother and grandmother, why she went to H&R Block, she exclaimed, "I want People!" She likes H&R Block because "they do the thing where they run everything so [you]'re guaranteed to get all the refunds you're supposed to and then if you get audited, if you buy the extra protection, their lawyers go and you don't have to deal with it." Gloria Diaz, a forty-two-year-old Costa Rican immigrant and divorced mother of a seventeen-year-old son and a nine-year-old daughter, works as a birth registrar in a hospital; she also paid extra to insure her return against an audit because "you just have to pay $29, and if the IRS say there is something wrong, [H&R Block] would go through with you and help you with the appeal or whatever you needed. . . . I mean, I shouldn't be afraid . . . but you never know. I just want to have peace of mind. In fact, I think that's what they call it." For both Tiffany and Gloria, using H&R Block frees them from worry; they are promised the maximum refund, and for just a few dollars more a trustworthy intermediary can be counted upon to deal with the IRS for them if necessary. In a world of widespread financial uncertainty, such protections are ardently desired.[24] H&R Block—along with other for-profit tax preparation firms such as Jackson Hewlett, Tax Man, and the dozens of mom-and-pop storefronts that advertise tax preparation services in a colorful array of languages all along Dot Avenue—is able to capitalize on poor households' aversion to risk with its range of services designed to ensure maximum refunds and provide audit protection.

A REFUND AT A PRICE

Like Cassandra, many we spoke with acutely felt the need for their refund right away. Sometimes it's because of a purchase they feel they just can't wait to make, like a badly needed used car. But usually filers' anxiety and sense of urgency can be attributed to a different source—the bill collectors who seem to be constantly calling and the threatening letters that choke the mailbox. H&R Block made the rapid refund, called a Refund Anticipation Loan (RAL), a household word—it loaned claimants the amount of their tax refund on the day they filed, saving families the suspense and the inconvenience of waiting seven to fourteen days to receive a refund check from the IRS in the mail. In 2007, H&R Block chartered its own bank so that claimants could receive these rapid refunds on an H&R Block debit card, the Emerald Card. The cost of the RAL depended on the size of the loan; for a refund of $2,000, the fee was $100, which translates to an annual percentage rate of 178 percent. The urgency that drives so many to claim a RAL despite these high interest rates reveals the tough financial straits that so many have fallen into by tax time, but it also hints at how they feel about the debts that they owe. They view themselves as workers—upstanding citizens—and often emphasized to us that they wanted to be responsible in discharging their obligations. The insistent ring of the telephone and the letters marked "urgent," "confidential," or "final notice" create a sense of pressure, tinged with shame, that few can bear with ease. Six in ten (61 percent) families we spoke with who filed their taxes with H&R Block utilized a refund anticipation loan, often for this reason.

H&R Block also offers loans on tax refunds that can be received in advance of tax season, under their Advance Holiday Loan program. Sometimes called a "Christmas loan," this program allows taxpayers to borrow up to $1,000 during December and have the amount deducted from their refund for a fee. Some parents find this option attractive because it means that they have money on hand to fulfill the ultimate parental duty—ensuring that their children "have Christmas." Kathleen Farmer, a thirty-two-year-old black preschool teacher, took out a Christmas loan for precisely this reason.

The past year has been extraordinarily tough for Kathleen and her two boys, Shane, sixteen, and Roland, eleven. Kathleen's mother is an alcoholic prone to violent outbursts, so Kathleen was raised by her aunt in the middle-class neighborhood of West Roxbury along with her brother, sister, and cousins. Until last year, Kathleen was living with her boys and her fiancé, Duane, in the basement apartment of her aunt's home. But Duane, whom Kathleen describes as a "jealous person," got upset because she went out partying one night. Their argument quickly escalated, coming to a devastating climax when Duane poured nail polish remover—composed of the highly flammable chemical acetone—on Kathleen and then set her on fire, severely burning her arms and chest.

Kathleen pressed charges against Duane following what she refers to as the "big incident," and he is now serving a two-year sentence for assault.

When the fire department came to the house in response to the 911 call, they discovered that Kathleen's aunt hadn't renewed the permit to rent a basement apartment and that the unit was not up to code. The family had thirty days to make the charred basement habitable and to pay all of the outstanding fees and fines for permit and code violations or the city would insist that the unit be vacated. It broke Kathleen's heart to leave her family and the house that she had grown up in, but she decided to go so that her aunt's family wouldn't be burdened with the cost of fixing up the basement. None of them had the spare cash on hand. Without money to go elsewhere, Kathleen took her boys to a homeless shelter. Once there, she got on the waiting list for a housing subsidy and, after three months, the housing authority's "preference" for homeless families qualified her for a unit in a public housing complex not far from her aunt's home.

On top of the trauma from the assault and the stress of living in a shelter, Kathleen's finances are in shambles without Duane's contributions to the household. She hasn't been able to keep up with bills, has no furniture yet in her new apartment, and scrambles to put food on the table for her growing boys. Even with money extremely tight, it was important to Kathleen to be able to give her boys a "nice Christmas" because the year had been so rough. They had actually witnessed Duane setting her on fire, Shane rushing to extinguish the flames that engulfed his mother while Roland called the ambulance. So Kathleen was enthusiastic when she found out that H&R Block "has that new thing where you can borrow money before Christmas." She took out a loan for $800 from H&R Block in early December and let her boys choose a "big-ticket item" for Christmas; each was allowed to pick one electronic game. The hefty fees Kathleen paid for this loan came out of her refund when she filed her taxes the following February, but, according to Kathleen, not letting her children down during the holidays was well worth it.

In response to widespread criticism of RALs' usurious interest rates, the IRS ended the practices that had enabled companies to offer RALs with little financial risk just after we completed our study.[25] H&R Block no longer offers such loans, though some of their competitors continue to do so. Recently H&R Block developed a new method of offering refunds, which are not loans but are instead called "Refund Anticipation Checks." In lieu of interest, the expense is in the added preparation fee. Still, only a minority of the lower-income families that we met felt that these types of charges were unfair. Since the fees were taken from the refund, there were no out-of-pocket expenses, and this dramatically eased the pain. When possible, we assessed how much they had paid in tax preparation fees by looking at the paperwork they were given after they filed, which specifies the amount. Yet families were often unclear on how much it cost to get an advance loan, or even to have their tax forms prepared.

NONPROFIT TAX PREPARATION

Some families decided not to use a commercial tax preparer and instead took advantage of a nonprofit tax preparer. In Boston, the Earned Income Tax Credit Coalition provides free tax preparation to low- and moderate-income families at twenty-eight Volunteer Income Tax Assistance (VITA) locations around the city. These sites serve more than twelve thousand taxpayers each year. They are often housed within local nonprofit organizations. The largest among these is Action for Boston Community Development (ABCD), an advocacy and service organization that has assisted low-income Bostonians since the 1960s and has offices in a dozen Boston neighborhoods. Such nonprofits typically offer a host of other services for low-income families—winter fuel assistance (via the federal Low Income Heating Assistance Program), emergency food, housing assistance, and ESL courses—and sometimes host sliding-scale child care centers or Head Start sites. Many of the families who utilized free tax preparation at a nonprofit in Boston were already familiar with the organization they approached and had previously used its services. A few had heard about the free tax preparation services through family or friends or through the mayor's advertising campaign leading up to February's tax season. Those who filed their taxes with nonprofit preparers were, on average, more economically disadvantaged than the families who filed their taxes with for-profit preparers.[26] This may indicate that those who feel they can afford the luxury of filing taxes with a company like H&R Block generally choose to do so.

Experiences at nonprofits were mixed. On the one hand, families that used them clearly appreciated that they did not have to pay to file their taxes. But on the other hand, those who volunteer at the nonprofit sites were seen as less professional, even though each volunteer must attend a lengthy training session and pass a test to be certified, and many have done so year after year. Those using VITA sites also worried that they might have trouble with the IRS due to preparers' mistakes or that a less experienced volunteer might fail to identify all of the deductions and credits for which they were eligible. What was most notable, however, were the ways in which their descriptions of filing taxes at some (though by no means all) of the VITA sites were reminiscent of the accounts they give of interactions with the welfare office, where many had had to go apply for TANF, SNAP, or Medicaid: long lines in drab buildings, impersonal or even rude treatment, and the heavy atmosphere of desperate people soliciting aid. This is obviously a far cry from the bright offices, neat as a pin, and the "specialists" at H&R Block—your "people," who treat you like a valued customer, just like every other taxpayer who chooses to file taxes there. While some families did rave about their experiences at the nonprofits, others related horror stories of taxes that were misfiled, untrained volunteers who didn't seem to know what they were doing, appointments not kept, or inordinately long waits.

We volunteered as tax preparers in two of the Boston VITA sites during the 2007 tax season, and, while one was well kept and deployed experienced volunteers—mostly agency staff who performed this service for clients year after year—the other was plagued by a lack of heating, particularly bracing on a cold February evening in Boston, electrical outages, computers that often failed to work properly, if at all, and erratic hours. While paying for tax preparation services may have been costly financially, it didn't exact the toll on one's time and self-esteem that some of the VITA sites did, underscoring how profoundly the method of delivery can affect people's perceptions of programs. In sum, for the majority, the for-profit firm was perceived as worth the cost, not only because families could access a rapid refund or gain freedom from worry over an audit, but also because the experience itself more closely aligned with their identities as workers.[27]

To illustrate how vital "experiences" were to offering these families the sense that they were "not poor," we turn to a story that is not related to taxes. One summer afternoon, one of us, Jennifer Sykes, visited the home of Penny McPherson, a white twenty-eight-year-old, in a South Boston housing project. While Penny was sharing with Jen the stories of her financial struggles, the air was suddenly filled with the jingle of an ice cream truck. Penny's four-year-old son ran to her, hand outstretched. She dug deep in her pocketbook and extracted a few dollars. The child ran toward the truck, shouting that he would buy a Superman Pop. Jen paused, curious about why the woman had so easily surrendered several precious dollars for this purpose, given her economic difficulties. Intrigued by how expectant the boy had seemed when asking for the money, Jen asked, "Does he get that often?" The mother revealed that this ritual was repeated at least a couple of times each week in the summer. "And it's even worse," she told Jen. "I have a box of these same Superman Pops in the freezer, right now. I buy them in bulk at BJs so they're only $.30 each. Costs him $2.50 at the truck!" When Jen asked why she would spend much more for the same treat at the ice cream truck, the mother replied, "For the experience. . . . I want him to feel like an ordinary kid."[28]

PERVERSE DISINCENTIVES?

Earlier we outlined a number of reasons why households seldom had a clear sense of how large their refund would be. Both researchers and policy makers have expressed concern about potential perverse incentives created by the EITC.[29] For example, once earnings place a worker in the program's phaseout, or benefit reduction, range, there is an incentive to reduce work hours, especially for two-parent families. In addition, the potential marriage disincentives are large: if two low-wage workers who each have a dependent marry and file as such, they can lose several thousand dollars in tax credits.[30] Further, having additional children can increase one's refund (with greater benefits for up to two children as of 2007; this was raised to three children in 2009 as part of the American Recovery and Reinvestment Act [ARRA], set to expire in 2017).[31] Each of these incentives and disincentives could, in theory, motivate behaviors that most Americans would see as deleterious. But, by and large, people tell us that they do not change their work hours, make marriage decisions, or decide to have a child because of these incentives.

In terms of work hours, the complexity of the tax code makes it difficult for parents to actually predict whether their households' refunds will increase or decrease with increased wages. But parents also point out that they have little control over their employment situations and must take what work they can get when they can. In most cases, their monthly bills are so pressing that they say they can't "afford" to game the system, even if they could figure it out. Marriage is described as far more a question of finding the right person than maximizing one's tax refund. As for children, parents wisely note that kids cost a whole lot more than an incremental increase in one's tax refund could possibly cover. Most important, though, are the moral claims that most parents make when asked these questions: in their view, to manipulate one's employment, marriage behavior, or childbearing is the kind of scheme employed by freeloaders, not by people who work for a living.

However, these parents *do* try to maximize their refunds in other ways: by manipulating how much is deducted out of their regular paychecks via the number of exemptions they claim, by negotiating who claims which kids on which tax return, and by using the tax filing status "head of household"—which is reserved for single parents and which counts only that one parent's income—even when married. Some of these strategies are perfectly legal, while others are legally questionable (although many are unaware that this is the case). These strategies can have sizable effects on refund amounts.

Labor Market Behavior

We asked parents directly if they would adjust their work behavior if they thought it would maximize their refund. All but two resolutely denied that they would do so. This is probably not just a matter of families trying to impress us—people admitted manipulating their taxes in other ways, just not in this way.[32] As indicated above, some said that it would be impractical to do so because their employment situations were too precarious or too difficult to control.[33] For example, twenty-six-year-old Rita Ramirez, a Hispanic hairdresser and mother to two kids, ages one and nine, sees her income fluctuate with the number of clients she has in the course of a week; in addition, her boyfriend, Gabriel, who lives and works out of state, contributes only sporadically to the household expenses. A few months ago he was laid off from his job at a plastering company; since then, he hasn't been able to provide much income. Rita has taken on a second job as a receptionist at a medical clinic to help cover the shortfall. Nonetheless, it has been difficult for Rita to keep up with her bills, much less help Gabriel out with the child support he owes for his son from another relationship. Given the pressure of getting by month to month, altering work hours to maximize a refund is not even on Rita's radar, let alone within her control.

Uncertainty with regard to how the refund is calculated also no doubt plays a role in the fact that households don't seem to work less when work disincentives kick in after earnings enter the EITC phaseout range. One parent notes that the refund "is great, but it's not everything," and another says, "You can't count on February." Yet some households say that they do worry a lot that, if their earnings grow too much, they'll lose their housing subsidy, SNAP, or government-sponsored health insurance. If income subsequently falls, they have to reapply for the program, and this does motivate some to limit their work hours. But most say they detest the idea that one would choose to work less to get a bigger benefit from any government program; they define themselves as workers and upstanding citizens and view such behavior as immoral. This disapprobation is yet another way such families draw a sharp distinction between themselves and "dependents" who would "game the system," a theme we will explore in the next chapter.

As indicated earlier, while manipulating employment to maximize a refund is not at all common, parents are eager to maximize their refunds through other means. "Claiming zero" is the most common strategy, and it's a perfectly legal one: these household heads claim no personal allowances or dependents on their W-4 forms, thereby prompting overwithholding—having more income withheld from paychecks for tax liabilities than what is owed. This money comes back to them via their refund at tax time, in the same check as their tax credit. To those who are especially averse to owing the IRS at tax time, "claiming zero" is also prized because it reduces the odds of receiving a tax bill rather than a refund at year's end.

Juana Vega, the thirty-six-year-old Puerto Rican mother of one whom we introduced earlier, lives in subsidized housing in the middle-class

Boston suburb of Arlington with her husband, Ignacio, and her eleven-year-old son, Milo. She is a Head Start teacher; Ignacio recently completed a mechanic's certification course but has been able to find only part-time work so far. Juana, the household's financial manager, is very frugal with money, putting aside enough each month to make sure that she can cover the basic bills. Ignacio is more cavalier with cash, insisting on things that Juana considers frivolous, like cable TV and a cell phone. So Juana has opened up a separate savings account in her name only so that she can save without Ignacio's either knowing about or having access to the money.

Each summer, like legions of Head Start teachers across America, Juana is laid off and must subsist on unemployment insurance. Despite the annual challenge to the family budget, Juana focuses with laser-beam intensity on accumulating some savings in that secret account—she insists that she'll manage to buy a house one day. Beyond the hidden bank account, she also claims zero because "it's like a saving account. I will have that money back for sure. . . . Because we struggle, this is a way to save." The money she lets the IRS hold would surely come in handy during those months that she is laid off each summer. But saving for the longer term is such an important goal that she is willing to suffer the stress of those summer months.

Claiming zero rarely comes without sacrifice. Some might point out that if these families had instead placed the extra withholding in a savings account they could have at least claimed some interest and, more importantly, could have accessed the money to alleviate a financial crunch during exceptionally hard times. But that is precisely the point—many of the families we spoke to are willing to trade off economic security for the guarantee that their "savings" cannot be touched.

Marriage Behavior

Researchers Adam Carasso and Eugene Steuerle have shown that the potential marriage disincentives in the EITC are huge.[34] Married couples do have a higher EITC earnings threshold than single parents, but in cases where marriage results in a dual-earner household the potential losses in tax credits are very large, even if the couple was already living together and sharing expenses before the wedding. Two full-time incomes make it impossible to get much from the credit. For example, a mother of two who makes $20,000 qualifies for an EITC refund of $4,269. If she marries someone who makes $25,000 or more, she will no longer receive any money from the EITC. If the couple simply live together and join their finances but do not marry, they can combine their $45,000 in earnings while she continues to receive her tax refund of over $4,000.

In 1984, libertarian author Charles Murray described a similar bind in the welfare program for a hypothetical couple, Harold and Phyllis.[35] By remaining unmarried, this fictitious pair could pocket both Harold's earnings and Phyllis's welfare benefits. Murray claimed that, through this "perverse incentive," welfare had caused the rise in single parenthood in the 1970s and '80s. A large volume of research largely disproved, or at least sharply moderated, Murray's claims.[36] Similarly, there is little evidence that marriage behavior has altered in light of these disincentives in the EITC.[37]

Our interviews with families offer some clues as to why. When we ask them how getting married would affect their refund, most have no idea. Many simply laugh at the thought of marrying, out of skepticism that they'll be in a position to get married any time soon. For example, when we ask twenty-six-year-old Gwen Bickford, a white mother of two, ages three and eight, who just lost her job, if getting married would make her refund go up or down, she exclaims, "I don't know. I have no idea! Those things are really so foreign to me!" The father of Gwen's two children is serving a long-term prison sentence, and, although they tried to make it work, the couple grew apart and eventually broke up. She's too busy searching for work to think about dating, much less marriage.

When we asked people directly if they would decide not to marry in order to preserve their EITC, some were downright offended by the question; like Gwen, some laughed at us. If only they could even be in a *position* to marry, some exclaimed, why on earth would they let a tax credit get in the way! But a handful of single mothers did indicate that they were aware of the penalties to marriage in a range of government programs and were thus reluctant to join their finances with someone else's legally. Interestingly, most said they would get married anyway and would simply continue to file their taxes separately, using the head-of-household tax filing status. It is important to note that they saw this as a perfectly legal option and were unaware that this is technically tax fraud. Many single parents have long seen themselves as "head of the household," a status they generally don't envision giving up should they marry. Filing as a single head of household makes intuitive sense to couples who do not pool finances, and few of our couples do join finances even when married (some even say they don't know how much their spouse earns). Filing separately would allow each person to claim his or her own income on separate tax returns rather than "pooling" finances with each other for tax purposes. This practice could make some appear eligible for the EITC, or eligible for a larger EITC than they otherwise would be.

Sharon Ingram, a forty-seven-year-old single black employee of Boston Water & Sewer, lives on a rough street in Dorchester where shootings are not uncommon. She worries about keeping her teenage son, Tyrell, safe and on the right track. Sharon has been a single mother since her two children were young; Tyrell and his older sister, Deja, have different fathers, who both provide occasional financial support. Yet for the most part, Sharon says, she has had to be "both mommy and daddy" since her kids were little. When we ask her how getting married might affect her taxes, she says, "It depends on his [employment] status, where he's at. You know, I mean, he might be [earning] over the tax bracket or whatever, then we could file separately. I could still be his wife but we'd file separate. He ain't messing up my [return]! I need that money regardless. . . . If it wasn't beneficial for me, I probably would file my own taxes. You can do that, even being married. So I'd keep *my* dependents, and we'd just do it that way."

Note that many of the single mothers we spoke with assume that, if they were to marry, it wouldn't be to their children's father, as those relationships have long-since soured, and that filing separately would allow them to continue to claim "my dependents." From their perspective, filing separately is the fairest, most logical way to proceed unless there is a clear benefit to doing otherwise. In justifying these views, mothers often drew on their own identities as the primary providers for their children. The label "head of household" simply fits the reality of less educated parents, for whom nonmarital childbearing is the statistical norm, the rate of multiple partner fertility is high, and marriage often comes later, after the prime years of childbearing are completed. In short, there are deeper dynamics underlying these patterns than a desire to game the system. Sharon thinks that it would be a bad idea to let a man "mess up" her refund. Though her understanding of the IRS rules is incorrect, in her mind tax-filing status is unrelated to actual marital status. If it benefits a couple to continue filing separately, they ought to do so. Choosing to file taxes separately also reflects her belief that spouses ought to each control their own finances and split the bills, rather than pool their resources.[38]

Childbearing

Children play an important role in determining the size of a family's refund, as most claimants know. In addition to receiving a child tax credit of up to $1,000 for each qualifying child, families with children also receive a larger EITC.[39] Because the CTC is available only to parents and the EITC is so much larger for those with children than for those without, families have a much clearer sense of how having children affects one's refund than they do for how earnings or marriage might change it. Approximately three-quarters of those we spoke with believed that having additional children would increase their refund. Many families lump together the EITC and the CTC when they describe what constitutes the refund, and both programs pay higher benefits for more kids. When we asked how they knew this, many explained that they had seen their own refunds increase after having another child, or that they knew friends or family members who had gotten a "huge refund" because they had several children.

Yet when we asked people whether they would have an additional child in order to receive a larger benefit, many offered the commonsense explanation that the extra cost of a child far outweighed the value of the potential increase in their return. Dominique Henderson, a twenty-three-year-old black teacher's aide and single mother to preschooler Tatiana, noted that having a child just to increase a tax refund would be "the dumbest move you could ever make" since "that's not even close to how much you spend a year to take care of them." Similarly, twenty-three-year-old black emergency medical technician Lawanda James, single mother to seven-year-old Deshawn, told us, "People who use that as a solution are not smart. It's like, 'Okay, money is tight, and I'm gonna have a baby to get some more money.' No. That's never been the thing for me." Note that Lawanda not only insists that this isn't wise but also does not want to be associated with that type of behavior—doing so is deemed not only financially foolish but morally dubious as well. In sum, most parents we talked with made strong claims that they would never base their decision about whether to have a child on maximizing their refund. Many expressed a sharp moral disdain for making any life decisions (how many hours to work, whether to get married, etc.) on trying to get a bigger refund, but their disapprobation was particularly pronounced when it came to the question of deciding whether to have a child.

The complexity of family relationships among America's lower-income households, including many of those in this study, offered some flexibility in who claimed which child on a tax return. Because there is a sharp increase in the EITC—potentially amounting to thousands of dollars—for claiming one dependent relative to none, parents sometimes allowed others to claim one or more of their children. They often expected a cut of the gain (generally half of the refund) in exchange for doing so, unless the beneficiary was already "providing"—paying a substantial portion of their household bills or a lot of child support. The IRS has a set of rules about who can claim a child as a "qualifying child" for the EITC: the filer must live with the child for at least six months of the year, the child must be under nineteen (or under twenty-four if a full-time student for at least part of the year) and must be the claimant's "child (whether by blood or adoption) or stepchild, foster child, sibling or stepsibling, or descendant of one of these."[40] No two individuals can claim the same child, so there is a complex set of "tiebreaker" rules governing which person can claim the child, based on their income and their biological and residential relationship with the child. Despite these guidelines, parents believed that they had a fair degree of latitude in this area, and some felt perfectly free to bend the truth when it came to what they told their tax preparer about who supported which children. Both live-in and nonresidential fathers who were contributing regularly toward their children's expenses were often beneficiaries, as were mothers' boyfriends who provided nurture and financial support to the children. But grandmothers, aunts, and sisters who helped to take care of the children sometimes benefited too. Some of these individuals, especially live-in biological fathers and boyfriends, could make perfectly legitimate claims that they met most, or all, of the requirements to claim a qualifying child. Still, our families almost universally believed that the decision was a mother's to make—she owned the right to decide who would get to claim each of her children and often deserved a substantial cut of the benefit gleaned.

Ashlee Reed, the twenty-nine-year-old white Head Start teacher we met in chapter 1, and her boyfriend, Adrian, who is out of work, have been together for several years and are raising their three children, ages, three, four, and five. Each year at tax time, Ashlee and Adrian file separately, as the law directs (they are unmarried), and each claims one or two of the children as dependents. The one who has earned the most money over the course of the year claims two, while the one who has earned less claims one. Ashlee explains that she and Adrian devised this strategy after she "started hearing more about the credit and the different things you qualify for based on income." She realized that "if you made more it would probably make more sense to claim the two because it would give more of a deduction ... so that we would be able to still qualify for part of the refund." Ashlee feels that it's fair for each of them to receive a refund from the IRS because "really we both take equal care of the kids; it's not like one of us does more and deserves the refund more." IRS rules specify that for Adrian to legally claim these children, they need to be his children or step-children; sharing an address, or even providing for a girlfriend's children financially, does not render one legally eligible to claim these children for EITC purposes.[41] Ashlee and Adrian's strategy complies with these rules, but even among those who do not, the sense that the manner of filing taxes should reflect the financial realities on the ground is pervasive.

SPENDING BEHAVIOR AND DEBT REDUCTION

As noted earlier, families are reluctant to count on the refund. Still, the majority describe earmarking a portion of the tax return for digging themselves out of debt. Generally, these debts accrue because regular monthly expenses exceed income, not because of extra spending in anticipation of the EITC. But, as noted earlier, a few do consciously choose to incur debt in the months leading up to tax time, intending to use their tax refunds to pay it off.

The most common form of anticipatory spending is to let the heating bill pile up—a reasonable trade-off for an economically pressed household to make in the winter because the utilities can't legally be shut off until spring. In Massachusetts, as in many other states, utility companies are prohibited by law from shutting off heat for families with documented financial hardship between November 15 and March 15. Coincidentally, families commonly receive their tax refunds just in time to pay their outstanding utility bills and prevent shutoff, but they pay for the privilege in late fees. These families are often very eager to get the National Grid and NSTAR utility companies off their backs, especially once March comes. Johanna Clark used this strategy; this white twenty-six-year-old medical assistant and married mother of two, ages four and seven, told us that "by the time that we get our tax money back . . . our heat bill is usually high because we pay like $350 a month . . . in the winter. . . . With Christmas with the kids, we don't pay a gas bill in December. But in January, it's like now they want seven hundred. You're like, 'Oh, we'll get taxes next month!' And then it's around $1,000." Anticipating the refund also makes some feel more comfortable with letting other bills build up as well. As Maureen Ellis, a thirty-one-year-old divorced white waitress with two young girls, told us, "I know that the tax refund is there, so I build up bills throughout the year. And I use the tax refund to help me dig out [of] the debt that I made."

Many of our households do not deliberately go into debt in anticipation of the refund, yet they accumulate debt because their household budgets are so frequently in the red. These households also eagerly anticipate paying off debt with their refund. Recall from chapter 1 that in a typical month most of these households run a deficit. But anticipating the refund is as much a psychological relief as it is a source of material comfort. Erika Norris, a black married mother of seven, constantly struggles to keep up with the bills using the money her husband, Douglas, earns from working part time in construction. Even when times are tough, Erika finds comfort in knowing that the refund is coming. "I've been getting a refund every job I've had. . . . There's [a] security [in that]. I can always know I'm getting this money. I know I could pay this [bill off because] I got this [refund] coming. . . . I can catch up on my bills. . . . If I can't pay a bill, I don't worry about it because I know I can pay it when I get the refund."

We heard a similar sentiment expressed by Tracy Sherman, a single twenty-eight-year-old white mother of two elementary school–aged girls who works as a medical coder, filing paperwork in the billing department of Boston Medical Center, for which she nets about $2,000 a month. Tracy tells us,

> I think about [the refund] *all year long*, you know what I mean, it's like, "Oh, I can't wait until I get my tax money so I can do this and that . . . !" You're thinking of all crazy things that you can spend it on—"Oh, I can get a bigger TV," or "I should go get a laptop," or, you know, stuff like this. But, I mean, realistically it comes at a good time, at that point where "Okay, I need to pay bills," and everything comes in perspective of what is a priority and what you really need.

For families like Tracy's, simply the thought of what might be done with the refund provides an escape from the daily grind, even if what *could* be done is often replaced with what *should* be done once the check arrives. The freedom to dream is one of the tax refund's rewards.

THRIFT OR SPENDTHRIFT

The new work-based safety net has its fans and detractors. Some say the lump sum feature of tax credits is ideal because this method of disbursement helps families to save. Many believe that they couldn't do so otherwise. In this way, it has the potential to boost the accumulation of assets by enabling large purchases or investments. This is important, as inequality in wealth is even larger than the already wide gap in incomes between the rich and poor. Others point out that the cash transfers offered through the tax code do nothing to address a fundamental flaw in the American labor market: fewer and fewer unskilled and semiskilled workers make enough to support a family.[42] Skeptics also worry that the poor will do what many Americans do with a windfall—they might "blow" the money on luxuries rather than securing the items that their children most need. As we've shown, families' actual allocation of the tax refund does not perfectly reflect the views of either its supporters or its detractors. Instead, these patterns reflect a more nuanced story. Families greatly value the sense of relief from financial pressure that the EITC provides, but they also strive to have, and to give their children, a fleeting taste of not being poor—via modest splurging. They especially value the chance to think big about the future.

We can think about these allocation patterns in various ways. If we use the logic employed by economist Timothy Smeeding and colleagues and define "improving social mobility" very broadly, including investments in traditional mobility channels such as schooling, as well as investments in durable goods and debt reduction, 63 percent of the refund is spent in this way (17 percent for savings, 21 percent for schooling and asset accumulation, and another 25 percent for reducing debt).[43] Yet, despite families' strong desire to save, less than one in five dollars was put in savings. And while many aspired to home ownership, only 3 percent of the refund went to home purchase or repair—perhaps less than it otherwise would be, since our families lived in one of the country's most expensive real estate markets.

Furthermore, what savings there were often ended up providing a rainy day fund to smooth income fluctuations—a valuable asset to be sure—rather than a nest egg for longer-term goals. Most families tapped into their saved refund dollars during the ensuing months—only 42 percent of the money initially saved, 7 percent of total refund dollars, remained in savings six months after tax time. Some were quite resolute about protecting their savings, yet felt compelled to dip into them when the car broke down, or when an injury or medical emergency generated unexpected debt, or when income suddenly fell because of the loss of a job or reduced hours, a gap in child support payments, or the rupture of a relationship with a parent or a boyfriend who had been helping out financially.

Others describe "pinching off" their savings little by little. Having these savings also means that they can pay all of their bills in full for a time instead of juggling them as they might otherwise do. Tanya Salazar, a black twenty-eight-year-old mother of three, lives in Dorchester with her husband, Angelo, and works at a T-shirt factory while Angelo sells hot dogs at a stand at Fenway Park, an under-the-table job. They also receive SSI for their son, Lorenzo, who has been diagnosed with severe bipolar disorder. The family used to have a housing subsidy, but they lost eligibility when Tanya received a small raise at work, pushing them just above the income limit. This past tax season, Tanya put money from the refund into college savings accounts she had set up for her children, twelve-year-old Lorenzo, eight-year-old Aisha, and five-month-old Manuel. "From there on," she tells us, the rest is spent on "what I like to call 'crackers and chips.' That's just like bullshit stuff."

Note that families did not succeed in allocating much of their refund to two purposes that might directly promote social mobility: moving to a better neighborhood with higher-performing schools or enrolling their children in a parochial or private school. Households spent an average of 2 percent of the refund on improving their own human capital through higher education. Spending on durable goods, such as car repairs and purchases (8 percent) and appliances and furniture (8 percent), was the most common form of asset accumulation at tax time.

For many families, the first step in getting ahead is digging out from under debt. As we have described, many have creditors breathing down their necks or are in danger of having services disconnected, having items repossessed, or even being evicted. As a result, many use the refund to pay off overdue bills and longer-term debt (see figure 4)—amounting to 25 cents out of each refund dollar. Families who spend refund dollars on debt reduce their debt burdens by almost 50 percent on average.[44]

But a big chunk of refund dollars (24 percent) goes toward what we call "current consumption"—meeting one's regular monthly expenses, which include paying one's bills in full and on time for a few months, plus stockpiling groceries and household goods and paying ahead on important bills like the rent. Michelle Tavares, a twenty-five-year-old black mother with a nineteen-month-old son, works as a clerk at an auto body shop, but even after she splits the bills with her husband, Jonah, who works as a cable installer, money is still tight. She was thrilled that she could pay off her many back bills with her refund. She recalls thinking,

> "I can pay my cell phone. I can pay my electricity. I can pay little things. I owe money on my son's insurance. I can pay that!" Just little things, you know. . . . Everything ended up going towards paying bills. . . . We had to do stuff that we knew would get shut off. I mean, you know you have other bills to pay, but you have to think of basic needs for your kid, you know. I have to think about his shelter and stuff. You go and pay your electricity because you want to have light.

Parents also explain how their refunds provide them with a cushion while the money lasts, so they don't have to worry as much about the size of their grocery bills or hold so tightly to the strict monthly budgets that they face the rest of the year. Luanna Fields, a white education coordinator who lives with her husband and teenaged son in Malden, a lower-middle-class suburb north of Boston, tells us that the refund "helps out a lot. It gives you that feeling that when you go to a grocery store you don't have to count every penny, you know what I mean? It's just nice to know that you have that extra money to be able to, you know, buy those things that you normally would turn your head on. . . . It's just nice to know that it's coming, that, you know, you can relax for a little bit and you have that extra money in your pocket." The real luxury here is not the few extras at the grocery store so much as it is feeling that you *can* buy a name brand rather than a store brand, for example, or that you don't have to worry quite so much every day about how you are going to cover the basics.

As we've noted, spending on "treats," like toys or eating out, constitutes only a small fraction of refund dollars (11 percent), but these expenses are among the most meaningful for families, allowing them to indulge some of their children's wants, rather than only spending on needs. These "wants" include the rare trip to TGI Friday's or Pizzeria Uno for a meal, a Dora the Explorer or Bob the Builder bedroom ensemble, a computer game, or, in rare cases, a pricey toy, such as a giant stuffed animal or a Nintendo Wii. Paying for small family vacations (a long weekend in New Hampshire, for example) and hosting a special event, like a backyard barbecue for family and friends, are also popular. Debra's family jaunt to the Connecticut Red Lobster was unusually lavish when compared to the practices of most families in our study.

Many parents eloquently describe how indulging in small luxuries such as these makes them feel like "real Americans" and makes their children feel like "ordinary kids"—even the Superman Pop from the ice cream truck carries an enormous symbolic weight.[45] Tamara Bishop, a thirty-three-year-old assistant teacher in a preschool classroom, is a black mother raising four children, who range in age from five to fifteen, on her own. With the modest amount of refund that remains after catching up with the bills, she relates the tremendous joy she felt in "treat[ing] the kids to the movies and get[ting] popcorn." That little bit of extra money in her pocket meant that she could just "let them have fun."

As we've described, previous studies, drawing on surveys or administrative records, have revealed that EITC receipt is tied to better mental and physical health and health behaviors among adults, better prenatal care and a lower risk of low birth weight among newborns, and, among children, higher test scores, as well as a higher likelihood of college enrollment and completion.[46] These studies, however, tell us little about *how* the EITC confers such benefits. Our study offers grounds for informed speculation about potential pathways. Improved finances may reduce material hardship, bring relief from stress, enhance one's feelings of efficacy as a parent, and bring pride in the status of "worker" and a sense of social inclusion. Finally, receipt of the EITC offers the peace of mind that may come from having money in the bank to weather the financial ups and downs that may lie ahead.

Each year though, once the refund is gone, "It's back to life," says trolley driver Ida Holmes, a fifty-four-year-old black divorced mother with a teenaged son. When the refund runs out, families return to reality—the struggle to cover their monthly bills with their wages or to cope with unexpected expenses. Corine Samuels, a forty-nine-year-old black administrative assistant who is divorced and cares for her four-year-old granddaughter, says that after the refund money is spent, "the bills, they just come so fast. It's like you got to rob Peter to pay Paul." The relief and comfort provided by the refund are palpable, but only for a few months. After the thrill of that lump sum in mid-February or early March, and the dreams that it inspires all year, most families have exhausted their refund by the time summer ends. But they've brought their budgets more into balance, given their kids a special treat, and invested in those durable goods—a used car, furniture, or a refrigerator—that increase their standard of living, items they could never have afforded in a regular month. Some have accomplished more: 7 percent of the refund remains in savings and 5 percent has been invested in homes or college savings.

As described, the financial stress households feel during the rest of the year is reflected in the popularity of the Refund Anticipation Loan. Families may plan all year for how to "invest" their savings in things that will ensure a brighter future, but when tax time comes many are in fairly desperate straits. Therefore, the fact that they manage to save at all—and manage to set aside as much as they do for mobility purposes—is, in our view, quite remarkable.

Despite their usually failed attempts to save or to invest meaningfully in their longer-term goals—a house, college for the kids, a nest egg for retirement—families continue to see the EITC as an opportunity to achieve their mobility goals. For most, tax time is their one chance to save, and they dream about what they could do if they could manage to save more of the refund next year. These dreams remain a source of hope for even the most financially strapped families. In this way, our work-based safety net may keep families psychologically afloat while they struggle to make it until February.

3   The New Regime
through the Lens of the Old

The story of the modern EITC, created in 1993 and fully implemented by 1996, must be understood in the context of the larger story of the landmark 1996 welfare reform. It was no accident that the two were forged during the same presidential administration. But converting a tiny tax credit into the program we have today—a pay raise for the working poor—was the brainchild of Harvard economist David Ellwood and a team of dedicated public servants who had worked on antipoverty legislation in Washington for decades.

Ellwood began his career as a defender of welfare after finding that its dynamics were far more complex than had been previously known. Most people claimed welfare for only short spells, suggesting that, for the typical recipient, it was a hand up and not a handout.[1] But, in 1984, Charles Murray's influential thesis—advanced in his book *Losing Ground*—gained strong currency: according to Murray, an increasingly generous welfare system caused poverty rather than alleviated it by creating perverse incentives to eschew work and marriage.

Suddenly, Ellwood found himself in the position of defending welfare against the likes of Murray. Though scholars roundly criticized Murray's statistical methods, and subsequent analysis revealed only a small negative effect on either work or marriage, the argument had broad public appeal. Because it fit so neatly into popular views of welfare recipients as behaving in reprehensible ways, it was a claim that was repeated at dinner tables across America as an incontrovertible truth.

Ellwood quickly found that there were few things less pleasant than defending welfare. Letters and phone calls came pouring in, decrying his views. Even welfare recipients were contacting Ellwood and calling him crazy for defending welfare. During those years, Ellwood recalls precious few friendly phone calls. Finally, he decided to change his strategy. As he puts it, "When everyone tells you you're drunk, lie down."

Given the ferocious reaction that Ellwood's defense of welfare had provoked, he came to the conclusion that America had to do something fundamentally different to support the poor; we couldn't merely reform welfare, we had to replace it. He took a step back and, along with Harvard colleague Mary Jo Bane, asked the following: What was it about welfare that ran so fundamentally against the American grain?[2] In his book *Poor Support*, published in 1988, Ellwood concluded that policy makers needed to devise a set of social policies to help the poor that would be consistent with American values—welfare clearly wasn't. Finally, the epiphany came—instead of asking how many poor people there were and what the government could do to help them, one should ask why people are poor and what it would take so that they wouldn't be poor, given what the government could actually control.

A key insight soon followed. The working poor were an obvious group of needy Americans that were being almost completely ignored. Cash welfare wasn't really helping them at all—AFDC punished those who worked, imposing an effective marginal tax rate on wages of nearly 100 percent. And most noncash benefits for the poor, like food stamps and Medicaid, were tied to cash welfare at the time. If you were working but poor, you couldn't win. Isn't it proposition one, Ellwood asked, that, if you work, you shouldn't be poor? More fundamentally, he wondered, how can the country justify helping some poor people when others who are undeniably playing by the rules and working—actions fully in line with America's bootstraps credo—aren't getting any meaningful assistance?

This small change in Ellwood's thinking made things fall into place in a different way. Working poverty is the one form of poverty that clearly went against Americans' beliefs; if you work, you shouldn't be poor. One would be hard pressed to find many American citizens who disagreed with that proposition; it was a simple idea that everyone could get behind. When Ellwood shared this basic notion with audiences around the country, heads would nod. After struggles with the value conundrums posed by welfare—that welfare did nothing to promote work, family, or independence, three ideals that Americans held dear—the idea of helping the working poor was immensely appealing. Work was central to the American ethos. Indeed, in America it was the equivalent of a badge of citizenship. A pay raise for the working poor was a policy that got the values straight for once. No conundrums. No more hate mail.

The trick was to identify the mechanism that could be used to fix the problem. Most economists had concluded that the strategy of raising the minimum wage wouldn't be targeted enough. Senator Russell Long had advanced this argument in the early 1970s, when alternatives to Nixon's guaranteed income scheme were being proposed. Besides, one would have to raise the minimum wage so high to fix the problem that the costs would be prohibitive—and, at that level at least, many economists believed that the consequences to the economy would have been too great.

A wage subsidy would have been ideal, Ellwood and others thought, but it was too complicated—too much information and oversight would have been required. Meanwhile, the government already had a program— a tiny tax credit that had been invented in 1975 in the wake of Nixon's failed guaranteed minimum-income proposal to offset high payroll and regressive sales taxes. The program (1) gave no money to people who were not employed and (2) was prowork: up to a certain point, the more you worked, the more you received. Why not transform this early incarnation of the EITC from a tax-relief policy into a pay raise for working-poor families?

In 1988, Democrats convened advisory panels that considered what to do about welfare, which they felt was in need of reform. Ellwood was on several of these panels. Then, at a meeting of the National Commission for Children (which Jay Rockefeller led, with Arkansas governor Bill Clinton as a member of the group), Ellwood presented a paper titled "Reducing Poverty by Replacing Welfare." His argument centered on three key ideas: (1) if you work, you should not be poor; (2) one parent shouldn't have to do the job of two; and (3) social policy ought to give a hand up and not a handout to the able-bodied poor. In his paper, Ellwood advocated for replacing welfare with "transitional," time-limited assistance, plus assured child support (ensuring that both parents did their share). Most of the paper, though, was devoted to championing the expansion of the EITC, a position that was growing in popularity. Then Ellwood presented the paper at the National Governors Association, with Clinton again in attendance. Clinton virtually rushed the stage, exclaiming how enthusiastic he was about the paper.

During the presidential campaign that followed, Ellwood didn't meet with Clinton directly, but he worked on the candidate's platform, talking repeatedly with deputy campaign manager Bruce Reed, so much so that many in the media began calling Ellwood Clinton's welfare czar. Ellwood kept a phone line open during the presidential debates—for the back-scene moment when either candidate made a gaffe and staff had to furiously construct talking points to fix mishaps or to sharpen attacks. But welfare was not discussed once during the 1992 presidential debates. Still, welfare reform was clearly on Clinton's radar; he wanted to sound like a different kind of Democrat—one that was not as out of touch with the American people as his "tax and spend" predecessors, who lost elections. The pledge to "end welfare as we know it" became part of his standard stump speech—a signature promise of his campaign.

After Clinton won the presidency, Ellwood waited for the invitation to join the administration—he had been called the welfare czar after all—but weeks went by without a call. Finally, on the Friday before winter break, just as he was leaving his office at Harvard's Kennedy School of Government on his way home for the holidays, the phone rang. He told his assistant, "Unless it's really, really important, I'm not here." It was the newly appointed secretary of Health and Human Services, Donna Shalala, offering him a job.

All along, Clinton had hinted he was paying attention to Ellwood's mantra about the working poor: "People who play by the rules shouldn't lose the game." In his speech accepting the nomination at the Democratic convention, Clinton had offered a friendly amendment to Ellwood's oft-repeated phrase: he said, "For too long, those who play by the rules and keep the faith have gotten the shaft."[3] Then Ellwood learned that Clinton's chief domestic policy adviser had been told to keep his paper "Reducing Poverty by Replacing Welfare" with her at all times. She had apparently done so, displaying to Ellwood a copy that had been photocopied so many times that it was barely legible. Ellwood offered to get her a clean copy.

Even before Ellwood was confirmed as the Department of Health and Human Services' assistant secretary of planning and evaluation, Clinton gave his first address—it was a budget address, because the State of the Union address doesn't occur until the president is in office for at least a year. In that 1993 speech, Clinton announced that he was going to dramatically expand the EITC, saying, "We will reward the work of millions of working poor Americans by realizing the principle that if you work 40 hours a week and you've got a child in the house, you will no longer be in poverty." Ellwood and Robert Shapiro (who invented the phrase "Make work pay") were given the job of determining just how exactly to tweak the EITC to fulfill Clinton's promise. They reworked the credit precisely so that a full-year, full-time, minimum-wage job would get a family of three out of poverty—almost to the dollar.[4]

Within days, Ellwood found himself making his first visit to the Oval Office, with the secretary of the Treasury, the undersecretary, and others in attendance, to present his plan. Clinton queried the group on the fine details of how the credit had been structured. The group turned to Ellwood to explain, and Clinton quickly saw the sense in what Ellwood had done. Ellwood walked out of that meeting thinking that he had accomplished a third of his work as undersecretary of Health and Human Services in the first week. What he didn't know was that this moment would be a high point; though a great deal would be accomplished, he would later oppose the president's decision to sign the Republican version of welfare reform, which Ellwood believed provided too few protections for families who hit the new time limits without finding a job.[5]

Any student of welfare knows that the years following 1996's landmark welfare reform coincided with the largest increase in work among single mothers in history, as well as the largest decrease in the welfare rolls the country had ever seen. Most have thus concluded that welfare reform "worked." Now, in hindsight, we have learned that the new EITC—the pay raise for the working poor—was probably a major reason why welfare reform succeeded.[6] A modest program with an innocuous name, originally crafted as tax relief for the working poor, had been called into service for a radically redefined purpose. Robert Greenstein, who was appointed to serve on the Bipartisan Commission on Entitlement and Tax Reform, worked behind the scenes, along with Wendell Primus, deputy assistant secretary of human services policy at the Department of Health and Human Services, and Bruce Reed, chief domestic policy adviser and director of the Domestic Policy Council, to get the new EITC through Congress in 1993. When they succeeded, everyone in this group knew it was a big win.[7] However, it was the 1996 welfare reform legislation—the Personal Responsibility and Work Opportunity Reconciliation Act, or PRWORA— that garnered all of the media attention, and this is the policy change that has been celebrated by politicians and the public. In contrast, the transformation of the EITC into the nation's largest antipoverty program for working families with children occurred with virtually no fanfare.[8]

Johanna and Mack Clark were just teenagers when the welfare system changed so dramatically and the modern EITC was born. For a time, Johanna was among the dwindling share of single mothers who went on welfare in the aftermath of that reform. The way Johanna, twenty-six, and Mack, twenty-nine, characterize that time offers a rich illustration of how profoundly the safety net has changed.

This white couple is raising Duncan, age seven, and Carrie, age four, in a well-maintained, four-bedroom apartment on the second floor of a triple-decker in the "Southie" neighborhood of Boston. The unit is just down the street from a bakery, an art gallery, and a health clinic, in a neighborhood of multifamily dwellings. In many respects, theirs looks like the typical American family home. Both children have their own bedrooms, with Carrie's decorated in Mattel pink, strewn with stuffed animals, and offering a TV and DVD player; they've made the fourth bedroom into a computer room for the family. The small kitchen has a sturdy table tucked against one wall, and the living room is dominated by a large TV and overstuffed furniture. The kitchen table and living room couch, side tables, and chairs have been purchased an item or two at a time each year when February rolls around and Johanna and Mack get their tax refund.

Duncan plays in his room and Carrie watches TV while Johanna and Mack sit down together at the kitchen table to tell us about their lives.

After dating for five years or so (it took a while for Mack's "cold feet" to warm up to the idea of marriage), Johanna and Mack were finally wed four years ago, after they had already had two children. Mack grew up as the baby of a family of seven children in Southie, and the Clarks still see a lot of Mack's family. Johanna had a completely different experience growing up. Because of neglect, she was removed from her mother's care when she was eleven and was shuttled between nine foster homes and a brief stay with her father after those placements failed. She met Mack when she was eighteen.

Johanna combines full-time work as a medical assistant and schooling—she is completing her prerequisites for a nursing degree—while Mack describes himself as a stay-at-home dad. Mack had been working, but he injured his foot on the job; while he was out on workers' compensation, Johanna found employment. Since they don't feel that they can afford day care and don't like strangers taking care of their children anyway, the two decided that Mack would stay home with the kids while Johanna took on the breadwinner role.

Johanna and Mack have tried hard to do the long-range thinking that they hope will ensure a more prosperous future. Soon after Duncan was born they came to the conclusion that they were never going to get ahead unless at least one of them furthered their education (both had dropped out of high school, and only Johanna had her GED). So they moved in with Mack's mother to save on rent, and Johanna enrolled in a training program that would certify her as a medical assistant. While in school, she spent six months on the welfare rolls. Once she earned her certification, she found a job and left welfare behind. Now she is taking the next step toward financial security, earning credits for a nursing degree a little at a time. But she's doing so while working full time.

With only one wage earner, the Clarks' budget demands belt tightening. Their monthly income from Johanna's regular pay plus overtime totals $2,463, which falls short of their $2,784 in monthly expenses. When Carrie begins kindergarten next year and Mack can go back to work, things will improve. This year, they had to use much of their $5,400 tax refund to pay bills they'd fallen behind on. Right now, it seems, there is not a lot of money left at the end of the month, but the Clarks are pretty happy in their current straits—anything is better than being on welfare, they say.

Like many others who have dealt with the cash welfare system—now officially known as Temporary Assistance to Needy Families (TANF)—Johanna and Mack feel they must "explain away" Johanna's days on welfare. Their strong need to justify her reliance on government benefits reflects their palpable desire to distance themselves from the unpopular image of welfare recipients. As Johanna and Mack think back on this time in their lives, we hear familiar themes: it was only for a short time; it was only because Johanna was going to school in order to better herself and to increase her ability to be self-reliant through work; it was for the good of their child; and it was a terrible experience that she would do anything to avoid again. Johanna exclaims, "I never want to be on welfare ever." Mack interrupts, "It's just no money." Johanna continues, "There really is no money, they basically give you nothing to live off of, which, I guess, is a good thing, because then it would make more people want to fend for themselves. . . . It definitely wasn't enough and I just didn't like the whole idea of being on welfare, like I didn't want to do it kind of thing, but you do what you have to." "She was on for such, maybe like six months, it was such a short time," Mack adds. "It was only while I was finishing up school," says Johanna. Mack interjects, "I think she might have been out of work." Johanna begins to sum up by saying, "I just didn't like the whole," and Mack completes her thought, "It's depending on other people, that's what it is." Johanna ends the discussion by asserting, "And I like to depend on myself."

In his book *Poor Support,* David Ellwood pointed to four value tenets that have shaped Americans' attitudes toward welfare for generations: self-reliance, the value of work, the primacy of family, and the importance of community. The Clarks justify Johanna's welfare receipt in astonishing correspondence to these values. Both Johanna and Mack assert the value of self-reliance through work; the implied contrast is with those who do not share the Clarks' dedication to American ideals but who are willing instead to sponge off the state. Both husband and wife work hard in this narrative to dodge the stigma that observers might attach to Johanna's spell on welfare. Such justifications, and the implied condemnation of less virtuous others, are nearly ubiquitous among those who have had any experience with government aid. This is an indication of the disreputable position of cash welfare in the moral hierarchy of government benefits—

and starkly contrasts with the pride respondents take in claiming that tax refund check each year.

In this chapter, we focus specifically on families' experiences with and perceptions of what remains of the old need-based welfare system, TANF. It will quickly become clear that, at least among the families in our study, TANF is vilified. Their discussions of TANF, or "welfare," as it's usually called, sharply contrast with the tone and texture of what they say about the refundable tax credits—the EITC and the child tax credit—that they receive at tax time. Importantly, as discussed in chapter 2, they do not see these as "welfare."

In Massachusetts, TANF goes by the name Transitional Aid to Families with Dependent Children (TAFDC). As of 2005, a single parent with two children could receive some cash benefits if her monthly income fell below the equivalent of $708 per month, her car wasn't worth over $10,000, and her other assets (excluding a home) didn't exceed $2,500. If the family had no earnings, TAFDC would cut them a monthly check for $618, for a limited time. The state, which collects child support on TANF recipients' behalf, would also retain all but $50 of any child support paid in a given month as partial compensation for the cash welfare benefits. If they had earnings, the first $120 plus 50 percent of their remaining wages would be "disregarded" (not counted) in the determination of their benefit level; for any additional income, they would forfeit about fifty cents in benefits for each dollar earned. Other government programs, such as SNAP and housing subsidies, would also reduce their benefits against these earnings.

The evolution of the social safety net can be seen in the falloff in the Massachusetts welfare rolls—in contrast to the rise in the number of EITC recipients, detailed in figure 5. Massachusetts's trends reflect the dramatic declines in welfare rolls that have occurred across the country. These changes are nothing short of astonishing when we consider that welfare reform was tried before 1996—repeatedly—but these attempts failed, moving hardly any families off of the rolls. In 1988, for example, with 10.9 million individuals on the rolls nationwide, President Reagan and Congress passed the Family Support Act, which made work requirements a core component of welfare.[9] Nonetheless, when then-presidential can-

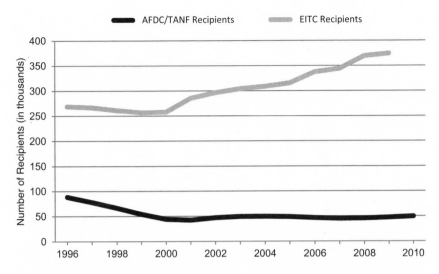

Figure 5. Number of AFDC/TANF and EITC recipients in Massachusetts, 1996–2010. Source: AFDC/TANF numbers from Office of Family Assistance (1996–2010). EITC numbers were obtained from Brookings Institution (2010).

didate Bill Clinton first promised to "end welfare as we know it" in 1991, there were even more welfare recipients than there had been three years before—12.9 million. During the next five years, when states were given freedom to experiment with their own versions of welfare reform, most focused on getting recipients into jobs, but again there were no dramatic declines. Though the number of welfare recipients had started to fall in 1994, it still stood at 12.3 million two years later, on the eve of the 1996 welfare reform. But by the time President Clinton left office in 2000 only 5.8 million people remained on welfare—a decline of 47 percent in only four years (see figure 6, which shows the changes in the total number of families receiving welfare), helped along by the booming economy of the late 1990s.

The financial crisis of the late 2000s had not yet hit when we interviewed families in 2007. Since then, many more families fell on hard times, and we revisit some of these families in the final chapter of this book to see how they have fared. But what was remarkable about the Great Recession from our point of view was that there was only a small

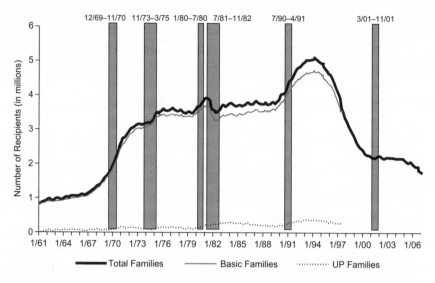

Figure 6. Number of families receiving AFDC/TANF in the United States, 1961–2007. "Basic Families" are single-parent families, and "UP Families" are two-parent cases receiving benefits under AFDC Unemployed Parent programs that operated in certain states before FY 1991 and in all states after October 1, 1990. The AFDC Basic and UP programs were replaced by TANF as of July 1, 1997, under the Personal Responsibility and Work Opportunity Reconciliation Act of 1996. Shaded areas indicate periods of recession as designated by the National Bureau of Economic Research. The decrease in number of families receiving assistance during the 1981–82 recession stems from changes in eligibility requirements and other policy changes mandated by the Omnibus Budget Reconciliation Act of 1981. Beginning in 2000, "Total Families" includes TANF and SSP families. Last data point plotted is March 2007. Source: Crouse, Huaun, and Rogers (2008, Appendix A).

uptick in the welfare rolls (see figure 7). This is a profound testament to welfare's declining role in the array of social programs aiding the poor and near poor. And this is in contrast to a marked increase in use of the Supplemental Nutritional Assistance Program—SNAP—(formerly called food stamps), which started to rise when President Bush championed changes that made the program more accessible, particularly for working families, and then swelled further during the years of the Great Recession.

After the spectacular declines in the welfare rolls that followed welfare reform in 1996, some commentators cautioned that the real test of the

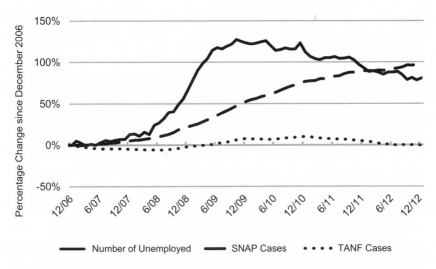

Figure 7. Changes in TANF, SNAP, and unemployment in the United States, 2006–12. Source: Center on Budget and Policy Priorities (2013a).

new system would come with the first major economic downturn. That time has come, and, clearly, TANF is no longer functioning as much of a safety net, even in very difficult times—as of 2011, only 1.1 million adults and 3.3 million children remained on the rolls.[10] The very modest rise in welfare evident at the height of the recession pales in comparison to the huge cuts in the number of recipients that occurred in the preceding decade—it is clearly no longer the "Plan B" for the poor that it was before 1996. A web of in-kind support—SNAP, along with WIC, government-sponsored health insurance, and, as mentioned earlier, for the 25 percent of eligible households lucky enough to get them, housing subsidies—now serves as the safety net to catch families when they fall. The EITC, in contrast, is designed to give them a boost once they already have some traction in the labor market.

Many families we spoke with have been struggling economically for years, if not decades. This is why a relatively high proportion—44 percent—say that they have used welfare sometime in the past. Only 8 percent, though, have claimed any cash benefits in the past year. Like Johanna Clark, most say they were on the rolls for only a short time, and under conditions of acute need. This is not surprising: it is rare, at least in most states, to stay on welfare for very long.

Although nearly half of parents say they've received benefits from welfare at some point, either TANF or its predecessor, AFDC, strong negative views of the program are rampant. Perspectives on TANF, in particular, and on means-tested assistance more generally, are embedded in larger American views of which behaviors are right and wrong, and who is deserving and undeserving. We will argue that the line that these households draw between the deserving and undeserving reflects what they believe it means to be American. In this chapter, we show that one kind of government assistance ("welfare" and its in-kind ancillary, SNAP) forces claimants to "cross the road that separated the community of citizens from the outcast company of the destitute," in the words of T. H. Marshall.[11] But another radically different kind of government aid, the EITC, can actually confer benefits and privileges.

In contrast, over the past eighty years the traditional cash welfare programs, like the Elizabethan Poor Laws that Marshall was writing about, have formed the great exception to the expanding sense of the social rights of citizenship, welfare rights that are not granted solely on the basis of need but based on one's status as a citizen. As David Ellwood so painfully learned when he tried to defend it—and what many of our families would have told him—is that welfare is perceived not as an integral part of the social rights of citizenship but as an alternative to them. To claim welfare, poor households must cease to be citizens in the social sense.

This is nowhere more forcefully communicated than at the welfare office itself. In the introduction to this book, we describe the gritty exterior of the old welfare office in East Boston, with the words "OVERSEERS OF THE PUBLIC WELFARE" emblazoned above the door, marking those who passed through its doors as dependents, in need of public supervision. Take that edifice as a metaphor for how it feels to be on welfare: for generations, researchers who asked recipients to relate their experiences at the welfare office collected stories rife with complaints about rude caseworkers who "treat the money as if it's their own," long lines, and impersonal treatment, insensitive to the tragedies that often drove parents to welfare's door.

By 1975, all recipients were required to comply with child support enforcement efforts as a condition of their benefits—thus caseworkers sometimes callously pried into the sex lives of the poor, often in cubicles that provided very little privacy. Since welfare reform, privacy has been further compromised by new requirements such as the drug tests that some states and jurisdictions have tried to implement. Even the Great Recession did not lead to a reconsideration of the idea that some form of need-based cash assistance that was not predicated on behavior (work) should be an entitlement during especially bad economic times, as it had been before the 1996 welfare reform.

Historian Michael Katz writes that in the 1700s American politicians of the time sought to draw a line between the "able-bodied" and the "impotent"—those physically disabled or otherwise incapacitated through no fault of their own—in determining who should receive limited public resources.[12] He chronicles how this division morphed into a focus on rooting out the truly needy from the merely lazy in the 1800s and beyond; moral judgments of deservingness accompanied these distinctions. As Katz explains, those who are not seen as responsible for their own neediness, because of disability, old age, or uncontrollable circumstances (like being widowed or laid off), make much more sympathetic figures and are judged to be more worthy of government help. On the other hand, those who are seen as engaging in immoral behaviors (for example, having children outside marriage or eschewing work) are considered undeserving of such assistance.[13]

This dynamic plays out in public opinion surveys. Political scientist Martin Gilens finds that the belief that welfare recipients are undeserving is the largest direct predictor of public opposition to welfare spending—more than other factors such as family income, political ideology or party, or beliefs in racial stereotypes.[14] Other survey research confirms this, showing that Americans are more likely to support progressive policies when the target group is seen as deserving (e.g., physically disabled) rather than undeserving (e.g., able-bodied); in addition, progressive policies are more likely to be endorsed when the responsibility for the group's poverty is seen to lie not with the individual but with society, or when the group's poverty is seen as being due to circumstances beyond individual control.[15] Public support, therefore, rests with programs that make assistance contingent on work effort.

Johanna and Mack's story, like the stories of many others in our study, reveals that this preference is not limited to the political realm and that these labels are not just applied by the middle class and wealthy to the poor. They are also ways in which those who believe that they are among the worthy poor try to distinguish themselves from the other poor Americans who are often deemed unworthy. Interestingly, work behavior, and not whether one must approach the government for assistance, is the basis for drawing the line. Indeed, some of our households claim more from the government each year than they could have if they had quit their jobs and applied for TANF. But among the array of government programs the EITC has a very special status. For while welfare and other means-tested programs available to the poor impose the mark of being undeserving—and connote visions of lobster-eating, Cadillac-driving social parasites—the EITC is a veritable certificate of deservedness. This sense of deservedness may be felt especially keenly if you claim it at the venerable H&R Block, which publicly confers the label "taxpayer." Alone among those programs targeted at poor families with children, refundable tax credits like the EITC are citizenship affirming.

WELFARE: "THAT'S NOT THE LIFESTYLE I CHOOSE TO LIVE"

As we saw in Johanna and Mack's story, lower-wage workers draw strong divisions between themselves and those whom they perceive to be living the "welfare lifestyle," which they characterize as choosing not to work, being on welfare for a long time, and, in general, getting benefits without being truly needy. They distance themselves from this definition as they describe their own experiences with welfare: parents routinely emphasize that they had no other choice but to go on welfare; it was only for a limited period of time; and they really needed it.

Though welfare benefits are calculated according to a stringent means test, welfare is most often discussed in moral terms, with judgments made about the values and character of those who claim it. These judgments are also made by parents who themselves have claimed benefits in the past. These parents pass judgment on others while insisting that they personally were not typical recipients; their use of the program was due to exceptional circumstances. Given their efforts to get and keep jobs, being on welfare does not give a suddenly needy mom or dad the feeling of being buoyed by the safety net; instead, it feels like a slap in the face. Unlike the EITC, which rewards work, welfare is perceived as rewarding the opposite: indolence and sloth.

Most charge that abuse of the system—claiming benefits that are not truly needed, or in lieu of efforts to provide for oneself—is the rule, rather than the exception, though none say they have been guilty of this charge. Marissa Lopez, a single Hispanic mother of three—ages five, eleven, and thirteen—in her early thirties who works as a medical assistant, describes her time on welfare as follows:

> I received it when Adriana was little, and, when I had had Jimena, that's when Governor Weld changed the law . . . [and] my two years was up when I had had Jimena. So that's when I went back to school and I got off of welfare completely, worked full time and went to school full time in the evening. . . . I was glad [I was working and going to school]. I didn't want to end up like everybody else, just sitting on welfare, getting welfare. . . . I could have sat on my behind and got the food stamps and the MassHealth, but my mother was like, "No, you're not going to. You're going to get up and get a job and support your kids." So I just didn't have the luxury of being able to sit on my ass.

Like many of the others we spoke with, Marissa takes pains to emphasize that she refused to "sit on welfare," opting to work and provide for her children herself. She portrays this choice as the more difficult option and details how hard she worked to get ahead. This is behavior that she says sets her apart from others who are content to depend on the government for a handout. It's interesting to note that Marissa draws this contrast even though she is aware that, since welfare reform, rules prohibit long-term benefit receipt and that in fact she herself left welfare only because she had "timed out" rather than of her own volition.

Penny McPherson, a white administrative assistant who lives with her fiancé and four-year-old son, is careful to offer a caveat to her critical evaluation of welfare recipients. Nonetheless, her views are similar to Marissa's. Penny gestures to the first-floor apartment across the street, saying,

> Like the family over there, they're on welfare, that's fine. Whatever. Everyone got to do what everyone got to do. But they take their check and spend it on

drugs and addiction. . . . So it's kinda like, it's going to the wrong hands. You
know? Like last year, they had a birthday party, and they took their kids'
birthday presents with the receipts. . . . They went and they returned the
kids' presents [for the money]. I'm not saying that all parents on welfare do
that. . . . But the ones who do . . .

Penny expresses the fairly common belief that those who receive government assistance are not using the money wisely and are engaged in an
array of immoral behaviors that speak to their lack of deservedness. As a
counterpoint, she offers a description of her own spending habits: "Give
me $100 and it's not going to me!" she exclaims, noting that she prioritizes
her four-year-old son over her own wants and needs. The implication is
that, while the government wastes its money on her undeserving neighbors, she would have put it to good (and morally appropriate) use: her son.

A short walk from the Fields Corner subway stop in Dorchester, we find
Alicia Robinson's apartment in a residential part of the neighborhood, a
good distance from the hustle and bustle of the shops along Dot Ave. Alicia
is a twenty-six-year-old black single mother and a current welfare recipient; until recently she worked as a personal care attendant but lost that
job. Alicia says she does the best she can for her daughter, three-year-old
Malia, whose photos are prominently displayed throughout their home.
The apartment's interior is in much better condition than one would guess
from looking at the building's shabby exterior. To enhance the homey feel,
she's outfitted each of the apartment's two bedrooms with colorful bed-
spreads and sheets. But evidence of her limited resources appears elsewhere in the house. The living room is all but devoid of furniture—a lone
table sits in the corner. The kitchen is also sparsely furnished, with just a
small table and a couple of chairs.

Alicia uses the opportunity to discuss her views of the welfare system to
condemn women who have more children just to get more money from
welfare, which she believes is a common occurrence. She then seeks to distance herself from other recipients by emphasizing her willingness to work:
"I just be like looking at these girls like, wow, you know, all these kids. . . .
They are going to cut welfare so what are all of you going to do . . . ? I'm not
lazy like that; I will get a job." Alicia names no one in particular in telling
her story but rather points to "these girls"—people she doesn't know but
sees on the street when she's out and about. She makes these claims even

though more than a decade has passed since Massachusetts put a "family cap" in place, which bars welfare recipients from receiving additional money if they have more children.[16] Alicia's views of the system, like those of many, are based more on supposition than on fact; she draws no obvious lessons from her own experience.

These perceptions sound remarkably similar to the stereotypes of shiftless, baby-making welfare moms that dominated the political debate prior to the transformation of the welfare system in 1996. In the pre–welfare reform days, one newspaper editorial declared, "Having babies while on welfare is wrong and we won't pay for it."[17] During the welfare reform debate in Massachusetts, Democratic state senator Michael C. Creedon claimed that "General Relief goes to people who are urinating on the floor in the bus station in Brockton and throwing up. They take that $338 and go to the nearest bar and spend it."[18] Bill Clinton, in his 1992 run for the presidency, called for an end to "permanent dependence on welfare as a way of life," despite evidence from David Ellwood and Mary Jo Bane that most welfare receipt was short term.[19] In the course of the national debates over welfare reform, some conservative congressmen compared welfare-reliant mothers to "alligators" and "wolves" in their speeches before Congress.[20]

As the proposed welfare reform legislation worked its way through the Senate in the 1990s, Republican senator Spencer Abraham of Michigan called welfare "the number one social problem in America today," and Robert Rector, of the conservative Heritage Foundation, referred to the program as "a system that promotes illegitimacy and destroys marriage."[21] It is notable that politicians have ascribed such wide-ranging powers to the welfare system, likening it to the use of a powerful narcotic.

For both Clinton and his conservative counterparts, taking a stance that was critical not only of the welfare *system* but also of the *people* who received assistance from it was a politically savvy move. In 1995, a nationwide poll revealed that 79 percent of Americans believed that those who were on welfare would never get off of it.[22] With the wide-ranging and fundamental overhaul of the welfare system in 1996, these stereotypes largely ceased to be the focus of political calls to action.[23] Nonetheless, they remain alive and well, at least among the families that we interviewed.

Massachusetts's TANF program, TAFDC, limits parents to twenty-four months of benefits in any given five-year period. Benefits are contingent on performing some sort of job search, work, or structured volunteer activity.[24] Despite the many dramatic changes in the system, meant to ensure that welfare aid is not a handout but a hand up, the program remains deeply stigmatized, and all of the old stereotypes seem to still stubbornly cling to the program.[25]

"THEY LOOK AT YOU LIKE YOU'RE NO GOOD"

Ironically, the families in this study have often been victims of the very stereotypes they impose. Angelica Rivera, a thirty-one-year-old Hispanic project manager at a health center and a married mother of three—two in elementary school and one in high school—describes her time on welfare as follows: "It was horrible. . . . They give you miserable money, and then you have [them] get on your case all the time. . . . 'Come in the office, come in the office, come in the office.' I think [the caseworkers] look at you like you're no good because you're on assistance. . . . I don't think she respected me. . . . They were making me look like a liar. . . . I think they [only] gave you enough [money] for like a bar of soap."

Bryn Gamble, twenty-eight and black, lives with her boyfriend and her five-year-old daughter and is now a buyer for a health insurance company. She is still outraged over the poor treatment that she received when she went to apply for welfare after her daughter was born. Her reaction is grounded in the fact that she identifies herself as someone who plays by the rules by working and supporting herself but just happened to hit a tough time and was therefore deserving of government aid. She says,

> That's why I think a lot of them treat people the way they do, because some people just abuse and use the system, so it looks, you know, it makes it worse for the people who really do need the help. And I was one of those, you know. Are you kidding me? I paid my taxes! Do you want to see my résumé? Do you want to see my paycheck stubs? I was so mad. It was disgusting. . . . I'm not lazy. I like [doing it on] my own. I really don't like for people to help me unless I really need it. . . . It was just so degrading and it was just so disrespectful.[26]

Tessa Morales, a thirty-year-old married white mother of three, ranging in age from five to fourteen, who works occasionally as a caterer, also felt judged by the welfare system. She describes her experience this way:

> Terrible. I'll never do it again. It was the worst experience. . . . I was sixteen, they told me [I had] to go back to school and put Philip into a day care [to get benefits]. [But then] I'm like "Oh, fuck this." I went and got a job and got off of it. Got off and worked ever since. . . . It was terrible. I'll never go back to them places again. Never. It's not for me. . . . They took me in a little office, in the welfare office, and they had me swear in front of a judge I was gonna pay [the] $42 [they overpaid me]. I was so embarrassed. I'm like, "You are wasting the taxpayers' money to throw me into this room with a *judge* and a swearing cop?" . . . I would never go back. . . . I swore I would work the rest of my life. I didn't care how I worked or where I worked, I would never go back there again. Never. And I didn't.

"I WAS TOO PROUD TO TAKE WELFARE, BUT THAT WAS THE ONLY CHOICE I HAD"

Chantelle Woodward, a thirty-four-year-old black medical assistant and mother of two, ages nine and fourteen, who is separated from her husband, really "needed" welfare; that's how she justifies her time on the rolls. She explains how her daughter had severely injured her hand, requiring trips for surgery and doctors' appointments. She had to take care of her child, which precluded her from working. "I had to take care of [my daughter]. I had to physically like bathe her and it was uncomfortable for her, but she couldn't use her hand, so I had to take a couple of months off [of work] for her . . . so at that point I did go on welfare. . . . I got all the documentation, everything that I needed so I was able to get welfare for my daughter." Chantelle's account is illustrative of a recurrent theme in people's stories about their time on welfare—they had no other choice. Furthermore, they say that they were doing it only for their children's sake, not for their own.

Chantelle continues on with her story: "I'm still gonna work. I just can't find myself sitting home all the time and not doing nothing and watching the same [TV] shows; that's not the lifestyle that I chose to live." She then draws on another recurrent theme—that leaving welfare and wanting to work are core credentials of a good parent. She says, "And not only that, but we have to survive, and I'm a role model for my daughter. I don't want them to get into that, to where it's okay to just stay home and don't work and don't think about responsibilities. I don't want that. I'm a role model for them, and I want them to know in order to get things in life and to get what you want you have to earn it, you have to go out there and get it, it's not gonna just come to you."

Fifteen years ago, researchers Kathryn Edin and Laura Lein found that, among those claiming welfare on the eve of welfare reform, there was a sharp tension between working and being a good parent; the two were often seen as being at odds with one another.[27] Although we do still hear about the difficulties of balancing work and parenthood, now many tell us that part of being a good parent is serving as a positive role model by working hard and staying employed. This sharp change in the view of work in relation to parenthood could, in part, be responsible for the strong distaste these lower-income parents have for welfare these days.

Lashara Redmond, twenty-six and black, describes her time on welfare as unavoidable and short-lived. This nutrition assistant and single mother to five-year-old Shadiah says, "I was only on welfare for a month, that's after I had my daughter, and I only did that so I could get a [child care] voucher. Because I could have [lived off of savings], but I just [went on welfare for a month] so I could get a voucher so I could get my daughter in day care because I wouldn't be able to afford that alone on my salary." For Lashara, it was okay to collect welfare because doing so is what allowed her to claim the child care subsidy that would allow her to work. Otherwise, she wouldn't be able to afford to take a job.

Maria Velasquez, a nurse's aide with a seven-year-old daughter, emigrated to the United States from Honduras as a child. She offers another Horatio Alger–type testimonial: "I try to live my life [with] whatever I have. . . . [In my country] they teach me, you have to work for whatever you want. . . . I don't like easy way. Sometime . . . I pray to God, 'Never [let me] go to welfare.' I know it [pays] nothing, but I know some people go over there and they don't need it." Maria believes that it is those who provide for themselves through work who deserve rewards. She knows that welfare pays little but suspects, nonetheless, that many people who receive it "don't need it."

In short, one's own past welfare receipt is seen as a regrettable necessity—only claimed in extreme situations—a source of intense shame, and woefully insufficient at the same time. These seemingly contradictory assessments of their time on the program aren't held by different groups but by the same people all at the same time. Take Tracy Sherman, a twenty-eight-year-old white single mother of two girls, ages six and eight, who works as a medical coder. She relates this story of how she ended up on welfare: "In the beginning I did it with my youngest when their dad [an alcoholic] had relapsed and I didn't want to put any of the burden on my parents. I felt like maybe I should go on it for a little while." Despite substantial misgivings, Tracy went ahead and applied for benefits. "I didn't feel good as a person, you know what I mean, like I come from a pretty good family, it's not like I'm struggling. I see people like in the lower end of Southie that really need it, and, you know, I was getting it and I could be working." Although Tracy believed that she could and should be employed, she had to sacrifice her self-worth for a while to attend to her parental duties. "[My daughter] was too young for me to go back to work . . . so I did it for probably like eight months, and then I got a job and my friend's mother did child day care inside her house, so she gave me a really good rate."

Even though Tracy believes that she did what she had to do in order to be a good mother, she claims she hated every minute of it.

> They gave me [cash] plus they gave me food stamps for formula and every-thing like that. And every time I used it, though, I felt like crap. . . . And constant appointments that you have to go to and you've got to bring in proof and you have to have people write you letters. . . . It was like they were constantly in your business. . . . And it's like, "Is it really worth it to just be getting, you know, $50 extra a week for formula and then like maybe $200 a week for assistance?" And I'm like, "I don't think so. I'd rather go to work and do it the regular way."

For Tracy, side glances at the grocery store when she pulled the electronic benefit card out—the form that food stamps, now called SNAP, come in—gave her sharp internal feelings of shame, as did having to prove repeatedly that she needed the money. And all for so little payoff. As Woody Allen once said, "The food here is terrible, and the portions are too small."

LEAVING THE OLD WELFARE REGIME BEHIND

Prior to welfare reform, Edin and Lein's research showed that recipients frequently worked without the knowledge of their caseworkers—often under the table for cash—in order to supplement their meager welfare benefits.[28] The new welfare rules have by and large eliminated this strategy. Because welfare recipients must be working, be involved in training, or serve as a volunteer to get benefits, they no longer have time to work covertly. In some ways, then, the package of benefits that welfare beneficiaries have to live on now is even lower than it was under the previous regime.[29] But as a result of the EITC that calculus changes dramatically when recipients leave welfare for employment. Full-time, full-year, low-wage workers with children are undoubtedly financially better off now than they have ever been before in terms of the assistance the government offers them.

The families whose stories we feature here come from widely varying backgrounds. Yet there is a consistent value system—a clear moral hierarchy—underlying their views of the acceptability of various government assistance programs. Collecting cash welfare and living in "the projects" are those forms of assistance that are most derided. The families disparage SNAP somewhat less (despite a relatively high earned-income threshold, receipt of this program is still quite "visible" because of the Electronic Benefit Transfer [EBT] card). The other main form of housing assistance, the housing choice voucher program known as "Section 8," which offers subsidies on market-rate apartments, is generally viewed as more acceptable than any of the programs above. This is probably because subsidized renters mix in with the general rental population. Unlike an address in a housing project (or even the use of an EBT card to pay for groceries), a Section 8 subsidy is largely invisible to outside observers, who have no way of distinguishing who among their neighbors has a subsidy and who does not. Government-sponsored health insurance programs (MassHealth, Medicaid, and the Children's Health Insurance Program, CHIP) hold virtually no stigma among the families we spoke with—perhaps because the programs are not restricted to the officially poor; children up to 300 percent of poverty are eligible for CHIP, for example.

The Special Supplemental Nutrition Program for Women, Infants, and Children (WIC) carries a status similar to health care, perhaps because it is limited to "nutritious foods" for pregnant women and very young children. Interestingly, at the WIC office mothers are encouraged to breast-feed, are weighed and measured to determine whether they are obese, and are given nutritional information. One might assume that potential claimants would find these intrusions offensive. Instead, many recipients welcome them. The practices even seem to add to their respect for the program, since they are "educational."

Child care subsidies and especially Head Start seem to carry no stigma either. Child care is enormously expensive in Boston, as in many other places. Nearly everyone we spoke with realizes the impossibility of paying for child care while working at a low-wage job. Besides, they say, a child care subsidy is what allows one to stay employed. In addition, Head Start (like WIC) is viewed as an educational program and draws some status from that designation. However, other than Head Start, all of these programs are to some degree seen as "welfare," while the EITC is not. As we've said, the EITC, by these households' lights, is the opposite of welfare.

Pundits and policy makers usually, though not always, agree on this view of the EITC. For example, while politicians on the right have made repeated claims that welfare perpetuates an underclass by discouraging marriage, few have made similar claims about the EITC or have even publicly worried about it. Nonetheless, as we have shown, the EITC does actually incur large marriage penalties in some cases. Americans have long been torn between judging the morality of our adult citizens (especially as evidenced by their work behavior) and wanting to provide assistance to the children in their care. The persistent critique of welfare we heard from the families in our study is based on the notion that welfare breeds immoral behavior (nonwork), which in turn breeds more poverty. To be a good role model to your kids, they say, you've got to be employed. Americans have long believed that providing support to able-bodied adults outside the paid labor force—even when they are raising children—risks the creation of a permanent dependent class. Recall that Ellwood and Bane's research had shown that this "way of life" was quite rare in reality, even back in the 1980s and '90s before welfare reform. Clinton and those who came after him castigated the system on this basis nonetheless.

The financial insecurity that lower-income families face creates a complicated relationship with government assistance programs. As we have shown, like their wealthier counterparts, the working poor hold sharply negative views of most government assistance programs. Nonetheless, many of these household heads claim SNAP or WIC, use housing subsidies, and enroll their children in Head Start or get a child care subsidy to bridge the gap between their wages and financial needs. As we showed in chapter 1, they believe that as working parents they deserve the hand up that these programs provide. The problem for the working poor is that many of these programs also serve those who don't have a job—people that they view as "undeserving." And this puts them on a moral tightrope when claiming these benefits. How do they distinguish themselves from those they deem the unworthy poor? The EITC's distinctiveness is that it offers low-wage workers an opportunity to secure government support without the baggage of the welfare label—no nonworker need apply.

Although a substantial portion of these families are not officially poor, it still rankles that their income from work isn't enough to cover their monthly expenses much of the time. The omnipresence of government assistance programs in so many of these families' lives vividly illustrates two key realities of the current labor market. First, jobs that many less educated American workers hold neither pay very much nor offer many avenues for meaningful advancement. Some Americans will spend years earning so little that supporting a family will require some form of government assistance—a housing subsidy or Medicaid, for example—much of the time. Others will come closer to the ideal of self-reliance most of the time, but an unexpected plunge in income—due to lost hours or layoffs, for example—or a sharp rise in expenses (a new baby arrives, the car breaks down, or a home repair just can't wait any longer) will prompt periodic need for government support.[30]

Turning our attention, as a society, to the working poor puts our cash assistance commitments more firmly in line with our other social support programs. Now cash benefits are seen as a right—a social right in a citizenship sense—only for those who are working and raising future citizens. Views of the EITC are most like those that Americans hold about Social Security's retirement benefits, which are also seen as a right because they are predicated on the past work behavior of the claimant or the claimant's spouse (those without a work history or without a spouse who worked can claim only a small benefit). Unemployment insurance is built on a similar premise, and importantly it requires that the job loss be involuntary. Social Security Disability Insurance, the federal disability program that serves those with a substantial work history, pays far more than its sister program, SSI, which is reserved for those without a sufficient work record. This latter program, like welfare, carries significant stigma and is viewed as problematic by our respondents, as well as society at large; the former has received much less public attention, even though the ranks of both programs are growing rapidly. Some have even charged that SSI is "the new welfare."[31]

Other forms of government assistance that are not viewed as welfare at all benefit legions of Americans; many of these are so beloved they are programmatic third rails—ones politicians would interfere with only at their own risk. The mortgage interest deduction for home owners is among the largest, along with other tax loopholes and shelters that often provide larger benefits to those higher up on the income ladder. The federal government and states also offer tax relief to those who engage in other forms of socially desirable behavior: the adoption tax credit, educational tax credits, home buyer tax credits, and credits to those who buy fuel-efficient hybrid cars are all recent examples. Like these benefits, the EITC largely escapes scrutiny, hidden among the complexities of the tax code and administered not by social service providers but by the IRS.

Economist Kenneth Boulding wrote that "social policy is that which is centered in those institutions that create integration and discourage alienation."[32] In other words, as they participate in social programs, recipients are endowed with personality traits that are the filter through which others come to see and treat them, and through which they may even come to see themselves. The EITC turns supplicants into taxpayers, even though they pay no federal and—in some states—no state taxes (except sales tax).[33] While "welfare" tries to divert potential claimants from its rolls, the EITC—often via the friendly faces at H&R Block—attempts to get the "customer" the largest possible benefit available by law.

4 Beyond Living Paycheck to Paycheck

Except for the small portion some manage to keep in long-term savings, our families typically fully allocate their tax refund in three months' time. For the other nine months of the year many find themselves living in the red, as the story of Ashlee Reed, in chapter 1, illustrates. With this in mind, it is quite remarkable that the typical household still manages to reserve nearly four refund dollars in ten for purposes they associate with getting ahead. Similarly, one in four dollars are devoted to paying off past debts, often with the goal of laying the financial groundwork for upward mobility. Most Americans would regard these as relatively sound financial decisions.

As we've argued in prior chapters, tax refund money is seen as special money. Accordingly, it is spent differently than regular monthly income—the income that families must live on during the other nine months of the year. During those nine months, families allocate very little, if any, of their resources to mobility goals or substantial debt payoff. Similarly, when Edin and Lein (1997) examined 165 low-wage working mothers' budgets in detail during the early 1990s, before either the modern EITC or the child tax credit went into effect, these mothers rarely reported that they used their earnings or other economic resources to pursue upward mobility. Nor did the 214 welfare recipients who also shared detailed budget information.

We've noted that many of our households explicitly associate the EITC with mobility goals. Dreams of upward mobility are pervasive, often fueled by the refund. We've argued that the meaning assigned to these dollars is part of why so much of the refund is directed to these purposes. This raises questions of what these families' asset profiles actually look like, what mobility goals they hold, and how they are deploying the refund to fulfill them.

For Jacinta Estrada, a twenty-six-year-old Hispanic mother of four who works in a hospital payroll department, saving money, much less building assets, is next to impossible in a typical month; she lives paycheck to paycheck. But she draws sustenance from dreams of a more secure economic future as a home owner. Jacinta and her boyfriend Luis have been together since they were thirteen or fourteen years old and share four children: two daughters, now three and eleven, and two sons, who are six and nine. They've been through a lot over the years, but the last few months have been particularly difficult. Luis attended a family gathering at his grandmother's house, and while he was relaxing on the front porch he was wounded, the random victim of a drive-by shooting. One bullet hit a nerve in his arm so he's been unable to work—his job as a mechanic requires heavy lifting and a level of manual dexterity he can't manage now. And it doesn't look as if he'll be able to work as a mechanic in the foreseeable future. He has applied for disability, but his eligibility hasn't been determined yet, so Jacinta is the family's sole wage earner. Fortunately, they have a Section 8 voucher. With Luis out of work, the share of the rent they must pay has been reduced from $680 to $240 a month.

Nonetheless, money is tight in the Estrada household. Jacinta gets paid twice a month and devotes the first check to rent and utilities while reserving the second for other necessities. She tries to set aside between $50 and $100 from that second check as a rainy day fund for unexpected needs, like "if we run out of groceries." These are the only savings she can manage right now. As for other assets, the only real estate she owns, she tells us with a laugh, is the "dollhouse that my daughter has." But Jacinta is determined to build a brighter financial future.

As we talk, she enthusiastically lays out her new savings plan, which she adopted from an AOL posting that claimed people could become millionaires by age sixty-five even if they started out with nothing in their twenties: "It said if you save from right now $148 a month, by the time you're 65 you'll have $1,000,000 . . . ! I was like, '$150? I probably spend more than that out eating!' Like [I felt] I could do it." A detailed examination of her monthly budget belies this claim. But she hasn't given up this goal. When Luis was working, both he and Jacinta received large tax refunds by filing separately, each claiming two of their four children on their tax returns, as is appropriate for unmarried couples under IRS rules.[1] When the next tax season rolls around, Jacinta is determined to save the entire federal portion of both refunds—far more than what she would have saved on the AOL plan. They'll spend only their state refund checks—usually a few hundred dollars each—catching up on bills and other odds and ends, Jacinta says. If they can put away this much each year for the next five years, she believes, they will have saved enough to buy their own home.

Jacinta has six credit cards with large unpaid balances. But it's been nearly seven years since she defaulted on the last of these cards. Like many other families we spoke to, Jacinta knows these offenses will no longer be counted against her after the seven-year mark. This is why she feels now is a good time to start saving for a home—she expects to have a clean credit slate very soon.[2] To help reach her goal, she intends to make use of a variety of programs she has heard about, especially the courses on financial literacy and home ownership that are offered by the Boston Housing Authority to families like hers, who have a housing choice voucher. Jacinta is convinced that becoming a home owner will mark the start of a whole new life.

She paints a vivid verbal picture of a home nested in the rural beauty of Vermont: "I'm the type of person that likes nice things, and I want to have my kids grow up in a nice neighborhood where I don't have to worry about them being outside. . . . In five years from now I want to see them in their own house, running in the back [yard]. [I see] family coming over and the kids—gotta call 'em because they're upstairs, you know? I don't want to see myself in an apartment anymore." Hers is a poignant picture of a boisterous family living and thriving far away from the violence of their current neighborhood—the drive-by that wounded Luis occurred just a few blocks from their current address. She envisions her family in a house with a second story, large enough to accommodate visiting kin.

But for now Jacinta scrapes by on her wages plus help from family. Her sister, who doesn't have any children, takes the four kids on outings a couple of times each month—to the movies or the video arcade, for example—and frequently stops by with toys, clothing, and school supplies. Jacinta also knows that she can look to her mother for help if need be, despite their rocky relationship. Before Jacinta landed the job at the hospital, times were even harder than they are right now. After paying the rent and utilities, she didn't have enough cash left over for food. During that time she took her kids to her mother's house "like every day" to get something to eat. She knows that if she were to get into that situation again her mother wouldn't turn her away.

Others in these situations rely on credit cards to get by, but Jacinta hasn't had access to credit for a long time. The six cards she defaulted on years ago represented only half of the credit woes she faced at the time—she managed to pay off the large balances on six other cards. Without access to credit, she has no real cushion—with Luis out of work and no word on his disability status, the family has to get by on her wages and SNAP. Over the past six months, her earnings plus SNAP have averaged $2,166 a month, but her bills and other expenses have totaled $2,858 in a typical month. Not surprisingly, she's behind on a number of bills, and with no other way to catch up, the much-anticipated tax refund is her only way out. In less financially lean years, the annual infusion of cash at tax time has allowed the couple to make vital, and otherwise unattainable, purchases. Last year they were able to buy a used car big enough for their six-person family. The $2,900 came straight from Jacinta's refund.

By the usual definition, assets include real estate, durable goods, and savings or other investments.[3] In this chapter we describe families' holdings in these domains. However, as was the case for Jacinta Estrada, low-wage workers are often short on these assets. For many of the households we spoke with, the IRS, which holds their tax refund until February or March, offers the only substantial savings account they have; as we have explained, many in fact explicitly view the annual check as a form of savings. As Jacinta's story vividly illustrates, no matter how beleaguered their financial histories, most still hold tight to their belief that the future offers the possibility of a good credit score, a nest egg in the bank, and, most importantly, a home of their own.

As we will show, substantial holdings in checking, savings, or retirement accounts are rare. Car ownership is not uncommon but carries with it expenses like fuel, insurance, routine maintenance, and fees for city parking stickers and emissions checks. When a less-than-reliable automobile breaks down, the shock to one's finances can be large. Only a handful of families in our study—10 percent—own homes.

But as was true for Jacinta, many families are motivated to save. They are sustained in bleak economic times by dreams of owning a home, with the accompanying possibility of a safer, more pleasant environment in which to raise their children. Often it is the prospect of a substantial tax credit—a large windfall—that allows households to believe they can save, thereby fueling these dreams. As we showed in chapter 1, to get by in the meantime people look to their network of family members, romantic partners, and close friends; these are folks who step in to buy treats for the kids, provide a bag or two of groceries or extend regular invites for a hot meal, and offer personal loans to cover unexpected expenses.

It's important to note, however, that pursuing assets is not without risks for lower-income families. For example, building up a good credit score requires spending on credit and then paying off these bills in a timely manner—often difficult for those with unpredictable incomes and expenses. Or one may buy a car to drive to a better-paying job but end up with more bills when that used car breaks down. The windfall nature of the EITC provides families with hope for building assets when tax time comes but leaves them without assistance for much of the year.

BEYOND INCOME

The Massachusetts Asset Development Commission defines assets as "financial resources (savings, 401k accounts, individual retirement accounts, equities), material possessions that have monetary value (house,

Table 5   Proportion of Respondents with Assets and Average Asset Values

	% with Asset	Mean Value
Savings account	66	$1,436
Checking account	78	$699
Informal savings	32	$167
Car	68	$6,675
House	10	$337,000
Stocks or bonds	10	$2,305
Retirement	23	$7,874

NOTE: N = 115. Mean values are for those who hold each asset type.

automobile, small business), and non-tangible resources (education, training, development of social networks). . . . While income is what families use to cover daily living expenses . . . assets make it possible to manage financial hardship, plan for the future, and provide opportunity for the next generation."[4]

Table 5 displays the average asset holdings among the families in our study. Although these are lower-income families, many do have savings and checking accounts and, as indicated above, own cars. However, homes, stocks or bonds, and retirement savings are not a typical part of our families' financial portfolios. They often have assets that are useful in the short term, like Jacinta's rainy-day savings—the amount she tries to set aside so she can buy milk and bread if the family runs low, pay a parking ticket, or purchase a birthday present. But these are not investments in the future, like homes and retirement accounts. Nor are such savings usually substantial. Few of our families have three months of income on hand to cover an unexpected job loss. This is the standard definition of having adequate assets; those not meeting this asset level are typically referred to as being "asset poor." Further, who does and does not save is not simply a matter of how much one earns. Motivation, skill in devising effective savings strategies, and luck all play a role in determining who builds a nest egg or buys a home and who doesn't.

Nationally, among the lowest-earning fifth of American families, only 10 percent have some retirement savings beyond Social Security, but 40 percent own a home, 65 percent own a car, and 76 percent have some kind of bank account (with balances averaging $600). But this bottom fifth of families holds assets that are worth 11 percent of those in the middle fifth of families and 2 percent of those in the top fifth. Every year, while about a third (32 percent) of the bottom fifth of families is able to save some money, more than half (56 percent) of the middle fifth and over three-quarters (78 percent) of the top fifth do so.[5] These trends reflect what we observed among those we talked to, except that far fewer of our families own homes (10 percent).[6]

HOME OWNERSHIP

Woven throughout workers' discussions of their financial strategies and plans is a recurrent theme: home ownership. Although dreams of home ownership may not often be realized, the dream seems to motivate disciplined financial behavior, especially debt payoff and savings. It is worth observing the various approaches deployed by those who have managed a home purchase, however—approaches that illuminate the obstacles that must be overcome in pursuit of this pinnacle of the American Dream.

Homemaker Lizann and insulation installer Donnie Moretti, a white couple in their early forties, managed to buy their home through family ties and lucky timing. In fact, by the time we met them, they had just paid off the mortgage and owned the house outright. Lizann explains the circumstances that allowed them to become home owners earlier than they had even hoped to, though the neighborhood they have ended up in is less than ideal:

> Well, [the house] was my mother-in-law's and she couldn't afford it anymore and she owed just a little bit on it [but] they were going to repossess it because she couldn't afford [the payments] anymore. So she gave it to us. We had been saving up to buy a home in New Hampshire and we had a good decent amount of down payment [saved]. She said to me, "Please, please before they take it." And I really didn't want to—I didn't want to be in the city. This was supposed to be a temporary stop . . . , just a temporary stop and we ended up getting stuck here. So we ended up paying off the note and we're here.

Now they are anticipating their eldest son going to college. As proud as they are that he will be the first in either of their families to attend, they are worried about how they are going to finance his education. Lizann holds out hope that some school might offer her son a football scholarship, but she also has a backup plan. "I was thinking just to take out a mortgage on the house . . . since we have home equity." As home owners, they have an asset to draw on that could help their son attend college. However, this may still be a risky proposition: even without the burden of a home equity loan, Donnie's $2,598 in monthly income is already a few dollars short of their $2,603 in monthly expenses.[7]

After years of carefully saving their tax refund, Jocelyn Bennett, a home health aide, and her husband, Marcel, both in their forties, had enough for a down payment on a duplex; it was a huge achievement for a family that had fled destitution in Haiti. Just before the Great Recession, when credit terms were generous, the Bennetts were able to secure a mortgage that required no money down and only the payment of closing costs, with a "teaser" interest rate. The house was in poor condition, so they used their savings to purchase the materials they needed to make repairs. Just after they bought the home, Marcel rehabbed the first floor. They are now renting that floor out while he tackles the second floor, where their family lives.

The two years since they bought the home have been a bit of a financial roller coaster, Marcel explains. "When we first buy this house and my wife have an account, a little money in the bank. After we buy this house, all the money gone. The house take all the money she got, you know? And material, everything, and sheetrock, shingle, everything we buy and I fix because I know how to fix. . . . And we continue spend, spend and, you know, we don't see where it coming from, we just continue to spend, you know? Sometime we hungry, sometime we angry, you know what I mean?"

With a $2,950 mortgage payment due every month on top of the expenses associated with home repair, Marcel says, "You know, [the house] suck all the blood." On top of that, there is the $542 due every month for the home owner's insurance and property taxes. Additionally, the rental payments from the first-floor unit are now counted as income and have rendered them ineligible for the federal government's Low

Income Heating Assistance Program, a resource they regularly drew on back when they were renters themselves. Wages from Jocelyn's two part-time nursing jobs and the rental income from the first-floor apartment just barely cover their house payments ($3,552 in income against $3,492 in outflow for the mortgage, property taxes, and home insurance). This is why they have had to empty their savings account to cover their other expenses. Despite these difficulties, Marcel is careful to add, "Sometime we happy, you know." Still, it is hard to see how this family isn't headed for financial disaster.[8] In one sense, the Morettis and the Bennetts are success stories, living the American Dream by owning their own homes. However, the Bennetts fall further into debt as they fix up their house, and, as we'll soon explain, the condition of the Morettis' home means they are unable to sell it; the reality, then, is that both families' hold on the benefits of home ownership, and the success it represents, is tenuous.

The power of the home ownership aspiration seems to come less from the house itself and more from the symbol of achievement and security it represents. Many parents we spoke with said home ownership was a goal; home ownership serves as an important motivator to get ones' finances in order, pay off debt, and make other sacrifices to this end, even if actual progress often falls short of their aspirations. We see this clash between hope and reality in the story of Dominique Henderson, a twenty-three-year-old black single mother of a three-year-old, who works as a teacher's aide in the public school system. For the past year and a half she has been involved in a program that is focused on helping low-income single mothers become home owners. The three-year program requires participants to be enrolled in a postsecondary education program of their choosing while it contributes $700 per month toward their rent, and it assists them in developing budgeting and savings strategies so they have a down payment once they complete the program. It also makes matched savings contributions on a participant's behalf to accounts that are designated for home-buying expenses. Dominique is enthusiastic about the program. She has already selected the condo complex in which she would like to buy a unit—it is in a suburb by a large, upscale mall.

Saving has been particularly difficult because Dominique's job is seasonal: she goes without a paycheck in the summer but can't claim unemployment insurance (as a teacher's aide in an elementary school, she is on a full-year contract but gets paid only during the school year). Three months of each year without earnings has stood in the way of generating sufficient savings for her home-buying goal. Now, halfway through the program, she has saved only $5,000 of the $13,000 down payment the program estimates she will need, despite dramatic cutbacks on spending on clothes and forgoing a car purchase. Even though going without a car leaves her walking around the city in the winter with her three-year-old daughter Tatiana in tow, she shrugs and says, "I'll take the bus—like I want a car so bad, but I'm like, 'Yeah, I am going to have a car, but in two more years am I going to be living out of my car?'" Although it is not easy to save, Dominique is still strongly committed to her dream of home ownership and willing to make the sacrifices required. What is less clear is how Dominique will manage the mortgage payment once she gets to the suburbs, where she'll likely need a car.

By carefully budgeting her monthly income and stashing away her tax refund checks, Genevieve Davenport, a divorced Hispanic preschool teacher in her early forties, has come closer to her dream than Dominique has. She has managed to save nearly $6,000 through a similar program. Next month she plans to use the money as a down payment on a condo, which she will purchase through the affordable housing program in which she is enrolled. She is getting her paperwork in order and has weighed her different mortgage options, choosing a single mortgage with a fixed rate rather than a "piggyback" or two-step "teaser rate" option. She is relishing her upcoming purchase: "It will be mine!" she exclaims, "and it will be for my children!" She sees this purchase not only as the culmination of her dreams but as the start of a whole new life and a legacy for her fifteen-year-old son and ten-year-old daughter. "I think that buying this condominium now is my first step, and then within time, you know, I might sell and then buy a house in the South, you know, in [a] quiet, peaceful neighborhood and live there peacefully, quietly . . . with a house that has a backyard so I can plant my flowers—my roses—[and] my tomatoes." For Genevieve and many others, a home purchase is much more than bricks and mortar. In their often richly detailed accounts of the better life they envision a home purchase providing, one can feel the warm air, relax in the garden's peaceful atmosphere, and smell the budding roses.

Many families say that tax time—with its big chunk of refund money and all the possibilities this implies—inspires both the desire to buy a home and careful consideration of how they might save toward that goal. But for a variety of reasons, most merely dream—they fail to take concrete steps toward home ownership. Angelica Rivera, a thirty-one-year-old Hispanic project manager at a health center, blames tight finances for her inability to turn her family's aspirations into actions. Not only are she and her husband "living paycheck to paycheck," but the hot housing market conditions of the mid-2000s also pushed prices out of their grasp. In five years, though, she hopes they'll be in a position to buy. Between now and then she plans to go back to school so she can get a better-paying job, and she speculates that the increase in earnings should allow them to save up for a down payment. But this is an awful lot to accomplish in just five years' time.

Recognizing Boston's high cost of living, many families link aspirations for home ownership with dreams of moving down south—perhaps to Florida—or north to New Hampshire where real estate is cheaper. Few, however, discuss concrete plans to make such moves. Thus those with the most tangible plans usually see themselves purchasing homes in Boston's less expensive neighborhoods or in working-class suburbs outside the city.

Like Angelica Rivera, Lanette Higgins, a twenty-nine-year-old black single mother to five-year-old Ebony, also hopes to buy a home in the next five years. Each step she's taken toward doing so, though, has proved frustrating. She has looked into several home ownership programs, but given the $27,000 a year she earns as a bank teller, she makes too much to qualify for the assistance provided to low-income families trying to purchase homes and too little to qualify for other first-time home owner programs. However, this bad news has not caused her to question whether it makes financial sense for her to save toward the purchase of a home. Nor has it dimmed her vision of the lifestyle she believes becoming a home owner will provide: "I want to stay in the Boston area. I don't want to go way out. There are a lot of historic places in Roxbury that I was looking at that are beautiful. . . . Like there are certain, like little streets here and there you see, you go down the street and you see beautiful homes and you talk with the people and it's quiet over there." Reflecting the importance of these twin desires—not only a home but a better life—Lizann and Donnie Moretti, whom we introduced above, are already home owners but remain unsatisfied. Their goal had been to buy a home in bucolic New Hampshire. Recall that Lizann had been reluctant to assume the mortgage on her mother-in-law's house—the tough neighborhood it was located in just wasn't what she had envisioned.

Three years ago, in fact, Lizann had had enough of the problems in their neighborhood, and they put the house up for sale as they shopped around for a place in the suburbs. They soon found a home that stole Lizann's heart. Initially, all the details seemed to be falling into place. They received an offer on their house and accepted it. But the buyer's home inspector discovered water damage, and, in the subsequent negotiations, the deal fell through. They had no other offers and were thus unable to purchase the home they had fallen in love with. Despite the time that has passed, Lizann still waxes poetic about the one that got away.

> Oh my God. This house was gorgeous. It was a huge, like, Victorian. It was unbelievable. . . . You walked into this long hallway. It was all wood. The floor was all wood. And to the left was the dining room, and it had these pillars—like these Roman pillars that were wood as you went into the dining room. . . . The doors opened up and it was a formal living room. It had this huge fireplace from floor to ceiling. . . . Then there was a staircase—a grand staircase that you would go up. And there was a level, like a platform [on the stairs], and that whole wall was stained-glass windows. . . . And then you'd go up [stairs] and there was my son's room, my bedroom with the fireplace, another guest room, and another kitchen. Just for the family.

Lizann had clearly mentally moved the family into the house before the sale fell through. But her account reveals that the house's setting, tucked away in a safe suburb, was just as key as its features—it would have afforded a quiet life where she could raise her children in the way she imagined. The strength of these sentiments, of the sense of loss at having the life you desire lying just outside your grasp, is key to understanding people's attachment to the idea of home ownership. It's not just about shelter; it's aspiring to a whole way of life. For home-buying dreamers, these hopes for a markedly different environment—not just a different address—seem key in motivating the short-term sacrifice required to achieve this long-term goal.

"I OWE MY CHECKING ACCOUNT $68"

To build substantial assets one must save; this logic escapes none of the families we met. And many families value saving in its own right, even when they have no specific purpose but a "rainy day" in mind. When Americans think about savings, they generally envision making deposits in a bank; indeed, most of the families we spoke with are "banked"—that is, they have at least one checking or savings account. But families near the bottom don't always see banks in the same way that middle-class customers do.[9]

When we ask Latrice Morris, a black woman in her late forties who works seasonally as a tax preparer and is the single mother of a thirteen-year-old daughter, how much she has in her checking account right now, she replies, "Like $800 something, you know, that's my in and out." The phrase "my in and out" reflects the function that bank accounts typically serve for our families. Rather than holding and accumulating money over time, these accounts are where paychecks (or refund checks) are deposited and from which money for bills and other expenses is withdrawn. Reflective of this fact, they rarely hold a great deal of money.

The $699 average amount in checking accounts shown in table 5 masks the wide range in these households' holdings. Fifty-five families—just under half of the sample—have less than $100 between their checking and savings accounts. Beyond safeguarding one's funds, a checking account may be beneficial insofar as it offers the possibility of direct deposit, a debit card, and the ability to pay bills online or over the phone. However, a checking account also carries with it the risk of overdrawing and being charged the accompanying fees. Rita Ramirez, a twenty-six-year-old Hispanic hairdresser and single mother of a one-and-a-half-year-old, puts it this way: "I owe my checking $68"—she has just overdrawn her account once again, a costly mistake. Unlike relying on money orders to pay bills, as the unbanked typically do, using a checking account requires an ongoing attentiveness to the timing of deposits against withdrawals. This can be particularly difficult for families living on the financial edge.

Like checking accounts, many of the savings accounts of the families we studied hold little money. Some families do manage to accumulate savings in these accounts (reflected in the $1,436 average balance for those with such accounts, shown in table 5), but this isn't the norm. Debra McKinley, a twenty-eight-year-old white mother of two, ages four and nine, lives with her fiancé and works on and off as a waitress. She explains that she usually has next to nothing in her savings account. "I put in what I know they're going to take out [from bill payments]—you know, maybe $10 extra just so I know [the cost of the bills is covered]. But nothing ever stays in there." For families like Debra's, who have little to no surplus at the end of the month, the account serves as a placeholder for where the savings could be.

Mack and Johanna Clark's $2,463 in average monthly income from Johanna's job as a medical assistant is outstripped by their $2,787 in monthly expenses. It is only at tax time that they can reconcile their financial accounts. Nonetheless, the Clarks, a white couple in their late twenties with a young son and daughter, have opened two savings accounts. They've designated one as their backup account—they aren't to touch it unless it's an emergency or the withdrawal is for something they've explicitly saved for (like a recent trip to California for a family wedding). This backup account holds about $300 right now. Mack explains the logic of having two accounts: "We always have [that second] account to fall back on, but we never want to touch it. We just try to use what money is in our checking and in primary savings [first], not the backup savings we've got." The Clarks regularly contribute to the backup account—$25 from each paycheck is directly deposited there. This account is with a small bank in a neighboring town that has only passbook savings and no online or ATM access. They've chosen this bank intentionally—they must go to the bank in person during business hours in order to withdraw any funds, and the lack of convenience is one of the strategies they're using to keep themselves from touching the money. Mack says their method is an "out of sight, out of mind kind of thing, [so] we wouldn't have to worry about [the temptation to withdraw] it." For most families though, the savings account sees a lot of "in and out."

INFORMAL SAVINGS

About a quarter of the households we spoke with keep money in informal savings, either in addition to or in lieu of bank checking or savings accounts. This money, kept in a closet safe or a designated jar, can range from just a few dollars to several thousand dollars but averages $167 among the families we spoke with (table 5). When thirty-year-old Angela Caponi, a single pregnant white assistant manager at an electronics store, claimed her tax refund check, she spent a portion of the windfall buying things she would need once her baby arrived, and she had parties for her older boys, eleven and thirteen, and her three-year-old, all of whom have spring birthdays. She says, "What I had left, I just put in my drawer, and took out money here and there when I needed things." She says she "pinched off" of this money for about a month to buy snacks or little dollar-store toys that her boys asked for.

Devonne Jefferson, a forty-year-old single black assistant preschool teacher, and her two teenage sons, Terrence and Seth, have a can they keep around the house that gets rechristened for every holiday or special event—it becomes a Christmas can, a Fourth of July can, or a birthday can. Devonne tells us, "Sometimes you could save $50 [in the can] and you'd be saying, 'Wow, I can't believe I saved $50!'" For some, like Angela and Devonne, informal savings is more a matter of keeping a little money on hand for little extras or a special circumstance than trying to build a significant nest egg. Others, however, really do accumulate substantial savings in this way. Realtor Shari Barfield, who is black and thirty-six, knows her husband keeps money hidden away in the house. Speaking in a whisper, out of her husband's hearing, this mother of three—ages one, five, and twelve—estimates that he has as much as $5,000 stashed away. However, such large balances are rare among informal savers.

RETIREMENT SAVINGS

Among the 23 percent of our households who have any retirement, holdings average $7,874. Forty-two-year-old Gloria Diaz, who immigrated to Boston from Costa Rica eleven years ago, has a 401k through her employer. Between her full-time job at a hospital and her part-time work as a Spanish-language interpreter at an area school, this divorced mother of two, aged nine and seventeen, earns about $2,916 per month. The hospital makes retirement contributions on her behalf, but she has not been paying anything into the account herself because her monthly expenses outstrip her income by nearly $200. Half hoping, half pledging, she says, "In a year or so I'm gonna do it." She believes contributing to retirement is vital, yet feels it just isn't feasible now. In contrast, Lanette Higgins, the bank teller, explains that between paying her share of the health benefit package her employer provides, which includes dental and vision insurance, and contributing to her 401k, her paycheck takes a big hit, but it is a sacrifice she's willing to make. She describes how she's planning on increasing her 401k contribution: "I started at 3 percent, but someone was telling me you should start at 6 percent now and it'll accrue more and keep it every year at that percentage or so and you'll be glad you did in the long run, so that's what I'm gonna try to do."

Retirement savings can also offer a vital resource for those who are otherwise credit constrained. Colin Fields, a fifty-three-year-old white grocery store manager, and his wife, Luanna, a coordinator at a local education program, recently raided Colin's retirement account, borrowing $25,000 to put money down on a home she was renting to own, to buy some furniture, and to pay for their wedding (these newlyweds are middle-aged—Luanna has a teenage son). Roughly $18,000 remains in Luanna's retirement account, and her husband has nearly $40,000 in retirement savings. He is quickly replenishing the amount they borrowed; he must pay $700 from each paycheck back into the account. Those without retirement savings lose out twice over—a potential asset to be deployed in the shorter term and comfort in retirement.

CAR

Similar to national figures for the bottom quintile of households, 68 percent of families in our study have a car.[10] Although cars are considered assets, they are also a burdensome expense—they incur costs for gas, routine maintenance, insurance, repairs, and—especially on Boston's congested streets—parking tickets. Those relying on public transportation do not face these potential financial burdens (though at $2 a ride the bus is far from cheap). Further, unlike many other kinds of assets that grow in value over time, a car's value only depreciates.

Because many of these families are credit constrained and have low monthly incomes, they often wait until tax time to purchase a car. Then they typically buy used cars that they can pay for outright or pay off relatively quickly so as not to have to shoulder an added monthly expense. Of course, cars costing only a couple thousand dollars are frequently unreliable and demand more maintenance than a more expensive car. For the past few years, twenty-three-year-old Laeticia Marshall, a black convenience store clerk and single mother of a toddler and a newborn, has spent her tax refund check in exactly the same way: another used car, registration, and insurance plan. Two years ago she bought her first car, only to see the transmission fail. The $1,400 it would have taken to repair it was too steep for her budget. With the car broken down and no money to pay a towing company to haul it to a garage, she ended up accumulating several hundred dollars in parking tickets. The following year, her refund was consumed by paying off the parking tickets on the old car, which she junked, and turning to the used car lot once again. Not that it's doing her much good: "I have a car now, but [I can't afford to have it insured or registered, and] it's having some mechanical problems, so I'm waiting to have to find out what's gonna happen with the car. Now because I had [baby] Kwame, I've [fallen behind in my financial situation a] bit further. So I'm just going to have to [save] all over again to try to have the financial money to get it [on the road]."

The parking tickets totaled a whopping $849, while the "new" used car, a '95 Plymouth Voyager, cost another $1,200. Soon, she thinks she'll be able to afford the $439 for six months of insurance and the $200 or so she'll need to spend to register the car. Until the car is insured and registered, she's not allowed to take it off the dealer's lot, where it has been sitting for several months. And then there are the "mechanical problems" she'll have to deal with. Right now, Laeticia's "asset" has left her riding the bus.

"HOW CAN I SAVE FOR A RAINY DAY? WHAT IS A RAINY DAY WHEN YOU'RE POOR?"

For most families, the following cycle is repeated: modest savings accumulate, only to be undone by a loss of earnings, a jump in expenses, or the month-to-month reality of bills that exceed the cash on hand. As families

Table 6   Respondents' Asset Holdings by Asset Category

Asset Category	%	Mean Asset Holdings
Limited assets	37	$78
Moderate assets	52	
Substantial debt	30	$6,685
Minimal debt	22	$2,040
Substantial assets	11	$14,038

NOTE: N = 115. Assets include the value of checking and savings accounts, informal savings, and retirement accounts.

try to save, money is generally tucked away into savings or checking accounts, rather than in other savings products like CDs, money market accounts, or stocks. But as illustrated above by our stories of those who have become home owners, there are exceptions.

As shown in table 6, families we spoke with exhibit one of three asset profiles: those with virtually no assets; those with moderate holdings; and those with fairly substantial assets and limited debts. Just under four in ten (37 percent) have almost no assets, taking into consideration savings and checking accounts, informal savings, retirement accounts, and property holdings.[11] In the middle category, sixty families (52 percent) hold some assets, but just over half of these families are also carrying at least $1,000 of debt.[12] Finally, thirteen families (11 percent) have relatively substantial assets and do not have heavy debt loads.[13]

As we have described earlier, some families try to save with specific long- or short-term goals in mind (a home purchase or Christmas presents, for example). Others have more nebulous motives—like Jacinta Estrada, some simply want to have some cash stashed away "just in case." As twenty-three-year-old LaWanda James, a black single emergency medical technician and the mother of an elementary schooler, says, "Just for a rainy, a real rainy day, a thunderstorm, blizzard, hurricane, I wanna save. . . . Just want to have a nice cushion of money." Lawanda has little savings at present.

No family we spoke with found that saving money was easy. Devonne Jefferson, the assistant preschool teacher who, like LaWanda, is among those with the fewest assets, notes that while friends and relatives advise her that she ought to be saving for "a rainy day," she counters, "What is a rainy day when you're poor? There's no rainy days when you're poor. . . . Like what would be a rainy day for me and my two kids when we're living day by day, check to check?" Devonne is especially adamant on this point at the moment—summer has just started, leaving this preschool teacher without a paycheck for three months; in fact, she can't even make ends meet on her wages during the school year, with $1,584 in monthly expenses and just $1,252 in income.

Homemaker Lizann Moretti, whose family falls into the middle category of asset holders who have substantial debts, expresses similar frustrations. "We always have intentions of doing something with money, [like] trying to save—but something always comes up. Always. . . . 'Ma, I need gas' and 'Ma, I need this.' So whatever little I was [saving], it disappears. With the gas bill . . . , I had them come at my door: 'We're here to shut your gas off.' 'Oh God,' [I thought]. 'How much can you give?' '$400.' That money I had [saved]? Gone." For many, attempts to save are foiled by a series of such setbacks—as the gas bill, a new baby, or car repairs demand immediate attention. In short, motivation is far from a guarantee of success. Nevertheless, families' narratives reveal that they place immense value on savings, both for building assets and for the safety net that savings can provide in difficult times. Being in the financial position to accumulate substantial savings is often an expressed goal—it is part of the lifestyle they aspire to.

Some families who have clear motivations or goals are successful at saving, despite their relatively low incomes. Carmen Sanchez, a forty-year-old Honduran preschool teacher who is separated from her husband and has four children, ranging in age from three to seventeen, is motivated to save by the fear that her employer may reduce her hours, which would mean she would default on her mortgage. "Right now, I [am] a little concerned because my boss tell me they may reduce my hours to four a day [from six] . . . and *that* is like . . . scary. I will not be able to pay my mortgage if that happens. And [after hearing this] I notice I don't have no saving just in case something like that happen in the *future*. . . . I don't need my children going to a shelter . . . and this is why I say, 'No. I have to save.'"

Carmen has resolved not to spend on anything extra this year—not even toys for her children at Christmas or on birthdays; the gifts this year will be limited to "a tie or socks . . . gloves, mittens." These austerity measures, she says, are "the only step" that can help her stay afloat.[14] Carmen works to save with a clear goal in mind. But many need more than motivation alone; they devise specific strategies or deploy mental "tricks" in order to succeed. Stay-at-home dad Mack and medical assistant Johanna Clark describe how they have developed better saving skills over time, motivated by their desire to purchase a home. Johanna admits that in the past, with "budget[ing], we weren't so good." Mack elaborates further: "We [decided we] don't need to go out to eat as much. We don't need to do takeout. We used to have every channel on cable; we [decided we] really don't need that, you know . . . ? I don't buy as many DVDs anymore. We just save, save. Like when we need things now we actually have money in the bank. Like our computer broke [last month], so we [were able to draw on our savings for] a new computer," which he explains they wouldn't have been able to do before. In addition to eliminating excess spending, they have another strategy that helps them save—directly depositing some money into that passbook-only savings account at a bank.

Despite their efforts, Mack and Johanna still struggle to save; in fact, they are in our lowest group of asset holders. Johanna explains why: "For some reason every time we go to Target we'll walk out spending $60 on toothpaste, you know." Her hyperbolic expression describes the experiences that so many families relate—their money almost mysteriously disappears with little to show for it other than "toothpaste." So while Mack makes grand claims about the passbook savings account—"We just leave it in there, we don't touch it"—the reality is that "if we need something and the money's there . . . " Their newfound determination to save has not yet transformed this pair of spenders into substantial savers.

Clever ideas for savings abound among our more motivated families. Some entrust the money to a sibling or other family member, asking them to "hold the money" so it will be harder to spend. Dominique Henderson, for example, the black twenty-three-year-old teacher's aide and single mother of a preschooler, deposited $3,000 of this past year's tax refund check into a joint bank account with her brother. Into that account she also deposited the $2,000 she had already saved through other means (including prior years' refunds), a step toward the goal of one day buying a home. If she didn't give her brother the money to hold, she says, "I knew I was going to pick here and pick there." Dominique is sure her brother can be trusted to act in her best interests. These savings come at a price, however. While she has been socking away money, she has fallen behind on several bills, especially during the summer months when she isn't employed. The considerable debt she has accumulated as a result, along with the attendant late payment fees, places her in our middle category: asset holders with significant debts.

Tamara Bishop, thirty-three, a black single mother of four—ages five, seven, thirteen, and fifteen—and an assistant preschool teacher, transferred a large portion of her tax refund into money orders. She says that having to cash a money order rather than simply withdrawing funds from a checking account will make her think twice before spending. And Tamara is a self-confessed "spender"—though her savings place her in our middle group of asset holders, her debts substantially outweigh them. Not having cash on hand makes spur-of-the-moment purchases more difficult and cuts down on frivolous spending. For Tamara, the convenience of a checking account is not necessarily a positive feature.

Home health aide Veronica Flores, a thirty-seven-year-old Hispanic single mother to two teenage boys, holds to the rule that she must have at least $1,000 in her checking account at any given time. This puts her among those who hold only a modest level of assets but have little debt—twenty-five of our families meet both of these criteria, about half of the moderate-asset group. She sets aside a portion of her tax refund for the summer months, when she knows using the air conditioner will cause her energy bill to spike. "I always like to have an emergency backup," she explains. It helps that her income of $1,856 from wages and child support more than covers her modest $1,479 in monthly bills—having more income than expenses in the typical month is relatively rare among families we spoke with. When her checking account falls to just $1,000, she says, it is like a stop sign for spending. "Then it's like, I stop spending—I don't go crazy with this or that or whatever. . . . I see that I'm at $1,000, I'm like 'Oh no! Wait!'"

Veronica's ability to adopt this rule and stick to it has put her on relatively stable financial footing, compared to many other families in the study. Along with the checking account rule, she has $20 of each paycheck directly deposited into a savings account she uses for small, unanticipated expenses. She aspires to save more over the longer term, "but I mean, there's only so much I can do." While her current strategies allow her stay in the black, she's not getting ahead. And should real disaster strike—job loss, for example—she won't be able to keep afloat for long.

Families' attempts to save are frequently tales of two steps forward, one step, or even two steps, back. The small minority who do build up substantial savings typically share three characteristics: they have sizable, stable earnings, often because they hold supervisory or unionized positions or are in a dual-income household (where if one loses a job the other still may be bringing in money); they report a concrete source of motivation; and they deploy at least one of the savings strategies described above. The desire to save for a specific purchase—a car, a home, or retirement—is the most common source of motivation, though a looming loss in income due to a seasonal job or a threatened cut in hours features too. As we have shown, savings strategies include setting up automatic deductions from paychecks, earmarking a particular account as "not to be touched," enlisting help from family to set up or maintain savings in an account that is hard to access, and, as was the case for Veronica Flores, adopting strict principles about how much money to maintain in the bank.[15] One additional lesson gleaned from these narratives is that many of our families view the convenience that banks advertise as requiring a warning label: beware if you want to save!

CREDIT

Credit can play the vital function of enabling households to smooth consumption in the face of a financial shock or to invest in a purchase now that may pay off in the future (like a car to access a better-paying job in the suburbs, or a stand-alone freezer, enabling bulk purchases of meat and other frozen goods). Credit also offers vital assistance to families making large onetime or seasonal purchases, such as household furnishings, a washing machine or refrigerator, or back-to-school clothes, because payments for such big-ticket items can be spread out over time.

However, as we show in the next chapter, credit can be a double-edged sword.[16]

Credit raises the risk of accumulating debt. Yet families generally know that they need to establish and use credit in order to increase that all-important credit score. Credit is most risky for families who face income fluctuations throughout the year—access to credit might keep the lights on or stock the pantry, but if one's financial boat doesn't right itself in a month or two, it can become hard to pay off the balance or keep up with the monthly payments. And missed credit card payments may bar families from accessing larger, and arguably more important, lines of credit for car or home purchases in the future. In addition, employers now routinely access credit reports when assessing the credentials of job seekers.[17] Indeed, those with poor credit scores can have difficulty finding a private landlord—at least one with a desirable unit—who is willing to rent to them; this can relegate them to the bottom of the housing market (public housing, or units in violence-ridden neighborhoods with poor-quality schools).[18]

This is not to say that lower-income families are ignorant of the importance of credit, and credit scores, in meeting their asset goals. Shari Barfield, the realtor, and her husband have three credit cards, two of which have zero balances. They reserve these cards for emergencies, but the third has a balance of $500 and a credit limit of $3,000. Shari describes their approach to finances as follows: when it comes to deciding which bills to pay first, they prioritize paying whichever are the highest (to keep balances from getting too unwieldy) as well as the credit cards "because you have to pay your credit cards down to keep your credit maintained." The Barfields are among the asset elites in our study, with $12,000 between Shari's checking and savings accounts (and some extra in her husband's account), two paid-off cars, and $4,300 available on their credit cards.

As the narratives we've related above show, standard strategies to build assets are of limited utility among many of the families with whom we spoke. Nonetheless, dreams of a brighter financial future and a better quality of life do animate financial behavior to some degree, especially for those with higher and more stable incomes. And the dreams may be of substantial value themselves. They may offer hope and enhance low-earning households' sense that they are part of the American mainstream.[19]

TAX REFUNDS

It would be hard to overstate the importance of the tax refund in generating savings and asset-building goals and helping families make progress toward achieving them.[20] Tiffany Grier, a white twenty-two-year-old single mother of two toddlers who works as a video store clerk, explains that she is able to put money into savings or invest in other assets specifically because the tax refund provides a lot of money all at once. She describes why she likes the "enforced savings" function built into the tax refund system in this way: "It's funny, 'cause people say . . . , 'All this is is them taking the money out . . . from your check.' But if they didn't, you know you wouldn't get that thousand-, couple-thousand-dollar check so [you] can go buy the new washer and dryer that's $3,000. . . . [The tax refund is] as good as putting the money in the bank. You just can't take it out when you want." For families like Tiffany's, who are in our lowest group of asset holders, the forced savings that comes with the EITC and other tax credits, plus any overwithholding, is very nearly the only asset they have. Like Tiffany, many of those we spoke to say the refund is what offers the chance to "save" for larger purchases. Rarely, a few families do use the tax refund to put a bit of money aside in accounts they have opened in their children's names, to pay tuition at a parochial school, or to finance their own college tuition or technical training, as described in chapter 2. The tax refund, a large chunk of money disbursed at one time, allows these lower-income families to make decisions about assets and savings that are unlike those they make at any other time of year.

As we have shown, for many, savings and assets are fleeting. A savings account can be wiped out by a spell of unemployment. A car is an asset until it breaks down, when it becomes an expense. Because so many of our families experience dramatic ups and downs in income and expenses over the course of the year, any savings a family may have tend to be deployed to smooth out drops in earnings and avoid hardship. In this way, savings rarely lead to long-term investments as they do for higher-income households; instead, they function as precautionary savings, put aside in anticipation of future problems. Nonetheless, our families' stories reveal that they want to save. Some are even willing to do so at the expense of meeting their routine financial obligations. They fall into debt, or further into debt, while they are saving. Some can't save because they do a poor job of managing their money. But an array of obstacles stands in the way of savings success for all but a select few. Some manage to summon up an impressive degree of financial discipline and successfully save, only to encounter an unexpected shortfall in income or an unanticipated expense that eats away at their gains.

Owning a home and a car and having a credit line and a bank account are good in principle. But building assets can be expensive, with banks' overdraft charges, the unfavorable and sometimes downright usurious terms of credit cards, unreliable cars that need frequent repair, and the inability of the mortgage holder to adjust living costs in the face of a sudden loss in income or an unexpected expense.[21] So while many families desire these symbols of financial well-being, their enthusiasm is often mixed with trepidation. Each of these resources carries risk—risk that families can have difficulty managing when they are living near the economic edge.

The standout group of thirteen families who have managed to accumulate relatively substantial assets without much debt share common features besides the state of their finances: nine of the thirteen are married couples. Marriage brings with it the possibility of a two-earner household as well as a man's earnings, which typically are higher than a woman's.[22] Of the four single mothers who made it into this category, two are living with their parents, showing the potential importance of network resources to bolstering someone's financial situation. Additionally, these household heads are a bit older than our sample as a whole, with an average age of forty (compared to thirty-five overall). They also tend to hold dependable jobs. For example, Ida Holmes works as a trolley driver for the state transit authority, Juana Vega is a disability specialist at a preschool and her husband is an auto mechanic, and Burt Bridges supervises a crew of workers at the local convention center. With such a small number of asset builders, we cannot draw strong conclusions about what allows some families to succeed in building assets while others fail, but these differences offer some hints about why so many others might struggle to get ahead.[23]

Just because families are nowhere near being able to save enough for a down payment on a home or a child's college education does not mean that doing so is not a cherished ambition—most dream of, and even plan for, such a financial future. Nor does it mean that dreams of savings and building assets do not profoundly shape families' behaviors. Even those on very shaky financial ground continue to aspire to improve their lot via these savings strategies and to set these as medium-term goals (over the next five to ten years). Some may open savings accounts in their children's names, making deposits sporadically at best, but will eloquently describe how with next year's tax refund they'll be able to contribute more regularly to ensure they can finance their children's college educations. Those not saving for a home at the moment hold onto the idea that they will begin to do so soon. They envision doing so through better budgeting, that long-awaited raise, the use of new savings tricks, and more careful safeguarding of the windfall provided by next year's tax refund. At best, the path toward asset accumulation takes place in fits and starts, but both dreams and goals are fueled by families' tax refund check.

5 "*Debt*—I Am Hoping to Eliminate That Word!"

The demise of welfare and the rise of the work-based safety net, most notably the EITC, has been nothing short of revolutionary. Working-poor parents are now better off economically than at any time in US history, given tax credits and in-kind benefits. We've described how they feel better off as well, as their status as workers has ushered them into the American mainstream. But there has been another revolution as well—a dramatic rise in consumer debt at the bottom of the income distribution.

Federal regulations used to make lending to the poor and near poor unattractive. Starting in the 1980s, Supreme Court decisions removed many regulations on interest rates and fees. These changes made lending to the poor more profitable, and a rising availability of credit to lower-income customers followed. Accordingly, the indebtedness of the poor, along with the not-quite poor, soared. For those inspired by the EITC to save, build assets, and dream of a better future, debt is the nightmare that could undermine all they hope to achieve.

Maureen Ellis was eighteen when she opened her first checking account. Several months later, while shopping with her debit card for clothes and toys for her newborn, she accidentally overdrew the account. At first she didn't realize what had happened, but after her card was repeatedly declined, she eventually made her way down to the bank to investigate. The teller had bad news: not only was there no money left in her account, but she owed the bank over $100 in overdraft fees. Maureen didn't have $100 to spare, so she stopped using the account, left the debt unpaid, and ignored the bank's subsequent notices. This hardworking waitress just couldn't see spending the precious dollars she earned to pay the bank back when, in her view, they should have simply declined the charges.

Maureen, now thirty-one, grew up in the Roslindale section of the city, one of Boston's largely white, working-class neighborhoods. She currently lives in the suburb of Dedham, which hugs Boston's southwest border. Her father worked for the Department of Public Works while her mother stayed at home to care for Maureen and her younger sister. She says her childhood was comfortable but not lavish: "[I had] exactly what I needed but never anything more. . . . [My father] gave me what I needed, but not what I wanted," she adds, implying he could have done better by his children.

By the time Maureen hit Roslindale High, she was struggling academically. She hung on for two years before trading school for a job waitressing at Friendly's—a New England restaurant chain. She spent what would have been her junior year living at home and working. But she was also busy seeing Sam, who worked construction and had his own apartment. Maureen wasn't really planning to get pregnant at eighteen, but she wasn't exactly against it either—she says she was "obsessed" with Sam. Her parents were opposed to her having a baby while she was still young and unmarried, and their disapproval drove her out of their home and into Sam's apartment. Pregnancy, however, wasn't the cure for what had always been a volatile union. Maureen and Sam broke up during Maureen's second trimester. Not welcome back home, she kept the apartment and struggled to make ends meet on her wages from the waitressing job. Once the baby came, her income wouldn't stretch to cover her bills plus child care. Maureen applied for a child care voucher and was baffled by what she learned—she couldn't get a voucher unless she was on welfare, and she made too much money to qualify for AFDC. "I wanted to apply for . . . the in-between money [for child care, but] they told me I had to quit my job [and go on welfare to get a voucher]! The system [made] no sense at all."

For the next two years Maureen stayed home with baby Kayla and collected welfare. The $500 or so in cash benefits fell short of her expenses, so she filled the gap by relying on credit. Maureen ran up large balances on two store credit cards from Walmart and Target. She purchased clothes for herself and her daughter. She bought groceries and cleaning supplies. She splurged on a few modest pieces of furniture to make the apartment seem more like a home. Maureen had no spare cash to pay off the balance on these cards, so the interest accumulated. Soon she couldn't even keep up with the minimum payments. This young mother didn't really think about the implications for her credit score: "I was totally stupid and ignorant to what credit was, and I screwed it all up," she recalls.

Then, when Kayla was about to turn two, the toddler died, an experience Maureen still finds too painful to talk about. The loss of their daughter brought Maureen and Kayla's father, Sam, closer, and he moved back in. Maureen and Sam had two more daughters together: Hillary, now eight, and Megan, who is three. Around the time Megan was born, Maureen and Sam got married, "mainly for me," Maureen says. "I wanted that ring on my finger. I was just brought up that way," referring to her Catholic upbringing and her family's traditional values.

After the wedding, Maureen got a promotion of sorts: she landed a waitressing job at a somewhat more upscale restaurant than Friendly's— Pizzeria Uno. Sam continued to work as a day laborer for a construction company, taking jobs whenever they came his way. During this period the two were able to stay afloat financially on their combined wages, but their marriage floundered, lasting less than two years. After a particularly vicious argument turned violent, Maureen moved out, taking the children with her. She had been squirreling away her tips and had just enough saved to pay for a two-week stay in a motel room. Maureen planned to remain there while she figured out where she and her girls could live permanently. She had put in applications at several nearby apartment complexes, but no private landlord would accept her because of her poor credit history, badly tarnished by the unpaid credit card and bank debt. Her only recourse was to apply for a government housing subsidy.

She had heard that the housing authority's waiting lists were shorter in the southern suburbs than in the city, so she applied for a subsidy there.

Maureen had been living alone with her kids for a year and a half when we talked with her. She is resigned to having to raise the girls without help from their father. The child support authorities have a hard time collecting anything from a casual construction worker like Sam. So she works full time at Pizzeria Uno to pay the bills while also taking courses at Mass Bay Community College part time. She just got her GED and is now working toward an associate's degree in human services. She claims that her determination to succeed in school this time is strong.

Maureen estimates that she earns an average of $1,300 each month in wages and tips. She proudly describes herself as a "discount shopper," frequenting Walmart, Target, Payless, T.J.Maxx, and other cut-rate stores for the family's clothing and household necessities—a skill she says she learned from her father, who "taught me how to be as cheap as I am right now." She funds her courses at Mass Bay through grants. In addition to her rent subsidy, she's managed to secure a child care voucher for Megan and SNAP benefits for her family of three.

Despite the long hours at Pizzeria Uno, her thrift, and her shrewdness in navigating virtually every government program she's eligible for—the rent subsidy, SNAP, the child care voucher, and student grants and loans—Maureen still struggles to cover her monthly bills on a waitress's wages. Her regular expenses include all of the usual necessities plus her cell phone, the Internet/cable combo pack from Comcast, and the insurance and gas for her car (which she needs to get around in suburban Dedham). Cigarettes are Maureen's main vice; the $5 pack she consumes each day adds up to $150 a month—more than a tenth of her gross pay. Occasionally she will spring for a six-pack of beer during football season when she gets together with friends to root for the hometown Patriots. When she is particularly strapped for cash, she can usually manage to get an extra shift at the restaurant. And her close network of girlfriends will come through with $20 here or there when she is in a pinch.

Meanwhile, Maureen's indebtedness continues to weigh on her. That bank overdraft fee that was levied when she was eighteen years old has now ballooned to over $700 between interest and fines. The stain on her credit has prevented her from opening a checking or savings account; she has been told she must repay the old bank debt before she can have any relationship with another banking institution. And those two credit cards she ran up when Kayla was a baby each has a $1,000 balance now, with the interest and late fees accumulating over the years.

However, she's not completely without access to credit if she's willing to live with the terms. Just a few weeks ago, she learned she had been preapproved for two cards. One had a credit limit of $300 and the other a limit of $125; both have interest rates of over 25 percent. However, there is also an annual fee of $150 associated with the $300 card—her first bill was for $150, before she had charged a dime to the card, and the credit remaining was just $150. Maureen maxed these new cards out almost immediately to finance a trip to visit family a few hours north in Maine. Now, with interest, she has over $500 of additional debt. On top of all this, she owes $1,500 to the dentist—that bill has gone into collections—and $2,000 in outstanding medical bills associated with Kayla's death.

How does Maureen cope? She pays a little on her credit card bills every couple months—between $20 and $50 each. But accumulating late fees and interest swamp these payments. Then, if things are particularly tight, she juggles the bills—she trades off the cable, electric, heat, and cell phone bills, not paying on one of them until she receives a shutoff notice; then she pays just enough to keep the service. But this practice incurs late fees: from 1.5 percent of the balance on her utility bill to 5 percent of the balance for Comcast. At tax time, she uses her refund to try to get caught up on all of her outstanding obligations.

Maureen's stance is that right now, since she's living from paycheck to paycheck, attending to debt is simply a luxury she can't readily afford. "The way I've gone through life, my basic motto has been 'You always have to pay for your rent and the necessities you need. Anything else, [if] you can't pay for it, you can't pay for it.'" Worrying over debt is a source of stress, but still, she says, it is "not my main concern. My concern is what [bill] do I need to pay right now." Maureen finds it difficult to prioritize getting rid of old debt when she has so many other pressing demands, like putting food on the table, keeping the lights on, and buying school supplies for the kids.

But Maureen also aspires to the consumer comforts that better-off families enjoy. And she has repeatedly used credit to finance a lifestyle that— while still quite modest—is one she can't really afford: new outfits each season for the girls, the trip to Maine, her cell phone, the Internet and cable TV package, the Marlboro habit, and an occasional drink with her friends. And, as with many Americans, a seemingly irresistible impulse to, as she says, "overly spoil" her kids takes hold at Christmas time and on birthdays. On these special occasions, she feels they ought to "get everything" that other children have. By living just a little beyond her means every year (and having little in the first place), Maureen has dug herself a hole that she now feels she can't easily escape. And her damaged credit score will almost certainly dampen her prospects if she seeks to move into a regular, unsubsidized apartment or tries to secure a car loan, much less someday buy a home.

"THE BILLS, THEY OVERWHELM YOU . . ."

With the easier access to credit that low-income families have gained over the past thirty years or so, credit has become a way to make ends meet, along with the budget balancing that is possible at tax time. These strategies combine to build an annual cycle of debt accumulation and repayment that may repeat itself year after year, as it has for Maureen. Historically, lower-income families have been severely credit constrained—thus they had few debts, even though experiences of hardship were common.[1] Then two Supreme Court rulings, in 1978 and 1996, weakened state usury laws that had provided consumer protection from very high interest rates and fees. These rulings made it easier for credit card companies to bring riskier borrowers into the market, allowing them to charge higher interest rates to compensate for the increased risk. Deregulation also ushered in an era of aggressive marketing and lower minimum payment requirements, accompanied by steep fees and high interest penalties for late payments. Partially as a result, between 1989 and 2001, Americans' credit card debt nearly tripled.[2]

The percentage of families making $25,000 a year or less (in 2001 dollars) who had credit cards increased from 20 percent in 1983 to 40 percent in 2001. One consequence of this newfound access to credit was that by 2001 over two-thirds of lower-income cardholders reported outstanding balances.[3] While the average family experienced a 50 percent increase in credit card debt over that period, low-income families saw their balances increase by over 100 percent. The proportion of low-income families with credit card balances that were more than twice their monthly incomes was less than one in thirty in 1983. It was one in eight by 1995. Low-income families were also hit hard by late fee and interest-rate hikes, the fastest-growing source of revenue for the credit card industry.

While credit cards have proven to be the downfall of many economically constrained households like Maureen's, she owes nearly as much in back medical and dental bills as she does on her credit cards. Medical debt among both the insured and the uninsured has increased dramatically in recent decades. Health care costs rose at double-digit rates through the 1990s and 2000s, and employers increasingly shifted rising costs to employees in the form of higher premiums and less coverage. In addition, the percentage of workers with employer-provided coverage has been slowly, but steadily, declining for the past decade, and experiencing periods without any insurance has become somewhat more common.[4] At the same time, many states have made substantial cuts in their Medicaid programs. Massachusetts is an outlier in this regard. Even before the federal Affordable Care Act, it instituted MassHealth, which mandates universal coverage, the year before we first talked with families for this study. But many were still struggling with medical bills from past spells when they had been uninsured or underinsured.[5]

Our families have gotten into debt for these and a variety of other reasons, which we will discuss below. It is worth noting, however, that some debts are taken on as investments—for example, cars, refrigerators and stand-alone freezers, washers and dryers, and educational expenses. These items can offer a return in the form of a better job, save money by enabling a family to purchase food in bulk, or save labor and time.

Maureen Ellis, whom we met at the beginning of this chapter, has the debt profile of the *average* family in our study (see table 7). She has the bank overdraft debt, owes several thousand dollars on her credit cards, and has $3,500 in medical debts. And Maureen is lucky in one respect— grants funded most of her community college education; typically, graduates of two-year programs have an average of $12,307 in education debt.[6] Even without the weight of student loans, Maureen shares feelings about her debt that are common among the families we spoke to: they can easily be large enough to feel insurmountable. If the interest rates are high, the

Table 7   Type of Debt and Median Debt Amount

Type of Debt	%	Median Debt Amount
Credit card	66	$1,945
Utilities	43	$900
Car	36	$7,500
Education	35	$4,000
Medical	14	$1,450
Mortgage	12	$306,000
Family/friend	7	$300
Bank	6	$700
Back rent	5	$4,000
Appliances/furniture	5	$750
Computer	3	$475
Child care	2	$175
Legal	2	$1,000
No debt	5	

NOTE: N=115. Median values are for respondents who hold that type of debt.

small payments that households do manage to make often barely cover the interest and late fees, so the odds of making any real progress may seem long.

Not all of our families were so heavily in debt. About a quarter owed less than $800, and a handful even had no debt. Eva Jimenez, a thirty-year-old single mother of two, moved with her parents to the United States from the Dominican Republic fifteen years ago. She finished high school and started taking college courses toward a degree in criminal justice but dropped out after her second daughter—now five—was born. Until recently, Eva paid the bills by doing clerical work for a construction company. But an allergy to dust made the job miserable. Right now, she's working informal jobs found through friends' referrals—mostly painting and cleaning. The clerical post had brought in about $1,200 each month. Now she's earning just a couple of hundred dollars from her side jobs. She gets no help from the father of her ten-year-old daughter, but her five-year-old daughter's dad contributes a small amount, about $100 each month. Her new boyfriend, Ronald, does not help out much financially either, but he does pay for Eva's cell phone so they can keep in touch.

Eva takes great care to keep her expenditures to an absolute minimum. She lives in subsidized housing, so she pays just $130 each month in rent. She gets $215 per month from SNAP, which she manages to stretch so that the amount almost entirely covers the family's monthly food bill. Usually, she doesn't spend money on anything extra for her children—no clothing, toys, or outings. She relies on friends and family members to provide these items. Unlike Maureen Ellis, she shuns credit cards, determined not to "spend money I don't have." She does not have a home phone, cable TV, an Internet connection, or anything she considers "extra." In the summer, she keeps her shades drawn during the day to keep the heat out and the utility bills low. If she cannot cover a bill in full for a particular month, Eva always pays at least something toward it, even if it is just $5 or $10, and she makes it a priority to pay that bill in full the next month. But Eva's exemplary financial management skills and her ability to forgo so many of the items that are virtual staples in American households (the Internet and cable TV, for example) put her on the far end of the spectrum.

At the other end of the continuum are families owing more than $8,000— making up a quarter of those in the study. Deena Albers, a white forty-six-year-old mother of four children who range in age from three to fifteen, heads one such family. She works part time teaching piano lessons at an upscale music school in the affluent suburb of Newton; her husband, Emmett, has spina bifida and receives government disability. The family lives in a public housing project in South Boston with grime and graffiti covering the buildings' exteriors. Beyond Deena's earnings—about $1,300 a month—her husband Emmett claims $300 from his military pension and $800 from the Social Security Disability Insurance program. Taken together, all of these sources of household income constitute quite a sum—$2,400— but a considerable portion of that is already spoken for—the housing authority requires its tenants to pay roughly a third of their income in rent.

In a month with no unexpected expenses, Deena can just barely squeeze by—or she could if it weren't for the enormous outstanding credit card bills, medical debt, and unpaid utility bills that are hanging over her head. Several years ago, Deena says, she "screwed up" her financial situation badly. Emmett had required surgery to prevent him from ending up in a wheelchair, and in the months that followed he was in a great deal of discomfort from the scar tissue that developed. His depression and outbursts of anger caused by the chronic pain strained the marriage. To ease her angst, Deena says she indulged in retail therapy; "I spent money like crazy. . . . I ran up every [credit] card we had."

Now she can't even remember what it was that she purchased. "Who knows?" she says, "I was immature." Nevertheless, she has a whopping $10,000 in outstanding credit card debt—more than a third of her family's annual income—to show for it. She has made no payments on this mountain of debt, and her credit rating is so damaged she can't even get a loan for a used car. Plus, there is the light bill that Deena has chosen to ignore in months when money is tight—it takes months for the utility company to shut off the service while other companies will discontinue service more quickly. As a result, she and Emmett owe over $1,800 to NSTAR, the local electric and gas company. She is now required to pay $150 each month for regular service, plus $200 toward her arrears, to avoid a shutoff.

Deena copes with all of this debt via her phone's caller ID, screening calls to avoid her creditors' harassing messages. When they happen to catch her, she puts them off—for weeks she has been fibbing to NSTAR that the "check is in the mail"—but she knows that this strategy is near its end. She is hoping that Emmett's disability will qualify them for a "hardship" exemption, which prohibits the utility company from shutting off service in the case of extreme health problems or demonstrated financial need.

While it is worth noting that it is possible to stay afloat on a low-wage job without incurring significant debt—like the Eva Jimenezes of the world—only a quarter of our sample can accomplish this feat through a combination of extreme financial discipline, help from family and friends, and luck. Furthermore, many people feel that they "deserve" to spend some of their earnings each month on small "treats"[7]—Maureen Ellis's cigarettes, trip to visit family in Maine, and splurges on the kids' birthdays, for example—as a reward for their labors as wage earners. When we consider those whose debt profile is nearer to the average, like Maureen, or those with debts that are especially high relative to their income, like Deena Albers, one or more of the following are usually to blame for their debt accrual: youthful inexperience, a habit of living a little beyond one's means, or financial shocks.

Credit Card Debt

About half of all the debt that our study's families carry is long-standing. Typically, these debts are accrued by young adults who have little experience with credit and don't know its dangers or rules.[8] Claire Haynes, a twenty-five-year-old white single mother of three young daughters who works in food service, told us that she no longer uses credit cards because "I learned my lesson . . . when I was eighteen!" Claire grew up in foster care, bouncing around from one home to another. As a result of all of the moving around, Claire says, she felt emotionally detached during adolescence and thus longed for a baby to love and care for. When she became a mother at eighteen, she immediately applied for welfare and a housing voucher. Claire used the voucher to move to an apartment in a run-down section of Dorchester near the mostly white enclave of South Boston where her family was from. To supplement her meager welfare check, she worked under the table from time to time as a waitress in a South Boston restaurant.

Welfare didn't pay enough to finance the crib, the stroller, and other things her baby would need. So when a flier came in the mail, she applied for the credit card advertised. Having had no experience with credit before, she didn't bother to read the fine print. She was delighted to learn that she qualified for a $300 line of credit—she had assumed she would be rejected because her last foster mother had put the phone and utilities in Claire's name to reestablish service after it was cut off, not an uncommon strategy among lower-income households who seek to evade repayment but want to retain service. Then the woman didn't pay the bill, leaving Claire's credit tarnished.

Claire never ended up using this credit card, however.

> [It started out as a $300 card, but] I didn't know better, and when I got it, [there] was like $40-something available. So you already owe them like $250 when you first get the card. . . . And there was a $35 late fee, and [an] over-the-limit fee. If you got a late fee, you immediately went over the limit. . . . They give you a $300 card, but they take out an $80 annual fee and they take out a onetime [activation] fee [of $170]. By the time they're done taking all the fees off the card, you only got like $40 to spend.

Now, seven years later, Claire has learned that she has an unpaid balance of $840, even though she never charged a penny on the card. When she had first gotten the card and learned its terms, she had called the company: "I'm like, 'You know what? I don't even want it.' And they were like, 'Well, fine, then don't use it.' But I didn't know [the interest on the fees] was still accumulating all this time. . . . I never knew they had cards like that." Claire is clearly outraged at what she feels is the company's pattern of deceit, starting with the activation and annual fees, the unexpectedly large first monthly bill of nearly $260, and late fees and interest that continued to accrue even though she had called and told the company she didn't want the card—not to mention the fact that she never actually used it. Claire's first experience with credit is not unique; it was a story we heard repeatedly among families in our study.

Tamara Bishop is a black thirty-two-year-old single mother who provides for four children, ages five to fifteen, on her modest $400 weekly salary as a preschool classroom assistant. Tamara accumulated significant credit card debt several years ago after one of her two exes suddenly stopped paying child support. Each of her children's fathers had been assessed $200 monthly in child support, and the payments came like clockwork each month, since they were garnished directly from each man's paycheck. But in a moment of weakness when she was on especially good terms with her youngest child's father, Tamara agreed to drop his formal order with the understanding that he would continue to pay her informally—outside the system. He even promised to pay more than the $200 he had been assessed by the child support system when he could.[9]

This agreement worked well initially. In fact, she sometimes got help with the bills on top of the $200. But then he got jealous after Tamara started seeing another man, and the payments stopped. "It just threw me off. So it's like I couldn't catch up, for some reason I just could not catch up," Tamara says. Like so many of the families we spoke to, it didn't even occur to Tamara to apply for welfare, and she was reluctant to ask kin for help, so she turned to her credit cards. Then Tamara's new boyfriend, who had been contributing to the household, lost his job, and credit cards also had to cover the bills he had been helping with. Currently, Tamara is waiting for a court date so she can reinstate that formal child support order, but she holds out little hope that that strategy will help much, since the father is now unemployed.

Access to credit is vital to many American households who need to smooth consumption during hard times—after a job loss, a family death, an injury, or some other unexpected event. Welfare has never been very successful in fulfilling this function. Despite its official name—Temporary Assistance to Needy Families—it was never designed to be responsive to shorter-term income shocks like the ones Tamara has experienced. But what is most notable about Tamara's story—and common among others in our study—is the strong preference for drawing on credit cards to deal with such contingencies rather than turning to kin. Asking for a handout from kin seems to impose significant psychic costs, while credit cards allow families to mask their need at least for a little while and avoid embarrassment.[10] Notably, though, in most parents' narratives about how they cope with unexpected financial shocks, turning to welfare isn't mentioned as an option.

But not all of Tamara's debt is due to this recent cascade of financial shocks. Truth be told, she has relied on credit cards to spend beyond her means for years. "I kind of live off of my credit cards," she admits. Each year, for example, she enrolls her sons in baseball camp and her daughters in dance classes, which not only charge a fee but also require a trip to Modell's Sporting Goods for a glove, cleats, and a uniform, or to the dancewear store for leotards and shoes. Plus, she likes to treat the kids to an occasional night out at the movies—a pricey outing for a family of five—and she usually springs for the expensive bag of movie theater popcorn. Her biggest splurge, however, is an annual trek to Miami to visit her father; she uses her tax credit to fund the airfare and charges the other expenses from the trip. She also has a weakness for brand-name clothes, though she indulges only occasionally.

As a result of these spending habits, plus the new debt brought on by the child support fiasco and her boyfriend's unemployment, Tamara has now maxed out nine different credit cards, including a $900 balance on a British Petroleum card, $700 on her Sovereign Bank card, $300 on her Old Navy card, several hundred dollars each on a Victoria's Secret card, two Visa cards, and a Fingerhut card, and a whopping $13,000 on a Bank of America MasterCard.[11] How will she even begin to dig herself out of this hole?

Banking Charges

While the middle class generally sees banks as institutions that promote savings, lower-income households often see them as sources of financial risk and potential debt. Many families we spoke with either had experienced trouble with a bank in the past or knew a relative or a friend who had. Debt owed to banking institutions most often accrues when our families (often inadvertently) overdraw their checking accounts. Less commonly, bank loans are taken on for personal reasons, or debts accumulate from borrowing against retirement accounts or home equity for big purchases like weddings or furniture.

At the time of our study, both ATM withdrawals and debit card purchases could prompt overdrafts, which resulted in a fee of $25 to $35 per withdrawal, depending on the bank. While overdraft policies vary considerably across banking institutions, most also charge an extra fee if the overdraft and associated penalty are not repaid within a certain number of days (typically an additional $20 to $35 if the original fees are not paid within five to ten days); some banks even charge a per-day fee. These fees are charged per transaction, so if people don't know that they have exceeded their balance they could make multiple transactions, each accruing its own fees, before they discover that they are short on funds.

Consumers are often angry that they have been allowed to overdraw their accounts, and they are even angrier at the substantial overdraft penalties; they say they'd prefer to just have the charge declined. Recall Maureen Ellis, who overdrew on her account while shopping for her newborn and had charged items at Walmart and several other stores by the time her debit card was finally declined. When she was able to get to the bank several weeks later, she had $100 in debt generated from what she saw as innocuous purchases for basic goods. Many banking institutions are changing this practice in reaction to the federal government's sweeping bank reform bill, passed in 2010.[12]

People also seek personal loans from nonbanking institutions like payday lenders and "loan sharks," who offer short-term, unsecured loans to individuals at high interest rates. These loans are not common among families in our sample, but the conditions that prompt families to seek these loans are especially unpleasant and pressing. The loan terms are unfavorable, with high interest rates and aggressive pressure from lenders to repay quickly. Those who seek out such loans often lack knowledge about just how usurious the loan terms are upfront but are also not usually eligible for more traditional lending options because their credit rating is so poor. Despite their strong reluctance to ask kin for financial assistance, most folks would rather turn to family or friends for help getting by until their next paycheck arrives than to use these types of loans.

Medical Debt

As described above, health problems and a lack of insurance (or sufficient insurance) are other common sources of indebtedness. In 2006, Massachusetts became the first state to mandate universal health coverage. The full ramifications of this bill, which include fines issued through the tax code for those without health insurance, had not been felt at the time of our interviews. However, fewer families were without health insurance in Massachusetts than in any other state, in part because of the generous provisions for lower-income families in the MassHealth program. Most low- to moderate-income children, and many of their parents, were receiving coverage through MassHealth (which encompasses Medicaid and the State Children's Health Insurance Program, or SCHIP) during the time we conducted our interviews.

Still, many were carrying old medical debts. Michelle Tavares, a twenty-five-year-old immigrant from Cape Verde with a nineteen-month-old son named Dillon, used to work as a clerk at an auto body shop but left that job during a rough pregnancy. Her husband, Jonah, installs cable service for Comcast, but he is a contingent laborer. He hasn't been able to get on as a regular employee, which would qualify him for the company's medical plan. Michelle was insured through her full-time job, but she has had only part-time jobs since the baby was born and has been without insurance at numerous points during this time. Meanwhile, she was hospitalized several times for complications related to her diabetes and accumulated $8,000 in debt as a result, some resulting from periods without insurance and some because her insurance policy didn't fully cover the services she received. For example, her last trip to the emergency room occurred while she was insured, but she hadn't understood the limitations of her policy and learned only later that not all of the services rendered were covered. Afterwards, the hospital "started harassing me because I had a humongous bill. I had this lady calling me and yelling at me on the phone telling me I had to send the money right away. . . . They wanted it to come from my pocket."

Just recently, Michelle racked up additional medical debt—this time for her son, whom she had thought was covered under MassHealth. He had to have eye surgery for a sty, but MassHealth denied the claim because Michelle had inadvertently missed the recertification period when new paperwork was required. This procedure left them $1,000 deeper in debt. Now Michelle has done what was required to reinstate coverage for the boy and has coverage for herself under another state plan. But she has almost $9,000 in unpaid medical debts.

Other families have medical debt due to workplace injuries. Thirty-four-year-old Chantelle Woodward, a divorced mother of two girls, nine and fourteen, worked at a local hospital as a nurse's aide and occasionally performed tests that required her to draw blood. One day she accidentally stuck herself with a used needle and was banned from returning to work until a battery of tests for disease—including HIV—came back clean. However, the hospital—which didn't offer her insurance as an employee—keeps sending her bills for the required tests. She believes that her employer ought to be responsible and is refusing to pay them; each time she receives a bill, she sends it back to the hospital with a note explaining the situation.

The back-and-forth has become a huge source of frustration for Chantelle; even though she feels justified in not paying, she worries about the situation, unsure of what she should do or whom she should contact to resolve the matter. She doesn't know anyone who might help her navigate these bureaucratic and legal minefields. Meanwhile, the unpaid debt—her only outstanding financial obligation—threatens harm to her financial future.

Student Loans

In a "college for all" era, community and for-profit colleges have become attractive destinations for high school graduates seeking to earn additional qualifications for occupations that pay a living wage. Community colleges are a particular draw to lower-income parents because they can enroll part time and complete a degree at their own pace, there are plenty of evening and weekend courses, and the cost is low. Proprietary programs provide similar certifications and typically have better job placement,[13] but the cost can be considerably higher.

Adult students, like those in our sample, often take out loans to cover expenses while they continue to work and parent. Those completing a two-year associate's degree at a public institution leave with an average of $12,300 in student loans, while debts for graduates of private for-profit schools are higher—over $17,000.[14] Some loans require that students begin repayment immediately, while others allow them to defer the payments while they are enrolled in school. But once enrollment ends, the bills start coming, regardless of whether the degree has been completed or whether the student has found a job using his or her degree. This mismatch between loan repayment requirements and working parents' ability to satisfy them can often spell disaster. Even if workers do get a job in their area of study, the bump in wages from technical certifications or associate's degrees is sometimes not enough to offset the increased monthly expense that loan repayment requires.

Juana Vega, the thirty-six-year-old Head Start teacher, lives with her husband, Ignacio, a part-time mechanic, and their eleven-year-old son Milo. Fourteen years ago, after earning her bachelor's degree in psychology in Puerto Rico, she moved to the United States. Payments on her student loans—totaling about $9,000—were due right after she finished the degree, even though she did not yet have a job. Only Ignacio was working and the couple were struggling to pay their bills. Not surprisingly, Juana couldn't keep up with payments on these loans. After she found the job at Head Start, she started paying on the loans each month, even putting several thousand dollars from her tax refund toward this end. But after two years at that job, Juana got pregnant with Milo. Once the baby came, she had a host of new expenses and had to cut back on her work hours. The loan payments once again went by the wayside. She has been paying on and off ever since, dropping a check in the mail when there is extra money and skipping payments when times are tight.

Even though she hasn't always been consistent in paying on these debts, Juana says she is constantly thinking about them, feeling a keen sense of pressure to pay them off. After fourteen years of on-and-off payments, she feels as if she's "been paying forever." Now she only has $500 left, and she recently authorized automatic deductions from her bank account each month to ensure that the loan is fully paid off. Juana is strongly focused on saving, especially since she adopted the goal of buying a house one day. In her view, paying off her student loans is a huge step toward achieving this goal, and this is what has motivated her to clear the student loan debt even though money has been tight.

Those responsible for collecting on student loans are often more flexible about repayment than other creditors. While it can be easier to ignore these loan payments when other priorities emerge, flexibility can also keep borrowers from defaulting altogether. Juana says, "I'm *slowly* getting it dwindled down. It's just one of those things that doesn't have to be taken care of right now, you know, it's more on the back burner than my other bills that I have, so they're just kind of paid when I could and [aren't] when I couldn't." Many other families took this approach to their student loans as well, making student loans a common long-term debt.[15]

Family and Friends

As mentioned earlier, most household heads in our study say they don't like to borrow money from family and friends and avoid doing so unless it's absolutely necessary. However, many say they have had to ask for help from family and friends over the course of the past year. As discussed in greater detail in chapter 1, this typically means borrowing $20 here and there to cover milk and bread or, occasionally, larger sums of money from parents or siblings for urgent needs like car repairs. The smaller sums are not usually considered "debts" that need to be repaid. Instead, respondents say they try to reciprocate and offer similar support when friends or family are in need.

Larger personal loans are another matter, however—they almost always come with the expectation of repayment. Allegra Mendez is a thirty-seven-year-old single Puerto Rican mother of three who lives in the Charlestown section of Boston. She dropped out of school at sixteen but earned her GED when she came to the mainland United States and now works as an assistant teacher in a preschool classroom. When she started at the school, she "really didn't have enough money . . . because I wasn't getting too much income from work. They were only paying me like $7, $8 [an hour]." Last year she borrowed money from two of her sisters to buy airline tickets to Florida, where Allegra's family now lives; she owed one sister $500 and her other sister $300.

When people owe money to family or friends they feel intense pressure to pay off these debts as soon as possible. Such debts are often a top priority when the tax refund comes. As soon as she got her tax refund this past year, Allegra paid back her sisters. She explains that she hates the feeling of owing money to relatives and friends, and she feels a tension in her relationships with her loved ones until the funds are repaid. Prompt repayment allows families to save face even when they've had to "go begging" to kin when things have gotten tough. Maureen Ellis, the waitress whom we met at the beginning of this chapter, said she does "not like borrowing money from people"—so much so that "if I borrow from somebody, I'll pay that off before I'll even pay my own rent." In sum, such debt carries no interest or formal sanction, but it still holds higher repayment priority than credit card or student loan debt.

As indicated earlier, even though the families we spoke with routinely borrowed from and loaned money to family and friends to make ends meet, almost no one said they asked for, or received, a personal loan to pay off outstanding credit card, education, or medical debt. People apparently feel it is inappropriate to borrow or lend for this reason. Perhaps this is because debt repayment is not immediately related to getting by and can almost always be put off (albeit at a price). Family and friends seem to be viewed as a resource for addressing tangible and immediate needs.

DEBT'S BOTTOM LINE

Getting into debt and trying to dig out of it were near-universal experiences for the families we met. As we have indicated, widespread debt among our families reflects increased access to credit for lower-income households in recent decades. Families accumulate debt for a variety of reasons: many lack basic knowledge of how financial instruments operate, or lack it at the critical stage when they first become adult consumers; others succumb to a desire to consume somewhat more than they can really afford; some make investments in human capital (via student loans) that don't pay off as expected; and most have little to cushion them when they suffer an unexpected financial shock—the sudden loss of child support, a health crisis, or a job loss. Beyond the financial dollars and cents, there are psychological costs to holding debt.[16] Debt struggles represent a relatively new element of life on the financial edge.

Even though our families' debt profiles vary widely—from just a couple hundred dollars to tens of thousands of dollars—their descriptions of how they got into debt reveal a common thread, a tension between aspirations and economic realities. Some debts, particularly those incurred via credit cards, result when desires for (often modest) consumer goods outstrip monthly incomes. As workers, parents often feel they deserve such goods and, in the moment, don't fully seem to consider the future consequences of their actions. Over the year, their finances tend to bounce around, but consumption seems to be influenced more by the high than the low end of that range, particularly when families have access to credit cards. Lack of knowledge about the terms of loans, fees, interest rates, and expectations for repayment is also a common cause of indebtedness, as households end up taking on obligations they find they cannot fulfill. Other debts, like student loans, reflect attempts to get ahead; families' inability to repay their student loans reflects the limited advancement sometimes reaped by these investments. Finally, some credit card and medical debt reflects holes in the social safety net that are revealed when families experience sudden drops in income or spikes in expenses. It seems that TANF—what remains of the old welfare system—isn't flexible enough to help families respond to these ups and downs; very few of our families draw on or even consider using welfare when facing sudden need, though they often do turn to other government benefits, such as SNAP.

PAYING OFF DEBT

What logic do families employ when making decisions about how to satisfy their obligations?[17] Tynetta Sanders, her husband, Alan, and Nyeshia, Tynetta's four-year-old daughter from a prior relationship, live in the city's Charlestown neighborhood. The black twenty-four-year-old works as a cashier at a CVS pharmacy, earning about $900 a month, while Alan clears roughly $1,500 a month at his job as a waiter. Tynetta collects about $250 each month in child support from Nyeshia's father. She saves money by keeping Alan's name off the lease so the housing authority doesn't take his income into account when determining her rent. Tynetta and Alan both have cell phones, and the family pays $150 a month for an Internet/cable bundle. They also spend $200 each month for Nyeshia's child care, the portion not paid by her child care voucher. And there is another baby on the way. This will bring new financial pressures.

Tynetta has outstanding balances on three credit cards totaling over $3,500. She claims she hates buying on credit, yet repeatedly ends up maxing out her cards because she "need[s] the money right now." But the urgency this statement implies doesn't always fit with her stories of how she came to be in so much debt. Recently, for example, she ran up a $300 balance on her Macy's account by buying furniture for her apartment. Macy's is a weakness, she admits. She loves shopping its sales, and a few months ago, she took advantage of a particularly good bargain and brought home a new set of pots and pans. Partly because she enjoys using it so much, she tries to keep the balance low on her Macy's card so that she can keep charging on it. She owes about $400 on that card right now. She uses a second credit card, from the Children's Place, to buy nearly all of her daughter's clothing—the girl is unusually petite and the pants there have adjustable waistbands. This is the one card on which Tynetta usually manages to pay off the balance every month. She remarks, "I don't mess up that card, because I know I use it all the time." Currently, she owes only $100 on this card.

But Tynetta's third store credit card, from Sears, has a balance of over $3,000, which she ran up buying furniture and households items after a move several years back. Until recently, she wasn't paying on this card at all—the bill was so large and so old and had such a high interest rate that she felt it was simply too great a burden. What would be the point of even trying, she thought. Instead, she focused on paying down the balances on her other two cards—the ones she still uses regularly. Sears' threatening phone calls were another reason she stopped paying on that debt. "I ended up changing my cell phone number so that [Sears] would stop calling me. . . . I keep telling them, 'You're calling to get your money. You don't have to be rude to me. That's gonna make me not want to pay you even more. . . .' I said, 'Lady, I don't have the money right now. I don't know what to tell you guys. When I get it, you'll get it. Trust me, because I want you to leave me alone. . . .' So I just changed the [phone] number to refrain from arguing." Tynetta also owes about $700 for a student loan from a program that would have certified her as a medical assistant. She had to drop out midway through because "money got tight." She stopped paying on that debt for the same reason she quit paying on the Sears card; she hung up on the rude woman who called last time because she was afraid she would "curse her [out] really bad" if she remained on the line. To her creditors, she offers some advice: "Speak to me in a civil manner, how you want to be spoken to; don't call me and disrespect me and then want me to pay you."[18]

Although many of our families are delinquent on one or more debts, few take a cavalier attitude toward these unmet obligations. Paying off debt is a pressing concern—it often weighs heavily on their minds. Debt must be considered when families make choices about how to manage their monthly budget, but it can become especially salient when they begin to formulate long-term financial hopes and dreams, especially for home ownership. But after necessary expenditures are made, there usually isn't enough money left at the end of each paycheck to make regular payments on every outstanding debt. So families deploy a variety of payment strategies that guide how they make trade-offs in assessing which of their various financial obligations to pay.

Juggling Debts

The most common approach to paying outstanding debts is to "juggle" them. Sometimes this involves paying on one debt in one month and on a different debt in another month. Other times, families may pay on one debt for a period of time, take a break and focus on other financial needs, and then resume payment on the debt; sometimes a household head may pay some portion of all obligations but none in full. Families often fail to make real progress toward alleviating their indebtedness with these strategies; interest and fines may equal or outstrip their efforts. However, juggling allows them to avoid going into default or collections.

Satisfying creditors is a secondary concern for a family living in the red. Tynetta Sanders says, "I'm telling you bills come so quick . . . , [they] overwhelm you. Food and things you gotta pay, and things you want for children. . . . As [the money] comes, it goes. I have a couple of things I've been trying to pay off [completely]. I told [the other credit card companies], right now I can't pay you guys [everything I owe]." As noted above, Tynetta has consistently tried to keep up with payments on the two smaller cards. However, her recent marriage and the pregnancy have provided new motivation to try and wipe the slate clean. So, for the last few months, she has let other obligations slide while devoting nearly $500 monthly toward that $3,000 debt on the Sears card. She thinks that if she can just get Sears off of her back she'll feel a huge sense of relief. Then she can focus on catching up with the smaller bills. This strategy has not brought her much respite yet, however. The creditors on those smaller bills are now calling "constantly," and they too are "rude, rude, rude."

When hit with a shortfall between incomes and financial obligations, prioritizing becomes necessary. As we indicated earlier, it is rare for families to say that they prioritize the debts with the highest late fees or interest rates as they make these trade-offs. Nearly across the board parents explain that taking care of basic needs, especially rent, takes precedence over all else. When debt payments are possible, often parents explain that they make the debt with the largest balance or the credit card they use the most their top priority—as we see in Tynetta's story—while letting others slide. This practice seems to offer some psychological benefits but presumably not financial ones, since they incur late payment fees (and possibly demerits to their credit rating) on several bills, not just one.

Working toward a Goal

Those families who adopted clear and disciplined plans—including cuts to current consumption—in order to get out of debt were almost always motivated by specific financial goals. Chantelle Woodward, who has the unpaid medical bills from the accidental needle prick at work, is determined to get her family out of public housing. She's also tired of the psychological strain of having a dark cloud of debt hanging over her head. For these reasons, she says she is putting every extra dollar into paying off her credit cards. She's "trying to get them bills down so I can get myself out of debt. I don't like owing, owing, you know, and the more you keep thinking and it stresses me—damn, I owe this, oh, I owe that. Then you start worrying about it. . . . I don't want to put myself in that predicament, so the best thing to do is just try to pay off what you can." Those who aspired to home ownership showed the strongest motivation to wipe out their debts. Adopting these goals was often a jump-start to a pattern of more responsible, often sacrificial, financial behavior. When we asked Juliana Soto, a thirty-two-year-old married Hispanic receptionist for a food manufacturing company, why she decided to put all of her extra cash toward paying off her credit cards, this mother of three—ages four, eleven, and fourteen—replied, "Because [we] really, really wanted this house. We figured the faster we get everything down to zero, the better chances we might have. . . . I wanted it at zero, and I cut up [all my credit cards] and I [called each credit card company and] said, 'Hi, I want to cancel my card, thank you!'" Efforts like Juliana's sometimes come at a real cost to current consumption.

When families take steps to educate themselves about how to secure a mortgage, they quickly learn that their unpaid debts are going to stand in the way of getting a mortgage or favorable loan terms or interest rates. To start repairing their credit, families often craft personal payment plans so they can make consistent progress on their debts. Monica Lourdes, a forty-two-year-old preschool teacher, has been living in a cramped three-bedroom apartment on the second floor of a triple-decker in the city's Jamaica Plain section with her husband, a housepainter, their son, sixteen, two daughters, both in their early twenties, and a son-in-law and a grandchild. She has decided that it's time to buy a home so the three-generation family can have the space they need. Recently, she announced to her husband, "At the end of this year, we should be looking into getting the house." But Monica and her husband owe roughly $4,000 on three different credit cards. When we ask about her plans for meeting her end-of-the-year goal, she explains, "*Debt!* I'm hoping to eliminate that word! I do want to get the home. I already took a home buyer's class. I looked into . . . the Credit Smart program [offered through the city of Boston], where you take the classes and they'll show you how to fix your credit, how to not fall into other traps, like credit cards, again. . . . I'm hoping and praying and, if everything turns out well, by December we should be looking into buying the first home."

Now, she says, they are "paying bills left and right, left and right." They have been trying to pay off their credit card debt and are cutting back on everything else to make this possible. All of the adults in the household go to a food pantry once each week to get groceries, they have cut back on providing financial support to needy relatives who come to them for aid, they have stopped spending on movie rentals and other entertainment, and Monica is even trying to quit smoking because she tallied up how much it cost her and was amazed by how much she could save. She is also looking into getting a second job. She becomes animated while relating these plans and then catches herself, and laughs: "You can tell I really want this house, right?"

Prioritizing Debts

Given that most of these householders have multiple creditors, which bills and debts they choose to pay involve trade-offs: Which do they decide to repay, when, and in what order? Families often give lower priority to debts that are not perceived as "legitimate," even if it would have made more economic sense to organize repayments in another way. Practices viewed as usurious or fraudulent serve to delegitimize some forms of debt and thereby discourage repayment. This is why certain credit card debt tends to fall at the bottom on most families' mental hierarchy of which debts ought to be repaid first. Many feel credit card companies took advantage of them, noting the hidden fees, fines, and high interest following lower "teaser" rates. We saw this in the case of Maureen Ellis and especially with Claire Haynes, both featured earlier in this chapter. Recall that Claire was enraged at being duped into accepting a credit card that had a substantial balance (the activation charge and annual fee) at the outset and that it continued to accrue late fees and interest charges without her knowledge even though she had never used it. Accordingly, she isn't paying on this bill. Likewise, Maureen Ellis, the waitress at Pizzeria Uno, refuses to pay on an outstanding debt to the bank because she feels the debt is unfair; she wouldn't have used her debit card if she had known that the funds in her account couldn't cover the charges, and she thinks the bank should have declined the charges, rather than overdrawing her account. In such cases, the perceptions of lenders' behavior lead parents to reject the legitimacy of the debt and allow them, at least psychologically, to absolve themselves of the responsibilities for repayment.

The way credit card companies typically interact with customers in order to get them to repay generates additional resentment. Such resentment was enough to prompt Tynetta Sanders to nearly default on the $3,000 balance on her Sears card. These hassle tactics no doubt work some of the time—credit card companies and collections agencies presumably wouldn't use them otherwise—but if our families are any guide, they can backfire too. To reiterate, many of our families cited these practices as the reason they stopped paying on certain debts altogether. They tell us that the hassling exacerbates feelings that paying off that debt is hopeless, which leads to a sense that it's useless to even bother making payments.

Though households sometimes prioritize their largest debt, even if it means neglecting other smaller obligations, there is definitely a psychological threshold that, if exceeded, can prompt families to give up on paying the debt altogether. Discouragement often ensues when, for example, after months or even years of meeting the minimum monthly payment in full, they fail to make a substantial dent in the principal. This is part of why large debts prompt an all-or-nothing reaction—either ignore them altogether or put every extra dollar toward them until you've paid them in full.

Nathan and Maryam Shirley tried to keep up with their debt payments but ultimately gave up. These Somalian immigrants live on the city's south side in Dorchester with their five children, ranging in age from three to eleven. Maryam stays at home with the children while Nathan drives a bus between Boston and New York City. Shortly after coming to the United States, Nathan obtained a credit card with a $2,000 limit. During the early months of their transition, he and his wife used it to fund all kinds of purchases for things they urgently needed—groceries, clothes for the kids, even the rent—but they had difficulty keeping up with even the minimum monthly payment. Then Nathan inadvertently exceeded his credit limit by $19, and the credit card company charged him an additional $49, a relatively small amount in dollar terms but a huge blow psychologically because he now felt even further behind. He kept putting at least some money toward the bill every month but wasn't able to make any progress on reducing the balance as the interest continued to snowball. Finally, Nathan gave up. "'This guy is never finished,' I said. 'Forget it; I'm not going to pay it.' [Now] I ignore them. . . . It's better not to pay."

Using the Tax Refund

For so many of our families, tax time is seen as *the* time to pay off outstanding debts. Recent research uses nationally representative survey data from 1988 to 1999—the period during which the EITC was expanded significantly—and finds suggestive evidence that single mothers use a portion of their EITC to pay down or avoid taking on unsecured debt.[19] Tax time seems to be an appealing time to tackle debt partly because the lump sum allows families to make large enough payments to enjoy the psychological relief of wiping out, or substantially reducing, a particular debt all at once. Many describe the wonderful sense of relief they experienced when they finally got their debt collectors off their backs at tax time and were able to start fresh with a "clean slate." Tynetta Sanders, the CVS cashier we met earlier who owes on nine different credit cards, looks forward to tax time because she can make large payments on several different cards all at once; it is a special pleasure when she can pay one of them off completely. She says, "I have a couple of things I've been trying to pay off, but like I told them, right now I just can't pay you guys. . . . If it accumulates, I'll deal with you when I get taxes. I'd rather just give you the money then, so that I don't have to keep worrying about you."

The promise of tax time appears to alleviate some of the discomfort and worry that the month-to-month financial juggle generates. But falling behind harms credit scores and incurs late fees. It is possible that the prospect of being able to resolve debts all at once at tax time prompts less responsible financial behavior during the rest of the year—weakening the financial resolve of those like Maureen Ellis, who lets her electric bill slide as tax time approaches. Despite the cost, putting bills off and then eliminating them all at once—at tax time—is a common strategy. Those who pay on their debts with the tax refund make substantial progress, cutting outstanding debts by an average of 50 percent.

Debt Assistance

Few families sought out help or information on how to resolve their debt; hardly any knew about public, private, or nonprofit resources they could approach for assistance. In part, this is because, at the time of our interviews in 2007, programs that addressed this need were quite rare. In our conversations, few families identified a government entity that offered such aid to general consumers. The city's nonprofit sector offered a patchwork of financial literacy courses, but most of our families either didn't know about them or felt that the curriculum was "condescending" because the information on offer was already within their grasp. Nonprofits and government agencies do sometimes provide home ownership programs for first-time or low-income home buyers, and these programs do offer some degree of financial literacy training. However, the only families who sought out such programs in our study were those who were already committed to buying a home.[20]

In this information void, a great deal of folk wisdom has arisen around the long-term legacy of debts. Family after family was certain that their debts would "disappear" after seven years. This seven-year milestone does actually hold for some debts, but it does not apply as automatically, or as universally, as many families assume. Only certain kinds of debts drop off one's credit report after the seven-year mark; this does not include unpaid tax liens, child support arrears, or student loans in default, for example. Six months to a year after one stops paying on a bill, the lender "writes off" or "charges off" the debt by selling it to a collections agency; state law governs the statute of limitations on the number of years during which a company can pursue repayment through legal means (e.g., suing to collect). Finally, this debt disappears from one's credit report seven years after the last missed payment. But this can occur only when a consumer completely defaults on a debt—something our families are hesitant to do. This is one reason credit card companies are so motivated to both hassle and make accommodations for families who are willing to continue making payments, no matter how small, on their accounts. This extends the period during which the company can pursue repayment.

Why don't families just declare bankruptcy? Simply put, they often can't afford it.[21] In fact, across the population, only a tiny fraction of those in financial distress pursue the bankruptcy option.[22] Filing for bankruptcy can cost upwards of \$1,500—a massive sum for a low-wage worker, even when payments are allowed in monthly installments over a six-month period. Further, filing for personal bankruptcy doesn't discharge certain kinds of debts, like outstanding educational loans, meaning it may not bring complete financial relief. Plus, the social stigma of bankruptcy adds the risk of being branded a financial deadbeat to the existing stresses of financial struggles—a prospect all are eager to avoid.[23]

The nonprofits that serve these communities seldom offer much in the way of debt counseling, outside the aforementioned first-time home buyer programs. Likewise, while family and friends may offer social support and practical assistance, we have shown that there appears to be a strong aversion to asking kin for a loan for the purpose of paying off debt. In short, the places where families commonly turn for help with other life challenges are often devoid of resources for dealing with debt. Still, as indicated earlier in this chapter, a small group of highly motivated and relatively financially stable families, like Monica Lourdes', were able to access home ownership and credit counseling courses. These courses seemed to offer useful tips for reducing their debt burdens and advice to keep from falling back into the same financial traps in the future.

DEBT'S DRAG ON MOBILITY

The burden of debt weighs heavily on lower-income families. It puts into sharp relief the gap between their aspirations—the kinds of lives they think a wage earner ought to be able to enjoy—and the realities of the low-wage labor markets in which they must try to make a living. The strategies we have described in this chapter are ad hoc coping mechanisms, many of which will incur concrete costs both in the short term (interest and late fees) and later on, as tarnished credit scores prevent parents from taking out a loan on a reliable used car, buying a home, getting a job, or even securing a lease on an apartment in a better neighborhood. The ability to get ahead, to realize the American Dream, depends not just on a stable income and the accumulation of assets but also on addressing debt obligations, which are clearly a heavy anchor holding many lower-income families down.

For these families, the expectation of the EITC is a double-edged sword. It encourages some to build up debt in the months before tax time by overspending or letting bills slide. But it also fuels aspirations that, in turn, motivate financially responsible behavior—saving, greater thrift, and debt payoff. The more positive behaviors are most evident among those with concrete goals for upward mobility, especially those who aspire to own their own homes. In the next chapter, we argue that one way forward is finding a way to capitalize on these positive functions of the tax credit, while also devising ways to minimize the debt families run up during the year.

6 Capitalizing on the Promise of the EITC

Throughout the late 1990s, when the economy was booming, many celebrated the success of welfare reform. But critics warned that such high praise was premature—the true test of the system, they said, would come when the economy took a turn for the worse, not when jobs were abundant. While the downturn of 2001 and the period of slow growth that followed took a palpable toll on the employment and wages of unskilled and semiskilled workers, many still didn't end up on the welfare rolls.[1] Just as we finished interviewing families for this book, the Great Recession took hold, offering a deeper challenge to the work-based safety net.

Many will wonder what happened to our families during the recession and its aftermath. Thus we revisited the households whose stories are featured at the start of each of our chapters four years after we had interviewed them the first time.

In chapter 1 we told the story of Ashlee Reed, a twenty-nine-year-old white college graduate, who lived with her boyfriend, Adrian, an unemployed cook, and their three young children. We detailed her difficulties making ends meet on an income that fluctuated throughout the year. The family had relied solely on her earnings as a preschool teacher for much of the year, experiencing a financial boom at tax time when her refund check arrived, and struggling through the bust when the school year's end meant that her paychecks stopped. It turned out that Ashlee's was the only family that we could not track down four years later. The phone numbers we had no longer worked, and letters went unanswered—understandable once a drive past her old house revealed that the building was being gutted. Our difficulties in finding Ashlee are not that surprising, given the frequent telephone service disconnection among low-income families. Researchers estimate that approximately one-third of low-income families see their phone disconnected during the course of a year.[2] Similarly, residential instability is common among low-income families. Just under a quarter of households say they relocated in the past year;[3] over a two-year period, around half of poor and near-poor families report a move.[4]

When we first met Debra McKinley and her fiancé, Sonny, profiled in chapter 2, they were getting by but feeling the pinch because Debra was in the late stages of her third pregnancy and couldn't work. Now this white couple, both in their thirties, have four children—including a one-year-old boy—and even less money than they did three years ago. Debra blames their financial straits on the recession. Both had been employed at a restaurant owned by Debra's sister, and, though she had held a five-year lease, the building's owner was forced to sell after he could no longer pay his taxes. The new owners had other plans for the building, forcing the restaurant to close. A new venue for the business has not been found, so Debra and Sonny are both out of a job. Debra says she is applying for every opening she can find but has had no luck. Sonny, whose career in construction had been sidelined several years earlier because of a back injury, has been able to claim disability. He has tried to use the time he's been idle to pursue an associate's degree program in computer drafting and design at a technical institute and will graduate in nine months' time. They hope the degree will secure him a job that pays much better than waiting tables. But returning to school has been costly. He has taken out $32,000 in loans so far. And, although Debra and Sonny don't seem aware of it, the job prospects for someone with Sonny's hoped-for degree are weak; the Bureau of Labor Statistics describes the job outlook for the field as "slower than average."[5]

In the meantime, they're living on the $365 that Debra's eight-year-old daughter gets because the child's biological father is permanently disabled. They also get $500 from Sonny's disability check. Debra, who worked under the table at the restaurant, did not qualify for unemployment. The kin they've relied on in the past—Debra's sister and mother—are no longer a source of financial support; they too were employed at the now-defunct restaurant. Debra and Sonny's housing subsidy, which limits their rent to 30 percent of net income, has been key to their survival. To get by, they have also had to rely heavily on SNAP, which covers roughly 80 percent of what they spend to feed their family of six. They also claim MassHealth (particularly important for Sonny, who has severe diabetes) and their tax refund check. Last year, most of the refund went toward getting their car back on the road—essential for the hourlong commute to Sonny's school. With money so tight, they've stopped making payments on their credit cards, with balances now totaling $7,000. This year they were grateful they could take advantage of a special program through Head Start, where their three-year-old attends preschool, which provided Christmas presents for the children. Otherwise, Debra says, there wouldn't have been any Christmas.

Debra and Sonny's story reveals the perils of relying on kin. In an economic downturn there can be no one with the wherewithal to provide that needed handout or loan. After Sonny's injury put an end to his career, Debra's sister and mother were able to buoy their finances for a while. But when the restaurant closed, everyone was left struggling. Further, their situation underscores how the EITC—which we often think of as a safety net program—doesn't actually catch you when you fall. When the hard times hit, the refund shrinks—and even disappears—along with one's wages. In the past Debra reveled in using a portion of her tax refund to make her daughter's birthday dreams come true—the glorious dinner at the Red Lobster plus the night in a Connecticut hotel. This year, though, she couldn't even finance Christmas; she also knows there will be no refund to look forward to next year unless she finds work soon.

We find Johanna and Mack Clark, a white couple in their early thirties, still married and living with their children, now eleven and eight, in the same Southie apartment. Johanna continues to work as a medical assistant, for $18 per hour plus benefits, and make progress toward her RN degree. She estimates she'll be done in the next year and expects that she'll have a job waiting for her at the hospital where she currently works. Mack, who'd been a stay-at-home dad, had planned to return to work soon after we met, but the recession stymied his employment search until just three months ago, when he landed a warehouse job driving a forklift. Last year, while they were still without a second income, they claimed a tax refund check of $5,500. Nearly half went toward the purchase of the car that Mack now uses to get to his new job, and what remained—$2,500—went into that passbook-only savings account. This special second savings account was depleted repeatedly during Mack's years of unemployment. In fact, without the refund check and their housing subsidy, which cut their rent to nearly half of the market rate when Mack wasn't working, they wouldn't have been able to make it.

When we first met them, the Clarks felt they had to justify Johanna's time on welfare. Now they're proud of their improved financial situation. Mack's warehouse job pays $13 an hour plus benefits. And Johanna's college graduation is under a year away, further proof of how far they've come.

In chapter 4 we profiled Jacinta Estrada, a Hispanic mother of four whose boyfriend had been shot in the arm in a drive-by and had been unable to work since. This had left Jacinta as the only wage earner in the household. When we talk with her again years later, not much has changed. She and her boyfriend are still raising their four children together, now ranging in age from seven to fifteen, and Jacinta is still the primary earner. Since we spoke with her last, her boyfriend's health has been further affected by a serious back injury. There is now no hope of his working as an auto mechanic, yet his disability case has been denied. While he tries to regroup, he works a day or two a week painting apartments for his uncle's painting company.

Meanwhile, Jacinta's work situation has also deteriorated. After getting laid off two years ago from her job in a hospital's payroll department, where she was employed when we first met her, Jacinta and her family got by on her unemployment. When those benefits ran out, she applied for SNAP and began to draw on her savings. After an arduous job search, she got hired on as a lunch aide at her children's school, but for only three hours a day. While it doesn't pay nearly enough to live on, she is grateful— it's better than nothing, she says. Her wages help tide the family over, and the hours leave time to search for a better job. Meanwhile, her boyfriend is studying for his GED, hoping that the credential will get him access to a job that isn't as physically demanding as being a mechanic. Because of Jacinta's tiny paycheck, the couple pay next to nothing toward housing—they have a subsidy—and they're eligible for $400 a month in SNAP, plus MassHealth and fuel assistance. But because of their joint spells of joblessness, they were unable to claim anything from the EITC this past year. That annual check had been the cornerstone of Jacinta's plans for home ownership when we first met, when she was so eagerly envisioning buying a two-story home surrounded by Vermont's safety and quiet in five years' time. Jacinta is far less likely to fulfill this dream now than she was just a few years ago.

Jacinta's story echoes those shared by so many other families: though they try to build a brighter financial future through assets and savings, any gains can be quickly eroded when financial hardships inevitably arise. Because so many families are in precarious financial positions, often with little to fall back on when tough times hit, any progress they make can quickly disappear. Jacinta had built up a small nest egg by the time she lost her job, only to see this savings rapidly spent down after her unemployment benefits ran out. As Jacinta's story shows, families of modest means may have the will to build assets and save, but not always the way to do so.

Maureen Ellis, whom we introduced in chapter 5, was waitressing and working toward an associate's degree when we first met her. Shortly thereafter, this white mother of two elementary school children traded her dreams of a college education for a four-month course certifying her as an emergency medical technician. Since then, she's worked full time in her new profession. Ironically, riding in the back of an ambulance doesn't pay quite as well as the waitressing job. Even worse for her bottom line, as a waitress, she didn't report her tips (which constituted the majority of her income) and thus could claim far more in SNAP benefits than she now can. Plus, she had qualified for MassHealth while at that job. Now she has to pay for her share of the health insurance plan offered by her employer. But still she thinks she came out ahead—working as an EMT feels more like a career than waitressing, which she considered just a job.

Maureen embarked on single motherhood when she left her husband after a violent fight. She's now living with a boyfriend who contributes some to the family finances. These days, though, Maureen is not so pleased with her new man. Several months ago, he was laid off from his job as a manager at P. F. Chang's, and ever since he's seemed content to rely on his unemployment. In Maureen's view, he hasn't put in nearly enough effort to finding a new job. This makes her nervous; she knows from experience how long it can take to find decent employment. Fortunately, Maureen's ex-husband has finally gotten a job and has started paying the $300 he owes each month in child support. Maureen is also looking forward to her tax refund check. Because of her steady yet modest earnings, her refund is typically large. Most years, she has taken out a $1,000 loan—an advance on the refund—in December, which covers Christmas gifts, but she has had to pay roughly $400 in interest and fees for the privilege; both are taken from her tax refund. This year she didn't feel she could afford that option. She waited to collect any money until tax time, which she put toward buying a used car, paying ahead on the auto insurance, and getting caught up on back bills. She reserved $500 as a cushion against any unexpected expenses, depositing the money in a savings account.

Maureen tells us that she's one of the lucky ones—the recession hasn't had much of an effect on her. It has always been hard to get by, she says, but she still manages to find ways to cover her expenses. This is the same attitude she had when we talked with her the first time; then, as now, she coped by forgoing any payments on her many credit card debts. For working-poor and near-poor parents like Maureen, carrying a relatively large debt load was common even before the recession.

Notably, even when times got tough, none of these families turned to welfare—even Jacinta, whose family was left without any source of income for a spell. This is reflective of national trends—while SNAP receipt rose substantially during the recession, TANF's rise was astonishingly modest even as poverty rates climbed.[6] This drives home a key point we've made throughout the preceding chapters: beyond the EITC, which benefits only workers, today's social safety net is a system largely woven from noncash benefits—SNAP, Medicaid, and, for a lucky few, housing subsidies, which cover only 25 percent of eligible households nationally, are the largest of these programs. The most generous cash benefits are not dispersed on the basis of need alone—as the "safety net" metaphor would imply—but are conditional on work behavior, like the EITC and other tax credits. The new safety net certainly promotes work in ways that its predecessor did not. But it leaves behind able-bodied household heads who aren't working, along with their dependent children.

The new work-based safety net was developed in the economic glow of the prosperous 1990s. Even through the doldrums that began in 2001 and intensified during the Great Recession, these benefits have become essential to the households that receive them. And the proportion of the population in tough financial situations has been growing: during the recession, the earnings of nearly one-third of working families were under 200 percent of the federal poverty line.[7] Today's approach to providing for the poor reflects the high value Americans across the socioeconomic spectrum place on financial self-reliance through work.

A majority of both higher-income and lower-income Americans maintain that the poor are at fault for their own penury. The United States is exceptional in this regard, at least in comparison to its European counterparts. While between half and three-quarters of Spanish, French, and German citizens agree that "success in life is determined by outside forces," just over a third of Americans feel similarly.[8] American workers up and down the economic ladder say that among the major causes of poverty are a lack of motivation and a decline in moral values; almost half, across income groups, list welfare as a major cause of poverty, even after welfare reform has shrunk the program to only a shadow of its former self.[9] Nearly three-quarters of Americans express concern that the poor are too reliant on the government for support,[10] and over half say too many government benefits go to those "who could get by without help."[11]

Nonetheless, across socioeconomic groups, Americans are highly supportive of government interventions to assist lower-income families who are *working*: 94 percent are in favor of expanded job-training programs, and 80 percent endorse increasing the tax credits going to low-income workers.[12] During the recent recession, surveys found that around two-thirds of Americans would prioritize government efforts to address unemployment over the deficit.[13] The rhetoric of providing "a hand up, not a hand out" rings true for Americans, who prefer not to help those who are not seen to be helping themselves; but they seem to hold tight to the belief that with hard work anyone should be able to get ahead in America.

Perhaps as a consequence of these public attitudes, the provision of cash assistance to nonworkers has been cut while those programs that serve as work supports have been expanded.[14] This lies in stark contrast to the original intent of the country's first federal welfare program established as part of the 1935 Social Security Act, Aid to Dependent Children (ADC), which explicitly sought to keep single mothers at home with their children, as they were ending up in orphanages because their mothers had to try to support themselves by working. At the program's inception, "deserving" recipients were those widows who were doing the "right thing" by caring for their children at home and not going out in the workplace.[15] Today's definition of "deservingness" has turned this notion on its head: while the general public is quite willing to support working mothers, women who are not working—even if they have children—are seen as unworthy of aid. This is not surprising, since middle-class mothers have now entered the labor market in large numbers. The expectation today is that mothers will work, even when their children are young; this sea change in mothers' work behaviors helps explain why there is little support for paying poor moms to stay home with their children, as the ADC program had originally intended. Although 2012 Republican presidential candidate Mitt Romney rousingly declared that "all moms are working moms" whether or not they had a paid job or worked in the home, he also proudly touted his tough-on-welfare record as Massachusetts governor, arguing, "Even if you have a child two years of age, you need to go to work. . . . I want the individuals to have the dignity of work."[16] Across our society, being a stay-at-home mom has become a luxury few Americans can afford.

Even receipt of cash welfare (through TANF) is now contingent on recipients' willingness to actively seek employment. Meanwhile, the EITC, along with the child tax credit and other state and local tax credits, has expanded over the past twenty years into by far the largest source of cash support for poor families. The federal government spent only about $16.5 billion on TANF in 2012—and only $5 billion of that amount landed in welfare recipients' pockets (the remaining funds are allocated to purposes such as child care vouchers and employment programs).[17] Meanwhile, over $100 billion was spent on the EITC and child tax credit alone, accounting for the federal government's outlays and forgone tax revenue.[18]

Very recently, politicians have been making louder calls for TANF-type work requirements to be instituted for SNAP and housing subsidies as well.[19] These proposals reflect the feeling among the general public and many policy makers that no one should get something for nothing: that is, assistance—whether cash or in-kind—must be contingent on work effort. Rearing children no longer buys one access to public sympathy or a check from the government; assuming the status of a working parent, however, can bring such rewards.

THE NEW SAFETY NET: SUPPORTING WORKERS, FUELING DREAMS

Despite the virtual demise of TANF, in the years since welfare reform the United States has actually expanded the cash support for the poor considerably through the tax credits that are available only to those who file taxes. In-kind supports have expanded as well, including the Children's Health Insurance Program (CHIP), as well as the extension of child care vouchers and Medicaid coverage to those transitioning off the welfare rolls. Unlike the old system's practice of paying parents not to work and docking their benefits when they did, America's new approach of supporting the working poor enjoys broad political support.

Toni Patturelli, whom we introduced at the start of the first chapter, would have received $670 a month in welfare benefits under the old welfare regime if she weren't working. Under the current system, she combines part-time work and child support, totaling $1,100 a month. On top of this, she claimed $2,550 from her tax refund. When she is able to work more, her EITC benefit will grow, putting her further ahead. And the potential benefits of the tax credits she receives extend even beyond Toni's bottom line: recall that research suggests that the extra money families get from the EITC is associated with improvements in children's educational achievement and health and with their parents' health as well.[20] So, even as Toni's family struggles, they are still clearly coming out ahead in the new regime.

Both economic sociologists and behavioral economists have made the case that one dollar is not interchangeable with the next; rather the delivery method, the source, and the meaning that is attached to each dollar can shape how it is spent.[21] Toni certainly wouldn't view the $670 she could get from the welfare system as equivalent in meaning to the $670 she earns in wages or to a $670 check from the IRS, her "tax refund." While the former are ways to keep a roof over her children's heads, and to keep them fed and clothed, she sees the latter as offering many more possibilities for transforming her financial future.

From its inception in the late 1930s until it was reformed in 1996, welfare enjoyed the legal status of "entitlement"—any parent who was below a minimum income level and met other program requirements was entitled by law to the money. According to the ideas advanced by this body of research, this label ought to have influenced how monies gleaned from the program were viewed. Sociologist Viviana Zelizer distinguishes between money from gifts, entitlements, and compensation and argues that recipients of entitlements have a stronger claim on a provider than do those who receive compensation; while a boss can fire an employee (choosing not to give compensation any longer), parents cannot similarly fire their children (choosing to no longer give the financial support to which they are entitled).

During the 1960s and '70s, the National Welfare Rights Organization (NWRO) and others fought to protect the right of single mothers, a group increasingly composed of the unmarried as opposed to the widowed, to receive benefits, especially in jurisdictions where African Americans were routinely denied aid because of prejudiced application of "suitable home" requirements and the "man in the house rule." They also fought to raise benefit levels and expand coverage for the poor. These battles were largely won—the rules that had led to improper denials were deemed unconstitutional, benefit levels were increased, eligibility was expanded, and the rolls more than tripled.[22]

Meanwhile, polls showed that few Americans had been convinced by the NWRO's argument that the mothers were truly "entitled" to government support, especially once large numbers of middle-class mothers began to work outside the home.[23] This is a key reason welfare carried such stigma. It was technically an entitlement, but it was out of synch with most citizens' moral sense of what people ought to be entitled to and under what conditions. And public opinion ultimately triumphed. The landmark welfare reform legislation of 1996 ended the program's entitle-ment status. States could by and large choose what level of support they would offer to the nonworking poor. The primary parameters the federal government set were limits on the maximum amounts recipients could receive. There were no longer any minimum requirements for what indi-viduals had to be provided.

The EITC is also technically an entitlement: you are legally entitled to it if you meet the requirements of the program. But the public supports it not because of its legal status but because it is *viewed* as a form of compensation—you *earn* it by working. The EITC is thus legally an entitlement, albeit con-ditional on work behavior, but is viewed as compensation—akin to earn-ings. The families in our study call it a "refund" and do not consider it a handout. This does not deny Zelizer's central point, that the larger cultural systems of meaning matter in shaping perceptions of money. In fact, it takes her argument a step further. Assessments of entitlements and com-pensation are also value-laden, altering the power dynamics accompanying each. In a culture such as ours that so highly prizes and rewards the moral value of work, being "compensated" may bring more power and social standing than being "entitled" by law. The high degree of public support for Social Security offers a parallel example. Though much of the money is redistributed from working taxpayers, its recipients—and society at large—regard it as savings from one's years as a worker. Again, we have an entitle-ment that appears to be compensation.

Indeed, the new work-based sources of assistance to the poor are not called, or even thought of, as "welfare." We spend roughly three times more supporting families through the EITC than we ever did on TANF, yet tax credits carry none of the social stigma of welfare; recipients of the EITC are proud to claim the status of worker, not dependent, despite the array of government programs from which many of them benefit. Because the EITC delivers benefits "invisibly" through the tax system, rather than the welfare office, and because it ties benefit receipt to work, it supports recipients' feelings of social inclusion, of being part of the mainstream and being workers just like everyone else.[24] All are treated as customers when they arrive at the for-profit tax preparers' offices to claim what they see as the reward for their labor. This clearly contrasts to the experiences some lower-income families have had at the welfare office. The families in our study who did try to claim welfare benefits at one time or another often said that their attempts were discouraged or greeted with suspicion. But any mistrust aroused among IRS personnel by one's tax documents occurs out of sight unless one is audited. Unlike the eligibility verification required of every applicant under TANF or its predecessor, AFDC, the auditing of tax filers' claims is relatively rare and can happen to anyone, at any income level. In fact, as we've mentioned, the parents we spoke with sometimes purchased "peace of mind" via the audit protection services offered by H&R Block. The sense of respect and protection that for-profit tax preparers often provide is the message behind H&R Block's memorable slogan "You've got people."[25]

Through the tax system, wealthier Americans may write off capital losses, middle-class home owners may claim mortgage deductions, and lower-income families may receive tax credits if they work. Though these benefits vary dramatically, such differences are hidden by their common method of delivery.[26] Claiming benefits through the tax system is a much less stigmatized and socially isolating experience than waiting in line at the welfare office. Working families can get help without paying a social and psychological price.

That lump sum from the tax refund can relieve the pressure of living paycheck to paycheck, at least for a few months. As we have described, families generally spend their refund money paying bills and back debts, purchasing durable goods, paying tuition, or putting some cash into a savings account for a rainy day or a long-term financial goal. They make real progress in paying down debt. Furthermore, the savings they tuck away help guard against financial shocks.[27] Very little is spent in ways the general public might perceive as "frivolous"—our research shows that nearly 90 percent of tax refund dollars go to these purposes and current consumption (which includes stockpiling goods and paying ahead on bills).

However, the modest amount of the refund that is spent on "wants" and not "needs" is of great symbolic importance. In February, in March, and on into April, not every penny has to be counted when that ice cream truck goes by or when a child longs for a Bob the Builder bedspread; a dinner out can be at a sit-down restaurant (like Friday's), rather than a fast-food joint; a dream birthday for a child who is struggling in school can sometimes be realized. The considerable benefits parents believe they—and especially their children—derive from small expenditures on treats should not be ignored.

Before the Great Recession, there was a consistent upward trend in the proportion of the public who viewed microwaves, clothes dryers, air conditioners, and other similar consumer goods as "necessities" rather than "luxuries."[28] Sociologist Allison Pugh finds that, among children, having the "right stuff" can be enormously important to feeling a sense of belonging among peers. Pugh, who conducted an ethnographic study of low-income elementary school children and their more affluent counterparts, finds that lower-income parents made extravagant purchases for their children precisely because of their symbolic significance among their kids' peers.[29] Our households make few such extravagant purchases, but the ability to purchase both "necessities" and some small luxuries carries important symbolic weight with them as well and may be necessary for these households to feel like "regular" members of society.[30] As the consumption of America's affluent continues to soar, what it takes to feel normal for those at the bottom seems to grow as well.[31]

The transformation of the US welfare state from a need-based to a work-based system has been truly profound, at least for workers. It does everything welfare does not. It creates feelings of inclusion rather than exclusion. It rewards rather than punishes. It gets people to behave in ways that are consonant with American values—they work. It ensures that if you play by the rules you won't get the shaft, to paraphrase Bill Clinton's famous phrase.

IT DOESN'T CATCH YOU WHEN YOU FALL

Today's lower-income workers confront working conditions that are unimaginable to some middle-class Americans. With little notice a retailer may cut a worker's hours when customer traffic is slow. Layoffs in the low-wage sector are so widespread that they are more the rule than the exception. Seasonal or temporary employment is common. Opportunities for upward career mobility are often limited, if they exist at all. Employees can be punished for even the slightest infraction with fewer hours or the loss of a job. There is little in current law that offers workers much protection. Accordingly, the Current Population Survey shows that income volatility is highest for those without a high school degree.[32] All this was true before the 2008 financial crisis, which has increased competition for even these "bad" jobs. In contexts such as this, a system of government assistance that is contingent on work can intensify, rather than counterbalance, the impact of earnings volatility. As we saw for Jacinta Estrada, losing a job is a one-two punch: one's earnings are lost along with that big refund check at tax time.

Employment and income instability were growing to dizzying heights among less educated workers even prior to the Great Recession. Over the last few decades, researchers have regularly surveyed Americans about their employment and income. In 1973, the chances that a man without a high school diploma would report being unemployed for two years in a row stood at 9 percent; by 2008, these chances had more than quadrupled, to 38 percent.[33] Economists estimate that the incidence of income instability among families has roughly doubled over this period of time. The proportion of adults who see their family incomes fall by at least half has more than doubled, with one in six workers now experiencing a loss of half or more of their income every year.[34] This volatility isn't usually due to those who "earn big" in one year falling back to their usual earnings during the next. Rather, America's families are experiencing sharp declines in their regular income. Financial instability affects much more than a family's ability to balance the books. Just as the resource infusion the EITC brings seems to benefit health and well-being, income loss is associated with negative health consequences for parents and children. Not only do such parents have fewer economic resources to invest in their kids, but parenting quality is also diminished in the face of the stresses of tough financial times.[35] Further, because the EITC has drawn less skilled parents into the labor force by offering a greater payoff for their efforts, employers have had a larger pool of potential employees; this creates downward pressure on the wages of less educated workers because of the increased competition for each job.[36] While refundable tax credits may compensate for this downward pressure on wages for those with dependent children, their childless counterparts and noncustodial parents are out of luck.

The instability now endemic to the low-wage labor market poses serious challenges for the work-based safety net. The low-wage labor market virtually promises instability and limited wage growth. The once-a-year windfall of assistance at tax time, and the strong cultural ideal that all Americans can and should work toward owning their own home, feed the dreams of home ownership so many of our families hold dear. The tax refund many look forward to each year makes it seem possible to put together a down payment in the not-too-distant future. Many of our households hold fast to the dream of home ownership. Yet it is renters who have the flexibility to move to a cheaper unit, live for a time with family or friends, or even apply for a housing subsidy when they hit tough times. Given their monthly mortgage burden, home owners have less agility when facing a downturn. Selling a home, even in a strong housing market, can easily take half a year or more.

The persistence of the home ownership ideal in the United States has proven resilient even in the face of the Great Recession, with its frightening headlines of short sales and foreclosures. In 2009, in the trough of the Great Recession, 90 percent of home owners still said that owning their homes was a source of comfort to them;[37] further, more than eight in ten Americans agreed that "buying a home is the best long-term investment a person can make," and more than eight in ten current renters reported that they would like to buy a home in the future.[38] Americans' long-term financial priorities also reflect the power of the home ownership dream. Home ownership was the goal Americans were most likely to list as "extremely important" and was described as "extremely" or "very" important by more than eight in ten in a recent survey. It came out ahead of other financial goals, like the ability to pay for a child's college education or to leave an inheritance for children.[39] In 2012, nine in ten of those surveyed insisted that home ownership is still a key part of the American Dream.[40]

This valorization of home ownership is no doubt furthered by government policies that explicitly, though perhaps subtly, promote it. The federal government eases and encourages home ownership by providing tax advantages to owners and by making it easier and cheaper to secure home mortgages.[41] Home ownership rates climbed fairly rapidly during the second half of the twentieth century, enabled by these policies. Yet some experts are starting to question the wisdom of these priorities.[42] Still, as one can see by the numbers above, faith in home ownership among the American public hasn't flagged. Ending tax advantages to home owners may reduce the appeal of buying a home for those whose incomes are limited and volatile. But would giving up on the centerpiece of the American Dream—a home of one's own—take away hope for the future and the motivation to get one's finances in order and start saving? Without Jacinta's dreams of a two-story home of her own in serene Vermont, would she still have been driven to cut costs and save?

Although dreams spawned by the EITC can motivate financially responsible behavior, such as paying down debt and putting money in a savings account, its benefit delivery through a once-a-year lump-sum payment may also potentially contribute to poor financial decisions. First, it sets in motion a boom-and-bust cycle in each family's annual budget. The tax refund shows up full of exciting possibilities once a year but quickly fades into memories for many, leaving only keen anticipation for next year. As economic psychologists have shown, people view and spend "windfall" money differently than regular income or incremental payments spread out over longer periods of time—it is more typically spent than saved.[43]

However, it must be emphasized that we find relatively weak evidence for this negative windfall effect with regard to the EITC. While it is true that only 17 percent of the refund is initially saved, most of the rest is spent on durable goods and debt payoff, stockpiling, and paying bills ahead (both captured in the category "Current Consumption" in figure 4) rather than on frivolous purchases. While economists have traditionally treated any dollar as equal to another, economic psychologists' research has shown that this is not how the rest of us view our money. We engage in "mental accounting," viewing different pots of money in different ways; as we detailed above, such allocation decisions are further influenced by the cultural meanings ascribed to different pots of money. One hundred dollars from one's regular paycheck is more likely to be allocated to bills or put into savings. One hundred dollars won from a scratch-off lottery ticket might be spent on treats.[44] The EITC seems to be viewed as a special kind of windfall. It has a set of special cultural meanings that direct allocation toward expenditures aimed at catching up and getting ahead.[45]

Still, these large annual tax refund payments may encourage some overconsumption; some families purchase items at tax time that they explicitly say they wouldn't have if they had gotten the money in smaller monthly increments.[46] The tax refund money is viewed not as "regular" money but as a happy "surprise."[47] While it does enable families to build a little wealth, in the form of some modest savings and durable goods, we also note that a few of our families do spend some of their tax credit in ways that are uncharacteristic, given their otherwise often-thrifty mind-sets. For a few, the tax refund leads to spending that is quite a bit more extravagant (a weekend on New Hampshire's Lake Winnipesaukee or even an expensive toy like a Wii, for example) than they might normally indulge in.

Nationally, more than two-thirds of EITC recipients file for their benefits through a for-profit tax preparation firm.[48] In one sense, the government has outsourced a portion of the old welfare caseworker job, but the recipients themselves foot the bill with a portion of their refund. Families do not usually seem too bothered by the fees accompanying such services, as they are relatively small given the large refunds they are set to receive. Because fees are often taken from the refund check directly, most don't feel the pain of cash leaving their wallets. They also value the experience of being treated as a customer, a benefit seldom experienced among those using nonprofit preparers. Not surprisingly then, the use of volunteer tax preparation is quite low nationwide—only 1.6 percent of all EIC schedules are filed in this way.[49]

THOSE WE'VE IGNORED: NOT WORKING, NOT ON WELFARE

In this new system, compared to that of the past, low-wage workers have come out ahead in a big way: the supports available to low-income households with a worker are without equal in the country's history. However, there were simultaneously cuts in resources for those who are not working and expansions for the employed, with less going to the deeply poor and more to those closer to the poverty line or just above it—that is, the somewhat more advantaged come out ahead.[50] While the safety net has expanded quite dramatically in terms of total dollars spent since welfare reform, and its reach is several times greater than before, the result has been a safety net with holes, and many of the desperately needy have fallen through.

The number of American families with children who reported no meaningful cash income—not from welfare, work, family and friends, or side jobs—in a given month has grown dramatically since 1996, the last year of the old welfare regime. By 2011, roughly 1.65 million households, including 3.55 million children, experienced at least one month that year living on less than $2 per person per day—a poverty threshold usually applied only in Third World contexts. This was more than double—up from 636,000 households—from where it stood in 1996. And roughly 2.4 million children spent a full quarter—three consecutive months—in these precarious economic straits, as compared to about 1.3 million in 1996.[51] What economists call "deep poverty"—families living below half of the poverty threshold—also grew quite dramatically starting in the late 1990s. This is due, in part, to the changes in the safety net brought about by welfare reform. Arloc Sherman of the Center for Budget and Policy Priorities has noted that, "if the safety net had been as effective at keeping children out of deep poverty in 2005 as it was in 1995, there would have been 1.1 million very poor children in 2005." Instead, there were more than twice that number.[52] Though we cannot be sure, it may be that under the old system many such families would have turned to cash welfare.

The families we talked with for this book, however, were only rarely suffering in these extreme ways in 2007, in part because we limited the study to households with relatively large tax refunds ($1,000 or more). To claim that amount, families usually had to have worked a considerable number of hours in the prior year. Despite their struggles, they were the winners of the new regime, which saw a fall in cash welfare for nonworkers and a rise in tax credits for the working poor and near poor. But just as we finished our conversations with these families, the Great Recession began to test whether the work-based safety net would hold. On one level, it appears that welfare reform has succeeded in reducing dependency—even in 2009, when the recession and jobless rates were at their height, only 1.2 million adults claimed anything from TANF. As we indicated earlier, in 2011, in the midst of a so-called jobless recovery, only 1.1 million adults remained on the rolls.[53]

In short, although not given a voice in the pages of this book, those who are without employment and without welfare have clearly been left behind by today's work-based safety net. While systematic research on how these families fared during the Great Recession is not yet available, evidence from the more mild recession in 2001 indicated that a growing proportion of people were leaving welfare and reporting no income.[54] Called the "disconnected," this group neither benefited from cash assistance nor was buoyed by the newer array of work supports now available. And so deep poverty (the proportion of Americans living under half of the official poverty line) and extreme poverty (the proportion of Americans living on $2 per person per day or less) have continued to grow. Our understanding of the successes of the work support system must be tempered by the knowledge of this group of Americans who are left on the outside looking in.

HEALTH, WELL-BEING, AND ACHIEVEMENT

As we have shown, the EITC not only eases the economic burdens of the working poor but motivates asset building and debt reduction. It does so in a way earnings or other forms of income our families receive usually do not. As a result, the EITC is uniquely positioned to boost parent and child well-being.

Earlier, we reviewed research showing that durable goods purchases increase during February, the most common month of EITC receipt. This research exploits the fact that the credit is paid out annually, rather than month to month, and looks at how spending patterns change around tax time. Another analysis using this technique shows that eligible households spend relatively more on healthy items, including fresh fruit and vegetables, meat and poultry, and dairy products, during the months when most refunds are paid.[55]

Economists have also examined the EITC's impact by assessing how various outcomes change after an expansion of the federal, or a given state's, EITC. Using this approach, they have found positive impacts on both health and long-term success. Mothers, for example, are less likely to smoke and have better self-reported mental health after an expansion of the credit than before. In addition they evidence fewer biomarkers that are predictive of future health problems, such as a heart attack or diabetes. Health benefits for children may also be substantial early in life, as the probability of prenatal care increases and the incidence of low birth weight declines. School-aged children also show higher test scores after a credit expansion. These benefits are in turn associated with better socioeconomic outcomes in adulthood, including higher rates of college attendance, higher earnings, and a lower teen birthrate.[56] These findings have led some economists to conclude that EITC expenditures are probably more than offset by the cost savings of these long-run improvements in health and socioeconomic status.[57]

What is it about the refund that boosts health among mothers and socioeconomic success among their children? The firsthand accounts in this book may shed light on this question. First, the EITC improves material well-being by increasing consumption of basic household necessities, at least for a few months. Parents allocate fully 23 percent of their EITC to current consumption, including stockpiling groceries and other household items and paying ahead on bills such as the car insurance and rent. Thus children are presumably more likely to have enough food on the table, adequate school supplies, and as so on. This may well boost their academic performance.

Second, we have argued that the benefits of the tax refund aren't just material but psychological as well. Our results suggest a role for the EITC in alleviating stress. In the months after getting the refund, parents say they don't have to worry as much about how they will pay the light bill, how they will feed their kids, or how they will keep their family from eviction or foreclosure. Stress can exact a heavy toll on one's health both directly, by raising blood pressure and cholesterol, and indirectly, by increasing the likelihood of unhealthy behaviors, like smoking.[58] Maternal stress during pregnancy increases the risk of a baby's being born preterm or at a low birth weight. Each is an independent predictor of future health problems for the child.[59] Thus, in addition to children benefiting from their lowered exposure to maternal smoking, the in utero environment in which children develop is superior when their mothers are less stressed.

Stress exacts more than a physical toll, however. It can also reduce one's capacity to make good long-term financial decisions. Recent developments in the field of behavioral economics, in particular Mullainathan and Shafir's book *Scarcity: Why Having Too Little Means So Much*, suggests that having too little consumes vital psychological resources, particularly what they describe as bandwidth.[60] Bandwidth is a finite resource and can be consumed by worry over day-to-day survival. A deficit of will-power, cognitive control, and attention in other areas of life, including financial decision making, can be the result. The laser beam focus the poor develop to deal with the challenge of material shortfalls has bene-fits—they are often unusually adept at managing on scarce resources. For example, as Edin and Lein's 1997 research has shown, such survival strate-gies can become honed over time, shared among neighbors, and even passed down from generation to generation; Edin and Lein found that second-generation welfare recipients, those living in high-poverty areas, and African Americans, a group disproportionately likely to be poor, were more skilled at living poor than their counterparts with more advantages.[61]

But the *Scarcity* research shows the dark side of this equation. When bandwidth is expended on survival, it is unavailable for other vital tasks. This may help to explain why those we meet in this book, while often adept at getting by, sometimes can't resist living beyond their means or make financial decisions that compromise future well-being and conflict with their longer-term financial goals. Mullainathan and Shafir's results show that the pressing nature of having too little "crowds out" attention to longer-term interests and exhausts the "muscles" of self-control.[62] Their research reveals that scarcity has these detrimental psychological effects on all who experience it—not just the poor. When dieters focus on com-plex diets—those requiring careful counting of calories, for example—they are actually more, and not less, likely to succumb to temptation when pre-sented with a piece of chocolate cake. The mental "tax" of worrying about the diet ends up—paradoxically—taking a big toll on their willpower. The poor are presumably more likely to experience scarcity in everyday life than other Americans. The consequences of reduced willpower, cognitive control, and attention may also be more severe for the poor than for the affluent, because the poor lack a financial cushion against foolish eco-nomic decisions they may make. Like those on complex diets who are con-sumed by the caloric trade-offs they must make, our households are often consumed by the task of juggling the bills.

In light of these findings, it may be surprising that EITC recipients allo-cate as little of their refund money as they do to treats and as much as they do to paying down debts and investing in savings and other mobility-related purchases. However, given how the psychological effects of resource scarcity appear to work, our research raises the possibility that the relatively disciplined and future-oriented allocations of the refund may be partly a result of the fact that the credit relieves psychological pressure. Receipt of the tax-time windfall may free up one's bandwidth, allowing longer-term thinking and more future-oriented behavior. This may be one reason why so few of our respondents "blow" much of the money, as one might have assumed a financially constrained household would do with a windfall.

In sum, the refund introduces some slack into budgets that are otherwise stretched to the maximum—recall that in our study, household earnings covered only about 70 percent of expenses. The three-month window of relief from financial strain might be the one time during the year when these families can lift their heads from the grind of mere survival and think ahead. Many of our means-tested social programs do not relieve scarcity, as they offer less than what is needed to get by.

For example, neither TANF nor its predecessor, AFDC, paid enough for families to survive on, at least if they wanted to avoid losing custody of their children because of neglect, as Edin and Lein's book *Making Ends Meet* showed. SNAP benefits are set so as to cover only a portion of families' food needs. A 2012 study showed that SNAP households routinely scramble for food for the last week or two of each month because their SNAP benefits have been expended and their earnings have been consumed by other pressing needs.[63] To the degree that these programs fail to alleviate scarcity's "bandwidth tax" for their beneficiaries, they could have negative consequences for decision making in other domains.[64]

Here again is another profound difference between the EITC and many other means-tested programs. While their benefit levels may be too low to fully mitigate experiencing scarcity, the tax refund gives households the funds to move beyond spending on basic needs. But there is a catch. The EITC seems to relieve financial stress for about a quarter of the year, according to the experiences of the households in this study. These families then struggle for the other three-quarters. Whatever psychological boost they may derive at tax time in the form of available bandwidth may not fully compensate for the losses in willpower and cognitive control due to their struggles during the rest of the year.

We have argued that the EITC and other tax credits confer considerable social benefits for families; they allow for spending and saving decisions that create feelings of social inclusion. This is a key sociological insight of this book, one that the economic psychology perspective misses. The cultural meanings of tax credits, which activate the identities of worker and parent, seem to guide how the families in this study allocate this money. That household heads file for the EITC at for-profit companies—where they are customers, not applicants—and receive it via the IRS-administered tax code—a universal system that serves those across the income spectrum— explicitly links the refund to work. This reinforces the notion that it is not a handout but a reward for work—the opposite of a welfare check. In addition, the households we studied often associate this lump sum with savings. In fact, it is sometimes explicitly described as such. Several specifically point to their anticipated refund as part of their savings. In this way, the EITC seems to have become strongly associated with possibilities for upward mobility. Accordingly, much of the credit is allocated to purposes of debt payoff (in part to improve credit), savings, and social mobility. Many families know they receive tax credits because they have kids; some even call it "the kids' money." Is it any wonder that a modest portion is reserved for kids' treats?

We've shown that the method of delivery reinforces the citizenship-enhancing nature of the tax refund—it confirms, rather than denies, a sense of being part of the mainstream. This has implications for income support policies in general: not all dollars are created equal, and the meaning and delivery method attached to the money matter a great deal. While the psychological benefits of the refund may enable parents to think more clearly about their future financial goals than is possible at any other time of the year, the social promise of the refund is equally powerful for those who receive it—the possibility that they, and their kids, can feel like "real Americans."[65] We know of no studies that examine the effects of refundable tax credits on civic engagement. However, existing research indicates that social welfare programs that create feelings of incorporation, rather than exclusion, among beneficiaries boost participation in political activities and civic organizations.[66] This raises the possibility that refundable tax credits for the working poor may also create a more engaged, prosocial citizenry.

It is worth noting that the "citizenship-stripping" nature of many other means-tested programs may have the opposite effect. The Special Supplemental Nutrition Program for Women, Infants, and Children (WIC) and Head Start are other means-tested programs our households identified as carrying very little stigma. Neither requires applicants to ever set foot in a welfare office. In contrast, those who wish to apply for SNAP must usually go to the welfare office in order to apply. As we've discussed, many feel shame in doing so. They must "cross the road" that separates citizens from "the company of the destitute," to use T. H. Marshall's imagery. [67]

MOVING FORWARD: BUILDING POLICY ON WHAT WE KNOW

The new safety net has developed in a time of widening income and wealth inequality.[68] At midcentury, family income doubled from one generation to the next; in contrast, the rate of growth slowed substantially during the last quarter of the twentieth century, with family income increasing only by a fifth over the course of a generation, even as more women went to work and more families could draw on two incomes to get by. The smallest gains in family income have been among those at the bottom of the income distribution.[69] Further, intergenerational mobility may have slowed over the last thirty years.[70] The United States, as compared to other Western countries, is particularly notable for its lack of mobility among those at the bottom of the socioeconomic ladder.[71] Fewer children are finding greater success, and more are experiencing greater instability, than their parents.[72]

Such financial struggles may be compounded by economic shifts and changes in family structure patterns over time. The decline of manufacturing and the rise of the service sector, as well as the increasing rewards of higher education, have meant fewer living-wage blue-collar jobs. And just as more families need to rely on two earners to make ends meet, divorce and nonmarital childbearing have resulted in large numbers of families headed by a single adult. Although divorce rates have remained relatively steady over the past thirty years, there is a sharp cleavage by class. Over this time more-educated Americans' marriages have actually grown more stable while less-educated Americans' marriages have become more likely to crumble. Meanwhile, more couples are living together and starting families outside marriage. In the United States at least, these cohabiting unions have proven to be far less stable than marriages, even among parents. While only one in ten married couples separates before their child's third birthday, fully half of cohabiting parents do so.[73] Child support payments, even when paid in full, don't fully compensate for the economic losses involved. Children and their parents inevitably end up with fewer resources when incomes have to be stretched across two households.

The rise in income instability at the bottom of the wage ladder may be exacerbated by changes in the economy, with fewer good jobs for lower-skilled workers, and rising family instability. But government policy, which now largely restricts cash aid to workers at tax time, may also be playing a role. The new safety net is built on the presumption that people can find and keep jobs. Yet unemployment is consistently higher among the least educated—coming in at 9 percent even prior to the Great Recession.[74] As social scientists Jacob Hacker and Elisabeth Jacobs note, "Total family income volatility for low-income families increased substantially . . . perhaps because of the move from relatively stable government cash transfers to the highly volatile arena of low-wage work."[75] In a world of growing income instability, depending on one's wages for survival—as well as for access to government assistance—has become riskier over time. The new safety net rewards work, but it does not provide a job or ensure a stable income.[76]

Moving backwards toward anything like the old welfare system, which paid parents not to work outside the home, is simply not an option. It was universally reviled before its demise, so even if it were a wise policy move, it is a political nonstarter. The overhaul of the welfare system, from AFDC to TANF, did little to soften Americans' views—public opinion data have remained remarkably consistent over time on these issues. Americans' distaste for welfare specifically, as opposed to aiding the poor in general, comes through in survey data: while nearly two out of three Americans believe the government spends too little assisting the poor, only one in five says the government spends too little on welfare.[77]

Therefore, new proposals to bolster the stability of working families' lives must be in line with core American values, with a focus on rewarding work and supporting self-sufficiency. To be politically viable, policies must follow the American credo that people should work, but work should pay. We make recommendations in four areas: raising incomes, stabilizing finances throughout the year, building savings and assets, and supporting education.[78]

Raising Incomes

Throughout this book we have illustrated the daily realities for working parents of trying to raise children on limited incomes. It is important to remember that many of these are families who do not fall below the poverty line—roughly half of EITC recipients have earnings that pull them out of poverty (before their EITC check), if only just barely.[79] But what these families' stories vividly illustrate is that being above the poverty line is cold comfort when your paycheck doesn't stretch to cover your monthly bills. As a society we need to decide to what extent we are comfortable with parents and children in our midst struggling in these ways, without "luxuries" many of us take for granted, like making a necessary car repair and still being able to afford a child's birthday present. If we conclude that we are not willing to settle for a nation in which so many working parents struggle day to day, month to month to raise their kids according to our current standard of living, then aiming to do more than eliminate poverty must be a goal guiding our policies. President Clinton declared that "people who work hard and play by the rules should not be poor." And in the years since, politicians on both sides of the aisle have echoed these words. Merely fulfilling this pledge for those lucky enough to stay employed full time, full year seems to fulfill the letter, but not the spirit, of his promise.

We can expand programs currently in place to better realize Clinton's pledge. We could make permanent the temporary expansions of the EITC that the Obama administration put in place in recent years;[80] we could enact expansions of the child tax credit;[81] and we could encourage the creation of refundable EITCs at the state level—currently offered in fewer than half of American states.[82] Low-wage working parents who remain beyond the reach of these policies could also be better served, perhaps through a more robust EITC. While we've discussed how much Toni Patturelli benefits from her EITC, we've ignored her ex-husband, on whom she heavily relies for his regular child support payments. Policy expansions could include the creation of federal and state EITCs for non-custodial parents like Toni's children's father, especially those who are up to date on their child support payments. New York City is currently experimenting with such a plan. Presumably, this would enhance the well-being of both fathers and children and would potentially provide an incentive for more unskilled men to join the labor force or increase their work efforts,[83] just as it has done for less-educated mothers. More generally, the EITC for workers who are not claiming dependent children (that is, both childless workers and noncustodial parents), which currently amounts to just a few hundred dollars at most, could be raised substantially.[84] We could also make it possible for divorced or unmarried parents who share custody of their children to split the EITC, avoiding the "winner-take-all" nature of the current setup, in which only one parent is eligible for benefits.

Helping families spend less is another way to help them stretch their paychecks. To this end, the provision of affordable, quality health insurance is of the utmost importance. For the lower-income working families we met in Massachusetts, the state's system of universal health coverage had taken many concerns about access to and affordability of medical care off the list of worries.[85] The Affordable Care Act will hopefully help address these concerns for lower-income working families across the country, although this is contingent on states opting in to Medicaid expansions.[86]

Stabilizing Finances

Beyond their low incomes, many of the other major financial problems families faced were caused by the ups and downs in their incomes and expenses. Some months, income was good or the bills were low, and making ends meet was possible; in other months, earnings plunged or were eclipsed by spiking expenses. Public policy should not only respond to families' levels of income but help them find ways to smooth the choppy financial waters so many must navigate. In our study, we saw that many families use credit cards as personal safety nets to fill these budgetary holes.

The move to the new work-based safety net occurred during a time of much easier access to credit for all, including lower-income families. As our families tell it, access to credit can tempt one to succumb to the lure of overspending—particularly strong when consumption seems to determine one's belonging in a culture that so valorizes it. Credit can also serve as a safety net in tough times,[87] but it carries the very real risk of long-term debt for those who routinely face budget shortfalls. The press of regular monthly expenses means credit card payments are often relegated to the back burner. Then the late fees and accumulated interest seem to take on a life of their own. Ironically, even though credit card debt carries both a literally and a figuratively steep price, making ends meet by buying on credit is not as stigmatized as receiving cash welfare or getting help from your relatives, even though all involve spending money you haven't earned.

The systemic problems of easy access to credit became clear once the economy started to collapse under the weight of subprime mortgages and other credit-related debts. It remains to be seen whether this national experience and the accompanying legal and market-based restrictions on credit will reshape how lower-income families think about and use credit. Even if such families face severe credit restrictions in the future, many will still be saddled with debt from past spending. While being credit constrained is one type of asset poverty, we need to recognize the dangers of access to credit that many of our families' stories speak to. Betting on the ability to pay off credit card debts in better times to come may be an unwise gamble for many, as they are using credit not to close a short-term income gap but rather to manage the routine costs of living.

Our proposal to help families experience smoother financial sailing relies on the current system of refundable tax credits. In the past, an Advance EITC option was in place, which allowed families to receive in regular installments a portion of the EITC they expected to collect at tax time; this offered the possibility of getting a more regular income boost than the standard "windfall" approach to delivering the EITC. However, take-up rates for the Advance EITC were very low,[88] with families enjoying the big annual check and avoiding the advance payments over worries that getting the money ahead of time could leave them owing the IRS on April 15—a financial shock all were eager to avoid.

Our proposal aims to avoid the pitfalls of the Advance EITC. We should explore an option that creates incentives for families to take *deferred* payments of their EITC.[89] Rather than being based on a tax filer's expected EITC—the way the Advance option worked—a deferred option could offer bonuses to those who wait to receive a portion of their EITC check. For example, rather than getting that big, one-time check in February, a filer could choose to receive half the check in February, with the remaining half paid out in regular installments—monthly or quarterly—over the next year, accompanied by a small bonus added to each of the installment payments. Ideally, saving half of the refund would be the default option, requiring those who wished to access the full credit right away to opt out. This would avoid the gamble in the Advance EITC that made families nervous about it. In other words, this approach would quell fears because it would involve deferring monies already "earned" rather than relying on mere guesstimates of future income and tax liability, as the Advance option did. In addition, because the deferred EITC would be optional and would offer a variety of installment options, families could decide from year to year what method of receiving the EITC made the most sense given their current financial situation.[90] A family in a financial crunch might decide to take the entire check all at once, while a family with a little more breathing room could opt to receive the bonuses and spread out the receipt of their EITC money throughout the year in regular monthly disbursements.[91] They could even defer withdrawing the money indefinitely, with interest, if they wanted to "save" in that way rather than save via a bank.

Given the ubiquity and low cost of benefit distribution via debit cards, deferred EITC payments could be distributed electronically and would not require the involvement of employers, as the Advance EITC did (it was distributed via employees' paychecks). The government already distributes benefits electronically for TANF and SNAP, so there is an existing knowledge base on which to build the bureaucracy for the deferred EITC. Further, for-profit tax preparers already offer these types of debit cards—like H&R Block's Emerald Card—to clients as a way of receiving their refunds electronically (rather than waiting for a paper check). Finally, the deferred EITC is consistent with the general direction the IRS has been moving in trying to make saving easier by offering filers the opportunity to split their refunds, including using a portion of the refund to directly purchase savings bonds.

Adding this deferred option to the current system of refundable tax credits gives tax filers a choice about what receipt option works best for them, while also offering an incentive to choose the option that has a longer-term benefit. The goals of doing so would be to ease families' monthly financial crunch, help them survive unexpected expenses or income gaps, and offer a regular income boost that could allow families to avoid accumulating (quite as much) debt.[92] Given the high interest rates on credit card debt, the fees associated with getting utilities turned back on, and so on, helping families avoid debt is a way of putting more money in their pockets in the long run. It is clear that families genuinely desire to have a financial safety net for themselves, but the refund gets quickly spent down when it arrives. A deferred option adds a modest commitment mechanism to encourage families in creating a reliable bump in monthly income—it is a way of extending the benefits of the forced savings function of the EITC throughout the year or beyond. Government funding of such policy experimentation would test various policy arrangements to discern the options in which families are most interested and find most beneficial over the long term; successful policies could then be scaled up to the national level.

Building Savings and Assets

Generally speaking, it can require considerable sacrifice in the short term for individuals to accumulate the resources to provide "self-insurance"—to create an adequate personal safety net. Publicly funded benefits such as unemployment insurance, disability, health insurance (for disadvantaged populations and the elderly), and Social Security have been designed in recognition of the reality that expecting families to build up enough personal savings to guard against every sort of crisis or emergency is not realistic. For this reason, our interest in aiding savings and asset building among low-income families is focused on smaller goals, like having enough money on hand to fix a car's worn-out brakes or to hire a plumber to snake a backed-up drain.

Individual Development Accounts (IDAs) are meant to support lower-income families in their savings goals. These matched savings programs typically allow participants to withdraw their saved money for paying tuition, purchasing a home, or starting a business. However, results of IDA evaluations have not been encouraging.[93] This is not surprising to us, as the findings of our research do not lend support to the thinking behind IDAs. First, families rarely have much extra money on hand to put in such accounts except at tax time. Second, these accounts are perhaps too prohibitive in how they allow saved dollars to be spent—only on education, home purchase, or a business venture. Most of our families are far more focused on attending to current bills and paying down debts than on starting a business, for example. While dreams of home ownership are powerful, they may not be prudent, especially if earnings are unstable or if saving for a home comes at the expense of getting rid of debt or paying for more immediate needs.

A deferred EITC would offer a form of forced savings that could help families weather short-term financial difficulties. The regular payouts from the deferred EITC could fill holes in a paycheck or be put toward unexpected expenses as they arise. We are not opposed to more creative thinking on IDAs that moves outside the existing box—for example, being less focused on long-term mobility goals and more focused on building up a rainy-day fund, paying off debt, or putting some portion of deferred EITC money directly into savings bonds or 529 educational savings accounts. However, we believe that any policy experimentation in this regard must be guided by two principles. First, it doesn't make sense for families to pursue savings goals while accumulating debt, because the interest rates on debt typically far outweigh those offered on savings. Second, program developers must fully appreciate the meaning of "frivolous" spending, like putting a few dollars toward buying a Superman Pop from the ice cream truck rather than the more economical choices available in bulk at the grocery store. Savings advice to families should be developed with the *meaning*, not just the *quantity*, of money in mind. "Cold" calculations about how to spend and save are unrealistic and perhaps sometimes counterproductive; so-called wasted financial allocations on kids' "treats" might be viewed by parents as vital, albeit modest, investments in their child's well-being. Likewise, small extravagances may go far in bolstering one's identity as a worker and in enhancing one's sense of inclusion in the American mainstream.[94] Savings programs should be built with such "meaningful" short-term spending, not just long-term asset building, in mind.

Supporting Education

The EITC provides incentives for parents to enter the labor force, even if it means eschewing additional education to take a low-wage job, and the "more you earn the more you get" feature of the program, for those in the phase-in range, creates incentives to work full time.[95] As we've seen, however, those low-wage jobs often provide little in terms of a career ladder or path to upward mobility. In today's economy, education is the key to unlocking these possibilities. Therefore, as part of a broader approach to strengthening educational opportunities and outcomes, we propose expanding the use of refundable tax credits as a way to support lower-income workers' investments in themselves or their children's futures via education.

We endorse a "cradle-to-retirement" approach to education. Early childhood education offers the possibility of better preparing children for later academic success,[96] while also providing high-quality, affordable child care so that parents can work without worry. Young adults must finish high school with a diploma and a set of strong math and literacy skills. We must make college and high-quality apprenticeship and training programs more accessible and affordable for both recent high school graduates and older workers seeking new skills. Vocational education programs need to be further explored, with a focus on those programs that are tightly tied to the needs of local employers, so that graduates emerge with not just a certification but a job. Graduates must be able to work independently and in a computerized environment; estimates are that eight in ten new jobs over the next decade will require some training beyond high school.[97]

Our community college system, currently the only potentially affordable option for many families like those we spoke to, is often of low quality; these institutions of higher learning are badly in need of attention.[98] Postsecondary educational institutions must be charged with getting students not only in the door but out the door in a timely fashion with diploma or certificate in hand.[99] They must also be focused on linking graduates to career paths that both justify the expenses they incur and pay a living wage. Joint ventures between the educational and business sectors can help to ensure that the newly minted workers will benefit and that their employers will have access to the skilled labor force they need.[100] In addition, by raising the skill level of workers without a college degree, we would be raising their value to employers, thereby creating incentives for employers to pay them higher wages and offer more generous benefits as a means of retaining workers and preventing employee turnover.

Finally, financing postsecondary education and training is a major issue. The existence of education deductions and nonrefundable tax credits is not all that useful to low-income families who have no tax liability. To this end, we advocate exploring the creation and expansion of refundable education tax credits, like the Lifetime Learning Credit and the American Opportunity Credit. At the very least, such credits might help to offset the disincentives within the EITC for those with low wages to cut back on work hours to attend college or complete a vocational degree.[101]

A FINAL WORD ON TODAY'S SAFETY NET

The fundamental overhaul of our country's approach to aiding the poor, with the vast expansion of the work-based safety net, has revolutionized the supports available to America's low-wage workers. Families are enthusiastic about receiving their tax refund checks each year. Without a doubt, today's system puts low-wage workers in a better position than the old welfare system did. Full-time, full-year work, in combination with tax credits, boosts families over the poverty line. The annual refund check gives a tangible reward to working a low-wage or dead-end job, while offering the more intangible benefits of hope for the financial future and a sense of social inclusion purchased through short-term consumption.

Fundamentally, however, this system does not alter the fact that many jobs offer wages too low for families to reliably pay their bills on time and in full, while also setting a little something aside in case of an unforeseen crisis. Further, many of our policy recommendations in this chapter rely on a return to economic growth and job creation—without jobs, a system of work supports is no system of assistance at all. Those who used to make ends meet through low-wage work and the EITC no longer benefit from either of these sources when they are out of a job. Only a few are turning to TANF for help.[102] Our swing toward supporting workers has left behind those least able to fend for themselves.

But for those who do feel its warmth, the new system of work supports is a boon. Despite the daily pressures of limited budgets and life on the financial edge, families continue to dream of brighter economic futures, in which they realize the American Dream: owning a home in a safe neighborhood and having a nest egg in the bank. These are *working* families, and, as one parent noted, "It's not like I'm poor." While their work buys them both government assistance and the aspiration for more, the labor market for less-skilled workers makes it unlikely they will realize their ambitions without help. Taken together, greater investment in skills so workers can claim higher-wage jobs, redesign of wage supplements like the EITC so that they both breed hope for mobility and bring stability to family finances, and enhancement of incentives to eliminate debt and save scarce resources will help families work toward a brighter future.

Introduction to Boston
and the Research Project

It's a blustery February morning in 2007 as we emerge onto Meridian Street from the low-slung concrete of the Maverick T station, one of the East Boston neighborhood's stops on Boston's subway line. We've been visiting tax preparation sites throughout the city as we try to learn more about the financial lives of lower-income, working families; at this time of year, tax offices are full of clients who are waiting their turn to have a professional tax preparer calculate the amount of this year's refund and file the forms. This is not a scene we'd find in Boston's tonier neighborhoods, in Back Bay, on Beacon Hill, or down Newbury Street. The enthusiastic hum around tax time is unique to poorer and working-class neighborhoods, where refundable tax credits deliver an enormous infusion of cash into the hands of workers and, in turn, to local businesses as residents use the funds to catch up on back bills or indulge in a few extras that are out of their reach the rest of the year.

Our first stop this morning is East Boston APAC (Area Planning Action Council), one of more than a dozen such neighborhood centers spread across the city. East Boston APAC is part of a network formed by the city's largest nonprofit, ABCD (Action for Boston Community Development), that offers area residents a variety of services, including fuel assistance, credit counseling, youth employment programs, and free tax preparation. In just the chilly tenth of a mile between the subway station and the warm retreat that APAC offers from a New England winter, the character of this East Boston neighborhood is apparent. The stores in the neighborhood reflect the changing history of the place as successive immigrant groups have shaped this corner of the city.

As we walk along Meridian, we pass the standard financial institutions of working-class neighborhoods like this one: East Boston Savings Bank, Sovereign Bank, and Boston Checkcashers. We can also see Braz Transfer just a little ways down the intersecting Maverick Street, which offers immigrants a chance to send a portion of their earnings back home. Glancing down the side streets gives a sense of the types of housing available in this part of the city; rows of triple-deckers in various states of repair offer apartment living without high-rises.

East Boston sits on the end of a peninsula surrounded on three sides by Boston Harbor and its waterways, and on the fourth by Logan International Airport. Its location between the ocean and the airport is appropriate to its evolving history. Wave upon wave of immigrants—Irish, Russian Jews, and Italians, followed by immigrants from Central and South America—have made their first American homes in East Boston, arriving initially by steamship and then by airplane.

The Irish were the first wave, Patrick Kennedy among them. He immigrated in the middle of the nineteenth century, and his four children were born here in East Boston. Joseph Patrick Kennedy, patriarch of the Kennedy dynasty, was born here in 1888. But nearly all traces of the Irish, most of who settled in Jeffries Point (the southern section of East Boston, next to the airport) are gone; this includes St. Nicholas, the first Catholic parish in East Boston. Another of the neighborhood's important Irish Catholic parishes, Most Holy Redeemer (founded in 1856), now features services in Spanish.

In the late 1800s, Italian immigrants and Russian Jews began to settle the area, with the Jews vying with the Irish for Jeffries Point while the Italians settled in Maverick Square and Eagle Hill (in the center and at the north end of East Boston, respectively). By 1900, East Boston housed more Jews than any other New England community and had seen the establishment of five synagogues; but such prominence in the neighborhood was fleeting. A fire in Jeffries Point in 1908 prompted the majority of

Jews to relocate to neighboring Chelsea. By 1915, Italians outnumbered the Irish, becoming the neighborhood's largest ethnic group. Our Lady of Mt. Carmel, founded in 1905, served as the center of the Italian American community in East Boston for the next century until its closure in 2004. Italians still cluster in nearby Orient Heights, but immigrants from Latin America are far more evident on streets like Meridian. These groups began settling in the area in the 1980s and '90s, along with a sprinkling of Vietnamese. Now the area is almost 40 percent Latino, hailing mostly from El Salvador, Colombia, and Brazil, which explains the plethora of culinary options now on offer.[1]

As we walk inside the APAC offices from the slushy streets, we see a small, square reception area with ten chairs lining the walls and partially drawn blinds covering the windows. We are greeted by Ana, the bilingual receptionist, who simultaneously welcomes tax filers and those who come here to apply for fuel assistance, passes out information to teenagers interested in summer jobs, and chit-chats, sometimes in English, but more often in Spanish, with everyone who comes in. Down the narrow hall there are four small, windowless offices in which staff and volunteers work through tax forms with clients. Some members of our research team have labored to learn complex tax preparation software, attended several hours of training, and passed a certification test to work alongside these other tax preparers. Today we're volunteering for the morning shift. As on most days, our clientele are largely young and single; some are navigating the tax system for the first time, while others already have files established from previous APAC visits. Some are older adults who, by virtue of the fact that they have no dependent children, are not expecting a large tax return. Others are immigrants who can expect little in the way of a tax refund but want to "stay legal" by filing taxes. None of these fit our research sample— we're seeking low- to moderate-income families with children who can expect at least a thousand dollars back at tax time from the government through their eligibility for a variety of refundable tax credits, including the hefty earned income tax credit. Some of APAC's clientele fit the bill, but we've quickly learned that most of the families we're looking for go elsewhere—usually to a for-profit tax preparer like H&R Block.[2]

Just before noon we leave APAC for our second destination—the neighborhood's H&R Block office. The stores continue to tell the neighborhood's story as we walk along Meridian past the Mi Rancho restaurant, Casas Home Realty, Los Primos Barber Shop, and the Caffe Italia Trattoria before turning onto Bennington Street. At Mi Rancho, the owner's son, a recent college grad who was raised in East Boston, tells us the customers in his family's restaurant are "a lot of people who just got to this country, Latin Americans, hard-working, working-class people."

We've selected H&R Block as our primary sampling site because around 70 percent of EITC claimants nationwide walk through the doors of a for-profit tax preparer to file their taxes.[3] But East Boston's H&R Block serves mostly white and Latino customers. Because we're interested in gathering information from even numbers of blacks, Latinos, and whites, we've also set up shop at the city's largest tax prep site, another H&R Block in the predominantly black Fields Corner section of Dorchester (another area of Boston), and at a Dorchester nonprofit offering the same free tax preparation services as the East Boston APAC.

The East Boston H&R Block we're visiting today attracts clients from the mixed population of the surrounding neighborhood plus various nearby communities. These include the North End (Boston's Little Italy) and Chelsea, in addition to Revere, Winthrop, and Everett—the destinations of many white working-class families who migrated from East Boston. These former inhabitants of the neighborhood—most living within a ten- to twenty-minute drive—still come back to shop, bank, and conduct other business in East Boston, including getting their taxes done.

Throughout the tax season, we set up in the small waiting area at the front of H&R Block at random four-hour intervals spanning mornings, afternoons, and evenings. On our first day, we lug a large poster board with us on the T (Boston's subway) and down Meridian to Bennington; it reads "Earn $10 for 2 minutes of your time." After that initial visit, the manager allows us to store the sign on site. We ask everyone leaving the facility whether they claimed the earned income tax credit, the federal refundable credit that is available to all households with children earning less than $36,348 during the 2006 tax year.[4] Our $10 offer has proven immensely popular—nearly all those who have filed for the EITC are eager to answer our short questionnaire,[5] which provides us with vital contact information. We ask all the respondents to estimate the amount of their expected return (also listed on the filing summary form they have just received from H&R Block) and how they plan to spend it. We also collect some basic demographic information, such as race, ethnicity, number of dependents, marital status, telephone number, and address. We'll use this information later to construct a sample for our in-depth interview study, which will commence in the summer. We continue to survey at random intervals throughout tax season.

Just after tax season is over we add another stop on our neighborhood tour of East Boston—one that takes us back up Meridian to East Boston APAC's Head Start site. Here, we post our placard inside the front entrance as parents drop their kids off for preschool. Again, we generate great enthusiasm, with parents happy to answer our simple questions for an easy $10. Roughly 30 percent of EITC recipients don't use a for-profit preparer like H&R Block but use a nonprofit, pay a friend, or file their taxes themselves. We hope that sampling at local preschools will aid us in reaching these latter two groups. We decide on Head Start centers because we know they typically serve the EITC-eligible population we're trying to find: low- to moderate-income families with children. To diversify this portion of our sample, we approach Head Start parents in a similar fashion at centers in South Boston, Charlestown, Roslindale, Jamaica Plain, and Somerville to capture the racial diversity of the city. In all, we gather our sample from more than a half dozen of the neighborhoods and inner suburbs in the Boston metropolitan area (see the map in the introductory chapter).

These neighborhoods contain a healthy dose of the Boston area's unique diversity. More than a quarter of the population in the metro area are foreign born (compared to just over 10 percent of the US population), and more than a third speak a language other than English at home. In the city, just over half of all residents are white (versus nearly three-quarters of the general US population), just under a quarter are black (compared to approximately 12 percent of the US population), and, as in the rest of the country, approximately 16 percent are Latino.[6] We purposely oversample blacks and Latinos relative to their representation in the metro area's population.[7] In this way, we can systematically compare the groups in hopes of capturing any differences that exist. Blacks and Latinos are more likely to be lower income, but many of the blacks and Latinos in the Boston area are not US-born. The city boasts high numbers of Haitians and Dominicans, for example. Because of the large number of immigrants from the Caribbean, our sample has relatively fewer native-born black and Latino families than the US population.[8] Thus the families we recruit though our short survey are a microcosm of the rich diversity of the city's lower-income residents.

A STUDY OF FINANCIAL LIVES

In June 2007, we draw 120 names at random from the roughly 332 surveys we gathered between February and April. Within each racial and ethnic group, we aim for one-third married couples with children and two-thirds unmarried parents (see table A.1). We send each of these families a letter informing them of the opportunity to participate in the in-depth portion of our study and then begin calling the home and cell phone numbers they provided us on the surveys and knocking on the doors of the addresses they provided. Along with a team of trained and experienced qualitative researchers, we spend the summer months moving between the largely black neighborhoods of Dorchester and Roxbury; the mixed-race housing projects of the otherwise all-white Charlestown and South Boston; and the largely white, but increasingly Latino, communities of Chelsea, Revere, Everett, Roslindale, and, of course, East Boston. In the end, we interview 115 of the 120 families originally selected for the in-depth interview sample (the remaining five families declined to participate). Interview respondents receive a $60 honorarium for their time.

We typically meet with these tax filers in their homes, where we are introduced to their children, spouses, and boyfriends, and they can point out, say, a living room set recently purchased with tax refund money. Those we interview are welcoming and generous with their time—our conversations with each family typically last two and a half hours (ranging from one to five hours long). We are served snacks, invited to dinner, offered financial advice, and told where to get the best Jamaican food in the neighborhood.

As the interview guide in Appendix B shows, we ask both closed- and open-ended questions. We collect detailed narratives of each household's routine and nonroutine expenses and all sources of economic support,

Table A.1   Stratified Sample of Respondents

Sample Characteristics	Number	Percent
Race/ethnicity		
White	40	35
Black	40	35
Hispanic	35	30
Marital status		
Married	40	35
Unmarried	75	65
Total	115	100

NOTE: Race is based on respondents' self-reports. *Marital status* refers to respondents' marital status reported to the IRS on their tax returns.

whether from income, personal networks of family and friends, or government assistance; this includes detailed questions about the EITC and how parents spent their tax refunds. We ask families about their banking practices, credit histories, and debts, and about their future financial goals and aspirations. In short, we learn as much as we can in a few hours' time about the financial lives of lower-income working families in twenty-first-century America in their own words.

All interviews are recorded and transcribed, with field notes written to accompany each interview. We use two analytical strategies in approaching the data. We make spreadsheets compiling responses regarding income, expenses, and the amount and allocation of tax refunds. The qualitative data are coded using inductive thematic codes, with additional subcoding conducted within the initial set of themes. These dual analytical approaches allow us to draw a picture of families' finances across our sample, as well as to understand the meaning and decision-making processes behind these dollars and cents.

APPENDIX B Qualitative
Interview Guide

1. Tell me a little bit about your family. (Get ages of all family members.)
2. Who all lives here?
   a. Let's start with the adults. (If extra adults not mentioned above, get ages and relationship to respondent.) What about the situation of other adults in the house? (Probe for work status, type, and hours and/or whether in school and what kind of program.)
   b. How about the kids? (If extra kids not mentioned above, get ages and relationship to respondent.) What about the situation of the kids? (Probe for whether in school, what grade, whether working.)
   c. What about people who live here part of the time, not all of the time? (If part-time residents not mentioned above, get ages. Probe as to how often and for what duration.)
3. Tell me the story of your life. What was it like for you coming up?
4. Tell me about your parents' educational background. (Probe for highest level of schooling completed.) Tell me about how they made a living. (Probe for mother's job and father's job while respondent was living at home.)

5. Some people say that their family struggled with money when they were growing up. Other people say that their family was pretty comfortable. How about you?

6. Tell me all about your situation right now. (Probe for work status, type, hours, and/or whether in school and what kind of program.) How did you find your job? (Neighbor, coworker, family, paper, etc.)

7. Tell me the whole story of how you came to live here in this neighborhood.
   a. (IF OWNING) How did you decide to buy a home in this neighborhood? When did you buy the home? How did you manage to get your down payment and closing costs together?
   b. What areas of the city are you thinking of when you think of your neighborhood? (Probe for streets and landmarks.)
   c. How would you describe this neighborhood to a family that was thinking about moving here?
   d. Tell me about what it is like for you living here in this neighborhood. What do you like most? What do you like least?

8. How much do you trust your neighbors?

9. Have you ever had to call the authorities on your neighbors? Like the police, child protection, something like that? Tell me about that.

10. To what extent do your neighbors get into your business?

11. Have any of your neighbors ever called the authorities on you? Like the police, child protection, something like that? Tell me about that.

12. Tell me a little more about your neighbors. What is the racial and ethnic makeup of the neighborhood? Mostly white, black, Latino, mixed, or what? How has this changed since you've lived here? Has this led to any problems? Tell me about that.

A. EITC INCOME AND EXPENDITURE

13. How did you choose where to get your taxes done?

14. What kind of refund did you anticipate before you got your taxes done?

15. Tell me how you wanted to spend that money.

16. What refund did you actually end up getting?

17. Tell me how you spent that refund. (See if items listed match items listed on survey. Probe any differences.)

    a. Let's talk about (ITEM 1). Tell me the whole story of how you decided to spend X amount on (ITEM 1). (Probe for who had a say in this decision, whose advice was sought. Do these people contribute money/some other resources to the household? Do they get a say in how other household resources/sources of household income are spent? Why do they get to give input into decisions over EITC refund spending?)

    b. Now let's talk about (ITEM 2). Tell me the whole story of how you decided to spend X amount on (ITEM 2). (Probe for who had a say in this decision, whose advice was sought. Do these people contribute money/some other resources to the household? Do they get a say in how other household resources/sources of household income are spent? Why do they get to give input into decisions over EITC refund spending?)

    c. What about (ITEM 3)? Tell me the whole story of how you decided to spend X amount on (ITEM 3). (Probe for who had a say in this decision, whose advice was sought. Do these people contribute money/some other resources to the household? Do they get a say in how other household resources/sources of household income are spent? Why do they get to give input into decisions over EITC refund spending?)

18. How much of your refund is left? Tell me how you plan to spend it. (Probe for how refund is stored—in a bank, cash under a mattress, etc.) (Probe for savings plans.)

19. Some people we've talked to have used some of their EITC to pay off debt. How about you? Have you ever thought about using your EITC for something like that? (Probe for specific types of debt respondent has incurred, such as credit cards, rent-to-own, layaway, car purchases, informal debt, or education expenses.)

20. Others say they've managed to save for a big-ticket item, like a down payment on a car or home, tuition for school, a move to a new neighborhood—things like that. Have you ever thought about using your EITC for something like that?

21. Do you know what portion of your refund was from a child credit? The federal EITC? The state EITC? (Look at tax returns if possible—federal [lines 66A and 73] and Massachusetts State [lines 38 and 44].)

22. Do you think you'll get a tax refund next year? Tell me about that.

23. Let's pretend that you get the same tax refund this year that you did last year. How will you spend next year's refund? (Probe in depth about all categories of planned expenditure, and the amount the respondent plans to spend for each. Also probe for respondent's motivation to spend in this area.)

24. Sometimes people tell us they spend more money in December and January because they know a tax refund is coming. Do you know anyone like that? Tell me about that. How about for you? (First probe in detail for usual patterns of expenditure, and then probe for how expenditures vary in anticipation of a tax refund. Get as many specific examples as possible.)

25. If you hadn't gotten your tax refund this year what would your financial situation be like right now?

26. Is there anything that you wish you could change about the EITC or taxes in general?

B. EITC KNOWLEDGE

27. So we talked a little before about the EITC. (If not married:) I'm wondering, if you decided to get married, how would it affect your EITC refund (refund check)? (If married:) I'm wondering, how would it affect your EITC refund if you divorced?
    a. (If the respondent has knowledge about this, ask the following:)
       i. (If not married:) How has that affected your decisions about whether or not to get married/stay together? (Probe for how financial concerns influence relationship decisions more generally.)
       ii. (If not married:) How do you decide each year who will get to claim your children on their taxes for the refund?
       iii. (If married:) How long have you been married? What made you decide to get married? (Probe for how financial concerns influence relationship decisions more generally.)

28. Tell me about how your EITC tax refund could be affected if you have another child.

    a. (If the respondent has knowledge about this, ask the following:) How has this affected your decision to have or not have another child?

29. Tell me about how your EITC tax refund could be affected if you got a better-paying job. What about if you got a job that paid less? What about if you worked more or less hours?

    a. (If the respondent has knowledge about this, ask the following:) How has this affected your decisions about what kind of job to take? What about how this has affected your decisions about how many hours to work?

30. What could you do to increase your EITC refund/ tax refund? Tell me about that. What would make you lose your refund? Tell me about that.

C. OTHER INCOME AND EXPENDITURE

31. So you told me that you worked at _____ and made \$\$\$/hour right now. Does your job come with benefits? (Probe more in depth for benefits, duties, and job tenure.) Tell me about any other jobs you've had in the past few years. (Probe in depth for wage rate, hours, benefits [including workers' comp, health insurance, dental insurance, retirement, paid sick time, paid vacation time, etc.], duties, and job tenure.)

32. How often are you paid? Weekly, twice a month, once a month, or what? How much does that total in a typical month? (Get take-home pay. Probe for earnings over the past six months *and* gross income for last year for respondent and partner.)

33. How did you spend your last paycheck? (Probe for expenditures in detail, trying to nail down what the money was spent for, when it was spent, and why it was spent in that way.)

34. Tell me about your other sources of income. (Probe for income from second jobs, informal jobs, overtime pay, and government benefits, including TANF, food stamps, and SSI.)

35. How about health insurance? Tell me what you and your family have for coverage. (Probe for co-pays for office visits, prescriptions, and other. Probe for health needs that aren't being taken care of and why.)

36. Tell me about your experiences with TANF. (Probe for AFDC history; when received and for what duration, whether they cycled on and off.)

    a. (If ANY TANF history:) What led you to apply? What was/is it like? Tell me what you like best about the program. Tell me what you like least.

    b. (If receive TANF:) In the last year did you get any lump sum payments from welfare for children's clothing, a new baby, or anything for the holidays?

    c. Tell me about the experiences of friends and family with TANF. What led them to apply? What have they told you about their experiences with the program?

    d. I've read a little about TANF but have never gotten it myself. How exactly does TANF work?

37. How much do you receive monthly in child support? Is this by court order? What do you spend it on? How much does dad help out besides child support?

38. What about your spouse/cohabiting partner? Tell me a little bit about the jobs they have right now. (Probe more in depth for wage rates, hours, benefits, duties, and job tenure.) Tell me about any other jobs they've had in the past few years. (Probe in depth for wage rate, hours, benefits, duties, and job tenure.)

39. How often are they paid? Weekly, twice a month, once a month, or what? How much does that total in a typical month? (Use last six months to help respondent estimate "typical" amount earned from pay. Get take-home pay. Also probe for amount cohabiting partner contributes to household.)

40. What about other adults in the household? How much do they earn? How much do they contribute to the household expenses each month?

41. What about anyone outside the household that helps you out financially on a regular basis? Do you have to pay them back? (Who, how much, how often?)

42. Let me make sure I've got this right. (Take out chart and along with respondent fill out income section of chart.)

43. So adding it all up, you have about $XXX to spend in a typical month. Is that right?

44. List your monthly bills. (Probe for amounts.) Once you've paid these bills, how much of your paycheck is left over?

45. What do you do with the money that's left over?

46. Does anyone borrow money from you on a regular basis? (Who? How much? How often? Do they pay you back?)

47. Let me make sure I've got this right. (Take out chart and along with respondent start to fill out the expenditure section of chart.)

48. Tell me about any time during the past year that you haven't been able to pay a bill on time. How did you deal with that problem? What bills do you pay first? After you pay those, how do you decide how to pay the rest?

49. Tell me about any time during the past year that you haven't had enough money to buy something that you needed. How did you deal with that problem?

D. BANKING, DEBT, ASSETS

50. Tell me about your experiences with
    a. banks
    b. credit unions
    c. check-cashing places

51. When you got your EITC check, did you put it in the bank? (Probe for where client cashed or deposited the check and why.)

52. When you get your paycheck, where do you go to cash it? (Probe for where client cashes or deposits the paycheck and why.)

53. How do you pay your bills? (Probe for whether client uses a checking account, pays in cash, uses money orders, credit card, etc., and why he or she uses that method.)

54. How did you pay for (ITEM 1, 2, and 3 in question 13)? (Probe for form of payment.)

55. Do you have any of the following? (General estimations are acceptable.)
    a. A bank checking account: Current balance
    b. A bank savings account: Current balance/whose name is it in?
    c. A car: Make/year/est. resale value
    d. Amount owed on car: Monthly payment, years to pay
    e. A house that you own: Value
    f. Amount owed on the house: Monthly payment, years to pay
    g. Stocks, bonds, savings bonds, IRAs: Value

  h. Credit cards: Available balance

  i. Amount owed on credit card: Unpaid balance/interest rate

  j. Any other debt (medical): Amount owed/interest rate

  k. Any other debt (educational): Amount owed/interest rate

  l. Any other debt (personal loans): Amount owed/interest rate

  m. Any rent-to-own accounts: Payments made/payments left/amount of each payment

56. Tell me about your housing. Do you own or rent? (If renting:) Is this subsidized housing? Do you receive any form of rent subsidy?

  a. (If renting:) What about buying your own home? Have you thought about that recently? Tell me about that. What is standing in the way?

  b. (If owning:) Tell me about how you were able to buy your home. How much was the down payment, and how did you come up with the money for it?

57. (If owning:) Tell me about things in your home or neighborhood that you feel increase your property values. (Probe: home improvements, new developments, gentrification, etc.) What about things that decrease your property values? (Probe: needed repairs, vacant lots, abandoned homes/buildings, trash in streets, neighbors' race or income, etc.)

58. Are you paying on any credit card debt right now? (Probe for total debt and typical monthly payment made over past six months. Also probe for interest rates. Probe for how much of this payment is for current expenditures and how much is for carryover debt and what is the current balance.)

59. Are you paying on your medical, education, legal, or personal debt right now? (Probe for total debt and typical monthly payment made over past six months. Also probe for interest rates.) (Add to expenditure section of chart.)

60. Some people say that they have to pay child support through the formal court system. Other people say that they do it informally. How about you? What about your partner? Have you been able to keep up to date on your child support payments lately? What about your partner? (Probe for total debt and typical monthly payment made over past six months.) (Add to expenditure section of chart.)

61. Do you put any money into some type of savings account right now? (Probe for total amount put into savings over last year. Also probe for informal savings.)

62. Do you plan to put any money into some type of savings account in the coming year? Tell me about that.

E. COOL-DOWN

63. Tell me about someone you know who is a great parent. (Probe for what qualities or behaviors make them a great parent.) Now tell me about you. How would some of your close friends describe you as a parent?

64. Who do you count on most to help you with the kids? Tell me about that. (Probe: How do they help out? Buying things for school or play? Babysitting?)

65. Tell me about what your kids do during the day.

    a. Are they at day care? Babysitter's? How is that situation working for you? (Probe for whether they'd choose another type of care if they had more resources.)

    b. What do the kids spend their time doing? (Probe for play time—what the kids play with most often.) What do you *want* to see them spend time doing?

    c. Tell me about the activities the kids are doing when they're not in school. (Probe: Clubs? Sports? Church?) Are there activities you'd like to get your kid(s) active in?

    d. In the summertime, how does your schedule change? (Summer camp?)

66. Raising kids can be so expensive these days. How do you decide what to spend money on for the kids? (Probe for how the respondent balances spending money on things her kids need versus things her kids want.)

    a. What's an example of a toy or game that you'd be willing to spend money on? What type of game or toy would you *not* be willing to spend money on?

    b. Do you give your kids an allowance?

    c. What things would you like to get for your child that you can't afford right now?

    d. If you were given $200 for each child and had to spend it only on the children, what would you buy?

    e. What did you buy for Christmas for the kids this year?

67. What do you think your financial situation will be like five years from now? Paint me the whole picture of what your life will be like then. What about where you'll live? (Probe in depth about moving plans, motivation to move. If they are *not* planning on moving, probe in depth for motivation as well.) How about ten years from now? (Probe for financial situation and whole picture of what life will be like as well as moving plans.)

68. If money was not a concern, where would you really like to live? Tell me about why you'd like to move there. (Probe for specific neighborhood, cross-streets, and landmarks.)

69. What could the government do to help working families like yours?

70. Now that the interview is over, how was the experience for you?

FIELD NOTES

After the interview has ended and you have left the respondent's home, remember to record your field notes as soon as possible. Your field notes should include a brief description of the respondent, the home and the neighborhood, any pertinent information that the respondent gave prior to turning on the tape recorder, anything unusual in this interview situation, and any background information that would help give context to the transcriber and researcher.

Notes

1. Seventy-one percent of earned income tax credit (EITC) filers use a for-profit tax preparation service. See Internal Revenue Service (2011, 47, table 19).

2. Boston Landmarks Commission (1994).

3. Greenstone and Looney (2011).

4. W. Wilson (1987).

5. See Fischer (2011, ch. 5).

6. Lampman (1969).

7. Hotz and Scholz (2003).

8. While the EITC is entirely prowork for primary household earners on the extensive margin, it may depress work efforts for secondary earners; in addition, it may incentivize working less among those in the phaseout range of the credit.

9. Tax Policy Center (2014).

10. Grogger (2003); Meyer and Rosenbaum (2001). However, some have argued that it was exits from welfare that drove the rise in EITC receipt, as opposed to the availability of the EITC tempting welfare recipients off the rolls (Mead 1999).

11. See Crouse, Hauan, and Rogers (2008, indicator 3).

12. Shaefer and Edin (2012).

13. For example, see Brown (2013); Eowyn (2013).

14. See, for example, Rank (1994); Seccombe, James, and Walters (1998).

15. Edin and Lein (1997, 139). These experiences persisted after welfare reform. One recipient told researchers, "Being on welfare you lose part of your dignity and your self-esteem" (London et al. 2004). Another complained, "It seems like somebody else is runnin' your life. And it doesn't feel like you're in control of your own destiny" (Grabowski 2006, 75).

16. Anderson (2001, 171).

17. Marshall (1950, 24).

18. See also Hays (2003).

19. Regarding the charge of freeloading, note, for example, the controversy over an interview with a welfare recipient on an Austin Radio station, which went viral on YouTube as *Welfare Recipient: "I Get to Sit Home . . . I Get to Smoke Weed . . ."* (2013).

20. The lone exception to that rule in their study was quite telling: a mother in Massachusetts—a state with unusually generous benefits—who played by the rules but was in the process of losing custody of her son to the child welfare system because he had only one change of clothing and often missed school because he lacked a winter coat and boots. Thus the exception proved the rule: you couldn't be a good mother and live on welfare alone.

21. Edin and Lein (1997).

22. Edin and Lein (1997, ch. 3).

23. Edin (1993).

24. Other studies have found evidence of differences among racial and ethnic groups in EITC knowledge and use, with Latinos less likely to either know about or use the program than whites or blacks (Phillips 2001). It should be noted that, as with all other studies relying on cross-sectional samples of EITC recipients, our study's sample probably overrepresents parents who experience longer spells of EITC receipt. That is, when benefits are calculated over time, most EITC recipients do not receive them year after year, but at any one point in time the EITC rolls are disproportionately made up of those with longer histories of program participation (Dowd and Horowitz 2011).

25. See Appendix A for more information about the locale and research study.

26. With the financial crisis that began in December 2007, economic conditions certainly have become even more difficult. While unemployment was 4.1 percent in the Boston metropolitan area in the summer of 2007 (US Bureau of Labor Statistics 2007), by the summer of 2010 it stood at 8 percent (US Bureau of Labor Statistics 2010).

27. American Fact Finder (2010b).

28. American Fact Finder (2010b).

29. See Appendix A for more information about sample recruitment and data collection procedures.

30. Across the nation, about 60 percent of EITC dollars go to single parents, while only about one-third go to married couples with children (the rest of the money goes to singles and couples without children). Likewise, just under one-third of our householders were married couples. The remainder were either cohabiting (15 percent) or not living with a partner (54 percent). (See Appendix A for more details.)

31. Of the thirty-nine white families—Toni's family among them—fourteen were married couples, six were cohabiting, and nineteen were single, though some were in dating relationships. Of the thirty-six Hispanic families, ten were married couples, six were cohabiting couples, and twenty were single or separated. Of the forty black families, twelve were married, five were cohabiting, and twenty-three were single parents.

32. In other publications drawing on these data, additional families are referenced by name. See, for example, Mendenhall et al. (2012); Sykes et al. (forthcoming); Tach and Halpern-Meekin (2014); Tach and Sternberg Greene (2014); Sternberg Greene (2013).

33. Since the time of our interviews, programs like MassHealth and, subsequently, the Affordable Care Act have worked to alleviate some of these cliff effects, as subsidized insurance is now available to those who earn too much to qualify for Medicaid or CHIP.

34. See Batchelder, Goldberg, and Orszag (2006).

35. One sign of the relative absence of stigma with regard to the EITC is that its take-up rate is quite high among means-tested programs (see Plueger 2009, 151–95). That rate increases to 81 percent when computed solely for eligible workers who live with children and who receive a much larger credit than those who do not live with children. (See also Dorn 2008; Government Accountability Office 2010; Leftin, Eslami, and Strayer 2011).

36. The title to this section is taken from Sykes et al. (forthcoming).

37. Bruch, Ferree, and Soss (2010); Campbell (2003); Lawless and Fox (2001); Mettler (2005); Mettler and Stonecash (2008); Soss (2000); Verba, Schlozman, and Brady (1995).

38. Edin and Lein (1997); Feeding America (2011); Food and Nutrition Service (2011).

39. Mullainathan and Shafir (2013).

40. Averett and Wang (2012); Baker (2008); Chetty, Friedman, and Rockoff (2011); Cowan and Tefft (2012); Evans and Garthwaite (2013); Hoynes, Miller, and Simon (2012); Michelmore (2013).

41. Shaefer and Edin (2012).

42. See, for example, Albelda (2001); Mink (1998); D. Roberts (2004).

43. See, for example, Rothstein (2008).

44. Bitler, Hoynes, and Kuka (2013).

1. FAMILY BUDGETS

1. In 2012, the Census Bureau adopted a "supplemental measure" of poverty that adjusted for things like regional variation of living costs, the value of tax credits (which are not counted in the official measure because they are after-tax income), and in-kind benefits.

2. Rector (2012).

3. Meyer and Sullivan (2009, 2007, 2003).

4. National Center for Children in Poverty (2010).

5. Jones (2007).

6. These general patterns held true for AFDC as well, though there was brief period of time—the late 1970s—when benefits were considerably more generous.

7. A unit renting at 40 percent of Area Median Rent.

8. Massachusetts is a best-case scenario—TANF benefits in the state are usually high, so TANF brings a family up to 50 percent of the poverty line (Finch and Schott 2011).

9. Rice and Sard (2009).

10. Ashlee Reed's net earnings are lower than we might expect because she overpays her taxes and opts to contribute 5 percent of her wages to a retirement program through work.

11. Boston Housing Authority (2010). See also Boston Housing Authority (2009). The first document says that, in a Section 8 tenancy, the tenant payment is the amount calculated under the 1937 Act (Section 3(a)(1)) as 30 percent of the family's Monthly Adjusted Income.

12. US Department of Housing and Urban Development (2014).

13. Child Care Aware (2012).

14. The average month has 4.33 weeks. Thus we multiply weekly wages by 4.33.

15. Unemployment benefits in Massachusetts provide approximately 50 percent of a worker's earnings, along with a $25 per child per week benefit. However, there is a one-week period of unemployment before workers become eligible for benefits and another delay of approximately three weeks before benefits get processed (see Massachusetts Executive Office of Labor and Workforce Development 2013).

16. This does not include Ashlee's cohabiting boyfriend's expenses or income. Prior to losing his job, Adrian contributed to the family household expenses, though not on an equal basis. For the most part, Ashlee says that he has his own expenses (his own credit cards, for example) but that he does chip in for household costs when she is short on money. During the time he was employed in the cafeteria, the rent on their Section 8 apartment was higher ($950), but after he lost his job the Housing Authority reassessed their rent and lowered it to $575,

on the basis of Ashlee's income alone. Adrian also has the following additional expenses, not listed in Ashlee's budget: $145 for car insurance, $173 in gas, and $50 for his cell phone. While he has been unemployed, Ashlee says that her paycheck has been stretched to cover all of his essential expenses as well.

17. Her boyfriend, Adrian, also has three credit cards with a total balance of $4,835.

18. Nationally, the median household income in the United States in 2007 (the year in which we interviewed families) was $52,673; in Massachusetts, the median household income was $64,815 (Semega 2009).

19. See also Edin and Lein (1997).

20. On the extent to which the stresses of poverty monopolize attention, see, for example, Mullainathan and Shafir (2013).

21. Income figures in this chapter refer to gross income, unless otherwise noted. We sought respondents' gross earnings figures, but in some cases they may have given their net income, resulting in an underestimation of gross income.

22. Because of how the American tax system works, cohabiting parents don't report their partners' income on their tax forms—this allows them to both pool income and enjoy a sizable credit. We count only the tax filing unit's income in our calculations.

23. The assistance received through SNAP would probably be substantially higher among a more disadvantaged group of families. Among families like those in our study, whose earnings are generally in the $20,000 range, SNAP benefits are more minimal than for those in more dire straits.

24. The Census Bureau estimates that the poverty rate would have been 2 percent higher without the EITC, rising from 15.7 percent to 17.7 percent (Yen 2011).

25. See Holt (2006); Meyer (2007, table 4).

26. The federal poverty line for a family of three in 2006 was an annual income of $16,600.

27. Albelda and Shea (2007).

28. Food and Nutrition Service (2013). Note that even the modest benefit levels these families receive from SNAP are quite sizable when summed over the course of the year. However, unlike the EITC check, SNAP benefits are parceled out monthly and can be used only for specific purposes. This means that $1 in SNAP benefits is not equivalent, in parents' minds, to $1 from their tax refund checks.

29. Benefits.gov (2013).

30. US Department of Housing and Urban Development (2013a, 2013b).

31. It is important to note that the EITC doesn't count against public housing rent, which is an added benefit for public housing residents of this form of income.

32. Massachusetts Executive Office of Health and Human Services (2014).

33. Social Security Administration (2014b).

34. Office of Policy, Office of Research, Evaluation, and Statistics (2007).

35. Social Security Administration (2014a, 6).

36. The measure of previous welfare use probably provides an underestimate, as respondents were not extensively interviewed about all of their government program usage throughout their adult lives.

37. Castner and Mabli (2010). The Consumer Expenditure Survey's measure of housing costs is broadly defined to include items such as furniture, while the figure for our study excludes items like furniture.

38. *Forbes* ranks Boston as the eighth most expensive city in which to live in the United States ("America's Most Expensive Cities" 2009).

39. These figures represent 2009 HUD Fair Market Rent for the Boston area (US Department of Housing and Urban Development 2009).

40. The 62 percent figure for those receiving some form of housing subsidy makes our sample stand apart from the common experience nationwide, where only one in four low-income households receives rental assistance (Sullivan 2013). Therefore, although our sample is exceptional in residing in a high-rent area, this disadvantage is balanced out, in a sense, by their greater likelihood of having some sort of housing subsidy.

41. Boston Housing Authority estimates (see Boston Housing Authority 2011).

42. Powers (2013).

43. Edin and Lein (1997).

44. Interestingly, one of the points many families make in claiming this status is that they pay taxes: that is, because they have paid into the system, they have, in a way, paid for their own benefits. This is based on a disconnect in their understanding of the relationship between the taxes they see taken from their paychecks on a weekly basis and the tax refund check they receive on an annual basis. For many, this refund check alone exceeds the taxes they have paid into the system, meaning that their discussions of paying for their own benefits (like SNAP or unemployment insurance, for instance) or their frustration at seeing less deserving people living off the taxes they pay through their hard work are based on a fallacy. However, this points out the psychological importance to people of feeling mainstream. From their perspective they are like other, more economically advantaged workers because they pay taxes; therefore, like these other workers, they are deserving, and their receipt of government support should not be stigmatized.

45. Some states have tried to introduce a degree of flexibility in the SNAP system to help households avoid a seemingly endless process of reporting income fluctuations. Nonetheless, for parents like Marissa who see sizable changes in income—in some months she is eligible and others she is ineligible for SNAP—reporting can still feel onerous.

46. See also, for example, Edin and Lein (1997); Pattillo-McCoy (1999).

47. Jayakody, Chatters, and Taylor (1993); Lee and Aytac (1998); Parish, Hao, and Hogan (1991); Sarkisian and Gerstel (2004); Swartz (2009). See also Harknett (2006).

48. For further discussion, see also Edin and Lein (1997); Stack (1974); Sternberg Greene, Boyd, and Edin (2010).

49. Such networks of support can help families in tough times but also have the potential to hold families back when times are good, weighed down by the needs of extended family. For example, Heflin and Pattillo (2002) find that having poor family members is associated with lower levels of asset ownership. This implies that programs that aim to help families build assets must think holistically of the entire family system or resource network.

50. Sternberg Greene, Boyd, and Edin (2010).

51. Baumeister, Vohs, and Tice (2007); Mullainathan and Shafir (2013); Shah, Mullainathan, and Shafir (2012); Spears (2011).

2. TAX TIME

1. Legally, as neither Lacey's father nor stepfather, Sonny is not eligible to claim her as a dependent for the EITC. In the past few years, the IRS has been making greater efforts to ensure that these rules are followed, including putting the onus on tax preparers for confirming that EITC claimants are legally eligible for benefits. Today it would be more difficult for Sonny to erroneously claim Lacey on his taxes were he and Debra still unmarried.

2. Internal Revenue Service (2014b).

3. For the year 2011 (Marr and Huang 2013).

4. US Census Bureau (2011).

5. Schott and Finch (2010).

6. As figure 1 shows, there are separate EIC tax schedules for married tax filers whose tax filing status is "married, filing jointly" and unmarried tax filers whose tax filing status is "head of household." Tax filers who are dependents on someone else's tax return or who file under the "married, filing separately" status are not eligible for the EITC. There are also separate tax schedules depending on the number of qualifying children on a filer's tax return. Children who count as qualifying children for the EITC must meet a relationship test (taxpayer's child or stepchild by blood or adoption, foster child, sibling or stepsibling, or a descendant of one of these), a residency test (lives with the taxpayer for at least half the tax year), and an age test (under nineteen at the end of the tax year, under twenty-four if a full-time student at least five months of the tax year, or permanently disabled). If a child can be claimed as a qualifying child for more than one taxpayer, there are "tiebreaker" rules that give priority to parents, the person with whom the child lived for the longest time during the year, or the parent with the highest income.

7. While a small "single adult" credit also exists for childless workers, the income limit is quite low (about $12,000 in 2006), and the maximum value of the credit is also low ($412).

8. About half of all states, including Massachusetts, have also implemented their own EITC; in this case, the state credit comes with the state tax refund. The Massachusetts EITC is calculated as 15 percent of the amount a taxpayer receives from the federal EITC.

9. This figure is for the total tax refund check, a combination of the EITC, the CTC, and the return of any overwithholding.

10. Expenditures in the debt/bills category include any payment on a bill that is late or past due and any credit card payment.

11. "Current Consumption" is categorized as regular monthly expenses, including all on-time bill payments or paying ahead on a bill (e.g., prepayment of a cell phone bill for a few months); groceries, toiletries, and household staple items; adult and child clothing; car expenses like gas or routine maintenance; public transit expenses; personal grooming, including haircuts; and routine child expenses, including diapers, medications, school supplies, and allowances.

12. Expenditures in the category "Treats" include eating out, entertainment (e.g., DVD rentals, going to the movies, or other family leisure outings); gifts purchased for others; vacations; toys, games, and gifts for one's children; alcohol and cigarettes; lottery tickets; and other personal splurges like jewelry or manicures.

13. Expenditures in the category "Assets/Mobility" include those related to purchasing or increasing the value of one's home, getting an education, starting or increasing the productivity of one's business, obtaining or repairing a car to make it functional, and obtaining durable home goods like furniture and appliances. We recognize that many people may not consider expenditures on cars and durable home goods to be assets, but from respondents' perspectives they are—investments in cars improve one's prospects for securing or maintaining steady employment, and investments in durable home goods (a dishwasher, a washing machine, a new bed for the expanding family) are seen as ways to improve the productivity and quality of life of the household.

14. Berube et al. (2002).

15. Zelizer ([1994] 1997, 211).

16. For example, Arkes et al. (1994) show that the way money is spent depends on whether it comes as a windfall or is part of one's regular income; see also Hodge and Mason (1995). Others have shown that a bonus is spent differently than a rebate in that the former is often spent, while the latter is more often saved (Epley and Gneezy 2007; Epley, Mak, and Idson 2006; D. Johnson, Parker, and Souleles 2004; Kahneman and Tversky 1979; Thaler and Johnson 1990; see also Shefrin and Thaler 1988; Thaler 1980).

17. Zelizer (1979, 1989, [1994] 1997, 1996).

18. Perez (2013).

19. Wiley (n.d.).

20. Further, because lower-income families are often involved in kin networks in which the sharing of resources is expected (Edin and Lein 1997; Stack 1974; Sternberg Greene, Boyd, and Edin 2010), "forced saving" offers a way to protect a pot of money from the claims and requests of relatives and friends.

21. The mystery around the tax refund check adds to its allure. The phaseout rate in benefits for some other means-tested programs, like SNAP, is not all that much higher than that of the EITC. However, the phasing down of benefits as earnings rise in these other programs is more visible; in contrast, it can be more difficult for families receiving the EITC to connect a rise in earnings in July with a fall in their refund check in February. Further, the EITC is distributed in combination with other monies, like the child tax credit and the return of overwithholding, rendering the connection in parents' minds between earning more and getting back less from the EITC that much weaker. Because similar processes are not at work with other benefits, like SNAP, parents have a clearer sense of how benefits decline as earnings rise for such programs.

22. Tax preparers rarely offer these loans anymore because of increased regulation but offer an alternative, called Refund Anticipation Checks (A. Johnson 2013).

23. Dowd and Horowitz (2011).

24. These fears of audits are not unreasonable. The IRS estimates that nearly 43 percent of all audits are of EITC claimants. Further, research has found that EITC filers who hire representation, rather than representing themselves in the audit, are twice as likely to retain the EITC rather than seeing their claim disallowed (J. Wilson et al. 2007).

25. While the IRS did not prohibit the practice of offering RALs, it no longer provided tax preparation firms with the information needed to determine the risk of making such loans to particular customers (such as whether their refunds might be garnished for nonpayment of child support or educational loans). For a discussion of these changes, see Holt (2011).

26. Mendenhall et al. (2012).

27. Indeed, research suggests that families are correct that it is worth paying to have a better tax-filing experience. While the identity of a "poor person" and being treated as such can be detrimental, affirmation of a positive, successful sense of self can actually boost the cognitive function and self-regulation of lower-income adults (Hall, Zhao, and Shafir 2014).

28. Sykes (2011).

29. Eissa and Hoynes (2006); Eissa and Liebman (1996). For a more detailed exploration of the issues discussed in this section, see Tach and Halpern-Meekin (2014).

30. Likewise, a marriage incentive exists—if a childless, lower-income worker marries a parent with little or no income, they will become eligible for a refund.

However, this promarriage incentive seems to worry critics and interest researchers less than its counterpart.

31. Internal Revenue Service (2013).

32. There were also some rare instances of workers not reporting all of their income, particularly income received for informal work or paid in cash, like tips, hairdressing, or repairing cars on the side. This was relatively uncommon, however, and, in general, cases of egregious tax fraud were rare among the families we met.

33. There is some evidence that the EITC is associated with a substantial increase in work participation among single mothers with limited education (Eissa and Liebman 1996) and a small decline in employment among married mothers with employed husbands (Eissa and Hoynes 2004; Eissa and Liebman 1996). In general, work effects of the EITC seem limited to work participation as opposed to hours worked: that is, it may induce some to enter or exit the labor force, but it isn't strongly associated with changes in work hours among employees (Hotz and Scholz (2003).

34. Carasso and Steuerle (2005).

35. Murray (1984).

36. See, for example, Edin (2000); Edin and Kefalas (2005); W. Wilson (1996). An additional study by Teitler and colleagues (2006) demonstrates that welfare does depress marriage rates slightly but that this effect is temporary and time-limited to the period of benefit receipt.

37. Dickert-Conlin and Houser (2002); Ellwood (2000; 2001, 157).

38. While a substantial minority of parents (about one-quarter) said that a couple could file taxes separately even once married as a way to preserve their refunds, most married couples in our sample did not actually do so. More recently, the IRS has put procedures in place—the EITC Due Diligence Law—to ensure that such erroneous filing does not occur by charging preparers with the task of checking for proper filing status.

39. At the time of this study, there were no additional increases to the EITC beyond two children, but in 2009 there was an expansion for three children as part of the federal stimulus package.

40. Internal Revenue Service (2005).

41. Internal Revenue Service (2014a).

42. See, for example, Bernstein (2002).

43. Smeeding, Phillips, and O'Connor (2000).

44. See Mendenhall et al. (2012) for a more detailed discussion of refund allocations.

45. Sykes et al. (forthcoming).

46. Averett and Wang (2012); Baker (2008); Chetty, Friedman, and Rockoff (2011); Cowan and Tefft (2012); Evans and Garthwaite (2013); Hoynes, Miller, and Simon (2012); Michelmore (2013).

3. THE NEW REGIME THROUGH THE LENS
OF THE OLD

1. These studies are summarized in Bane and Ellwood (1994).

2. Bane and Ellwood (1994).

3. Clinton (1992).

4. In 1996, the minimum wage was raised from $4.25 per hour to $4.75. At $4.75, a full-time, full-year worker would gross $9,500; together with an EITC of $3,556 for a working parent of two, this would be a total annual income of $13,056 against a poverty threshold of $12,641 (for a family of three that includes two children). Of course, most household heads earn a bit more than the minimum wage. Ellwood recalls that they purposely made the per-child adjustment small to get a little more cash into families' pockets. Today, the minimum wage is no longer high enough that full-time, full-year earnings combined with the EITC would boost a family above the poverty line.

5. Green (2000).

6. However, some researchers have maintained that the causal arrow was reversed—the success of welfare reform, which led women to leave welfare for work, drove up EITC receipt by expanding the pool of low-wage workers (Mead 1999).

7. And they had learned a big lesson about politics. Observers now wonder whether anyone could have predicted how large the EITC would grow; but the new version of the credit started out large—at a whopping $30 billion, an unbelievable amount for a new antipoverty program. AFDC cost only about $12 billion at the time. Ellwood claims that if he had tried to get even half that amount—another $15 billion—for welfare, the response would have been, "Do you want to give up WIC and Head Start?" But in budget discussions, especially when big tax reform is on the table and huge amounts of money are at stake, $30 billion is not a large number. Working through the tax system involves a different set of committees and people with different priorities in mind—and a much better sense of what the scope of the federal budget actually is.

8. The credit underwent significant expansions in 1986, 1990, and 1993, and temporary expansions were made in 2009 as part of the federal economic stimulus package.

9. Ultimately, this regulation lacked the teeth to revolutionize the system, and its work requirements were rarely enforced. However, this marked an important step along the path toward the overhaul of AFDC.

10. Shaefer and Edin (2012).

11. Marshall (1950, 24). *Social inclusion* is a term more often used in Europe and the rest of the English-speaking world than it is in the United States. In this view, full inclusion in society is possible only for those who are not economically marginalized and are therefore able to conduct their lives in keeping with the

community's standard of living. For example, while telegrams or letters were once the standard communication modes of the day for those who did not live in close proximity, today someone would be excluded if deprived of a telephone or access to the Internet.

12. Katz (1993).

13. Gans (1995); Jencks (1992).

14. Gilens (1999).

15. Appelbaum (2001).

16. Many with whom we spoke used the term *cap baby* to describe a child for whom you cannot receive government benefits. For example, current welfare rules stipulate that if you have an additional child while already on welfare you do not receive an accompanying increase in your benefits. Prior to the 1995 welfare reform in Massachusetts, a family on welfare would receive approximately $90 more per month for each additional child they had.

17. Richard Cohen (1995).

18. Sack (1992).

19. Clinton (1991).

20. Toner (2002).

21. Toner (1995).

22. Gilens (1999).

23. Toner (2002). However, during the 2012 presidential campaign, this issue resurfaced when Republicans sought to portray President Obama as weak on welfare for allowing states to apply for waivers from current federal welfare rules; their charge was that Obama was removing the work requirements from welfare, an argument not well supported by any available evidence.

24. The welfare reforms instituted in Massachusetts, which occurred in the year prior to the federal overhaul of the system, were known to be particularly strict and were deemed among the toughest in the nation by the National Governors Association (Wetzstein 1995). If Governor Bill Weld had had his way, the reforms would have been even more stringent; he proposed ending welfare benefits to unmarried teenage mothers, saying, "Well, we think a hundred-plus dollars a week for that stuff still makes teenage motherhood look like too much fun" (Hennrikus 2006).

25. As Robert Asen notes, "PRWORA did not end welfare as we knew it because the legislation did not—indeed, could not—repeal the contrary beliefs, competing values, and malevolent images that historically have plagued deliberations of welfare policy. Public suspicion toward persons as cheats and shirkers and public anger with governments unable to correct their pathological behavior did not end with the repeal of AFDC" (2002, 225).

26. The sense was not uncommon among families that, because they were paying taxes, they had, essentially, paid for their own benefits. In fact, taxes paid by families in the lowest income quintile (less than $3,000, on average) are far

outstripped by the transfers they receive from programs like TANF, WIC, SNAP, housing subsidies, Medicaid, and the EITC; even families in the second income quintile receive as much in government assistance as they pay in taxes. Despite their strong identities as working taxpayers, most families in this study were benefiting more from government assistance than they were paying for (M. Dahl and Perese 2013).

27. See also Michalopoulos et al. (2003); London et al. (2004); Scott et al. (2001); Scott et al. (2004).

28. Edin and Lein (1997).

29. Although some states have raised their "pass through" rates, or the rates at which welfare recipients can retain their earnings from reported jobs while still receiving benefits, these rates are obviously much lower than the 100 percent of earnings respondents were able to keep from jobs performed under the table.

30. These realities are reflected in the balance of taxes families pay versus the government benefits they receive. Among nonelderly households in 2006, the bottom income quintile received far more (approximately $13,000) in cash, near-cash, and health transfers than they paid in taxes. However, reflective of the reach of work-supporting benefits and need among those higher up the income spectrum, even those in the second income quintile saw the taxes they paid basically balanced out by the government assistance they received (M. Dahl and Perese 2013).

31. Office of the Inspector General (2013); Raab (2013).

32. Boulding (1967, 7).

33. In addition to sales tax, families may pay property tax (either directly or as part of the cost of rent) and payroll taxes, even when they pay nothing in income tax. For further explanation of the taxes paid by lower-income families across states, see Newman and O'Brien (2011).

4. BEYOND LIVING PAYCHECK TO PAYCHECK

1. This unmarried couple files separately as single household heads, each claiming two of their children; there is a limit on the number of dependents for whom a household head can "get credit" (the last time they filed, two children was the limit). By filing separately, they can claim almost an additional $2,000 in tax credits. As Jacinta explains, "We [are] splitting [the kids] because, that way, it helps him out with whatever he needs and it helps me out with whatever I need."

2. Once the statute of limitations on a debt is reached (a time period that varies from state to state—extending six years in Massachusetts), companies can no longer sue to recover unpaid debts, although it is not uncommon for them to continue efforts to get debtors to pay voluntarily (this is often done by the companies

to which the original creditor has sold the debt). However, the time period during which a credit gaffe still counts against one's credit score typically extends longer than the statute of limitations—seven years from the date of the last payment—before no longer being factored into one's credit score (Welsh 2011).

3. Sherraden (1991). This list includes the types of items Sherraden classifies as "tangible assets."

4. See Massachusetts Asset Development Commission (2009, 6).

5. Carasso and McKernan (2007).

6. The Massachusetts Asset Development Commission notes, "Housing costs rose steeply in Massachusetts between 2000 and 2005, outpacing income growth for both renters and owners. Overall, the state ranked third in the nation in 2005 in terms of monthly expenses for homeowners with mortgages, with approximately one-third of them paying 30 percent or more of their income for housing" (2009, 7). This put home ownership farther out of reach for many in Massachusetts than elsewhere in the nation. Further, as urban residents, our respondents do not have options available to lower-income families in more rural locations—like purchasing a mobile home.

7. In fact, it seems their financial situation has worsened since we met them in 2007; our follow-up research into public real estate records reveals that the Morettis had two instruments of taking filed against them in 2008 and a writ of execution on their house in 2009. By Massachusetts General Law, an instrument of taking is pursued by local tax authorities and allows the government to take land as a way of collecting overdue taxes (M.G.L. ch. 60 § 54). A writ of execution is a court order allowing for the seizure of property because of nonpayment of taxes. The Morettis' tight finances seem to have prevented them from keeping up with their taxes, leaving them in danger of losing their home and the accompanying assets it could leverage, like affording their children's college educations.

8. Sadly, the Bennetts have not been able to hold onto their home; in early 2008 an instrument of taking was filed against them, and, by the fall of 2008 foreclosure documents had been filed on the house into which Marcel and Jocelyn had put blood, sweat, and their life savings. That both the Morettis and the Bennetts, two of only a few families we met who owned their own homes, were both at risk of losing this key asset gives us a window into how the economic crisis may have affected these working families. A tight budget and few other assets leave people with little room to maneuver when times get tough; losing the family home, and all that's been invested in it, can be the result.

9. For example, more than two-thirds of people who are currently unbanked have had a bank account in the past; common reasons for not having a bank account include bank account fees being too high and banks requiring too large an initial deposit in order to open an account (each mentioned by nearly one-quarter of respondents) (Caskey 1997). Previous negative experiences with banks and credit are also commonly mentioned deterrents to using a bank account and

demonstrate the risk involved in using one—as the possibility of bouncing a check or accumulating difficult-to-pay fees is quite real (Berry 2005).

10. Carasso and McKernan (2007).

11. These families typically have less than a few hundred dollars, combined, across all these asset categories. We count a family as being in the lowest asset category even if they own a car, so long as the amount they owe on it is as much as the car is worth (meaning they could not sell it for money). Averaged across these families, holdings in checking, savings, informal savings, and retirement accounts are $78.

12. They hold this much debt even after excluding money owed on cars or mortgages (save for the amount owed over the worth of the property) and excluding educational debt (save for educational debts that are in default). The thirty-five families with debt in this middle category average about $6,685 in assets across checking, savings, and retirement accounts. The remaining twenty-five in this middle category who have limited debts average about $2,040 in holdings across checking, savings, and retirement accounts; in addition, fifteen own cars, two own small pieces of property in their countries of origin, and seven currently have available credit on their credit cards. The higher asset holdings among those with greater debts seems contradictory, but we again see that the opportunity to accumulate debt (which is more readily made available in the form of credit to those with more assets) is all too commonly realized among these lower-income families; asset building may be risky business.

13. The asset holdings in the highest asset group, between checking, savings, and retirement accounts, are $14,038 on average. In addition, eleven families own cars (the other two families lease their cars), four own property, and eight have credit available on their credit cards.

14. Carmen is trying to save, even while falling behind on her monthly expenses—even now, her wages are less than half of her reported expenses ($2,090 against $4,670), and she has a substantial amount of credit card debt as well ($5,260).

15. Families' attempts to earmark money for particular purposes, changing the meaning of money as a sort of savings strategy, can be further understood through Viviana Zelizer's work on the social meaning of money (1989, 1994 [1997]). She explains that while in financial terms one dollar is equivalent to any other this is not how money is understood in "real" life. From where or who money comes from and for what it is designated can change the meaning of one dollar compared to another.

16. For further discussion of views of credit use among low-income families, see Sternberg Greene (2013).

17. See Kiviat (2013); Traub (2013).

18. It is important to note that we talked to families before the recent financial crisis and the resulting limitations on available credit lines as well as the changes in regulations governing credit cards. While it is possible that these

factors could change the stories families would tell today, understanding their approach to credit, at the very least, gives insight into attitudes that played a part in the financial crisis and highlights the fact that many families are having to weather the recent economic storm with substantial nonmortgage debt as a result of the deregulated credit market.

19. See also Sykes et al. (forthcoming).

20. For more information about people's aspirations and the EITC, see Sykes et al. (forthcoming) and Romich and Weisner (2001).

21. In fact, for those dealing with income instability, home ownership may simply not make sense, since the likelihood and consequences of running into trouble keeping up with the mortgage are so high.

22. While cohabiting families could also garner these benefits, the lower level of "enforceable trust" in these relationships makes it a riskier proposition for partners to invest heavily in them (Cherlin 2009).

23. Although race is strongly correlated with asset holdings in the population overall, within our truncated sample race does not seem to be associated with being in the highest level of asset holders; five families are black and four each are white and Hispanic.

5. "DEBT—I AM HOPING TO ELIMINATE THAT WORD!"

1. Draut and Silva (2003).

2. Draut and Silva (2003).

3. All the statistics in this paragraph are from Draut and Silva (2003).

4. US Department of Treasury (2009).

5. Medical debt accounts for up to half of personal bankruptcies in the United States, but low-income families are much less likely than their middle-class counterparts to resolve their debt through bankruptcy (Himmelstein et al. 2005; Warren 2003, cited in Warren and Tyagi 2003, 194).

6. FinAid (2012).

7. Sykes et al. (forthcoming).

8. This happens with young adults across the economic spectrum and is not unique to the lower-income population (Draut and Silva 2004). A key difference is that the upwardly mobile are better able to dig themselves out of debt once they have secured well-paying jobs.

9. In Massachusetts, it is possible for custodial parents to release noncustodial parents from child support orders if the custodial parents are not receiving public assistance (SNAP, Medicaid, or Transitional Aid to Families with Dependent Children [TAFDC]) and if the fathers have no arrears for prior child support payments.

10. See also Sternberg Greene (2013) for further discussion of credit use in this sample of families.

11. Store credit cards, like many of the cards Tamara holds, can be especially tricky for consumers and present an even greater risk of racking up debt. This is because retail credit cards often carry particularly unfavorable terms—a 0 percent introductory interest rate that disappears if a balance is not paid in full, accompanied by a retrospective application of a high interest rate and the associated back interest. For families who juggle debts or who wait for tax time to pay off their credit card bills, therefore, store credit cards may be particularly problematic (Ellis 2013).

12. In the summer of 2010, President Obama passed a bank reform bill, which, among other things, has imposed new fees and restrictions on the nation's biggest banks and has created a new Consumer Protection Division to monitor mortgage and credit card products. The Federal Reserve Board also ruled that banks must reform the way debit card overdraft fees are assessed. Many banks have instituted new regulations for overdraft fees that require account holders to formally "opt in" to bank practices that allow them to overdraw on their accounts.

13. Rosenbaum, Deil-Amen, and Person (2009).

14. FinAid (2012).

15. If families forgo payment for too long on a government-financed student loan, tax refund checks will be garnished, and this sometimes occurred among the families in this study. Michelle Tavares, who received an associate's degree from Boston's Bunker Hill Community College in psychology, had thought about transferring to a four-year college so she could complete her bachelor's degree, but "just wanted to work and then I ended up having a kid and next thing you know I'm home for a little while." Last year, Michelle filed taxes as head of household (even though she is married but separated) and was due to claim a $4,000 refund, mostly from the earned income tax credit. She filed her taxes at the Dorchester H&R Block and got some of the money she was owed in the form of a rapid refund. However, once her taxes had been processed, her student loan default was discovered and the entire tax refund was garnished. To make matters worse, she now owes H&R Block $500 for her filing fee and refund anticipation loan, expenses that would have been subtracted from her refund check if it had not been garnished. Because Michelle had so many debts from so many different sources, she had put her student loans on the back burner. The surprise garnishment of her refund was a big financial blow—her budget was already very tight—and to her felt unjust: "They don't even care what circumstance you are in. They don't care if you need [it]. I needed the money to pay my bills and stuff. I wasn't lookin' for the money to go shopping. I was looking for the money to just pay bills."

16. In fact, researchers have found that debt holdings are positively associated with depressive symptoms, particularly for adults with less education (those with a high school degree or less) (Berger, Collins, and Cuesta 2013).

17. For further details on the ideas in this section, see Tach and Sternberg Greene (2014).

18. Credit card companies have an incentive to use harassing methods to get debtors to make payments because it lengthens the amount of time before the debtors default on the loan, which typically occurs after one year of nonpayment. Once this occurs, debtors can declare bankruptcy or settle their debts, often at a substantial financial loss for the credit card companies that must accept a smaller repayment than they were owed.

19. Shaefer, Song, and Williams Shanks (2013). This research suggests that EITC recipient households may hold less unsecured debt because they are able to pay down existing debts or have enough cash on hand to avoid taking on new debts.

20. These include the Section 8 Homeownership Program and first-time home buyer courses offered by nonprofit home ownership agencies. Many of these programs offer financial literacy resources for low-income families.

21. Gross, Notowidigdo, and Wang (2012); N. Martin (2005); N. Nichols (1994).

22. White (1998).

23. Thorne and Anderson (2006).

6. CAPITALIZING ON THE PROMISE OF THE EITC

1. TANF receipt continued to dwindle, leaving fewer than one million adults and three million children on the rolls by 2007 (Office of Family Assistance 2010). For a review of the effects of the downturn on unskilled and semiskilled workers, see Edin and Kissane (2010).

2. Henly, Danziger, and Offer (2005).

3. Kushel et al. (2006).

4. Rebecca Cohen and Wardrip (2011).

5. Bureau of Labor Statistics (2012).

6. The number of TANF recipients rose to 1.9 million families during the recession—compared to 5.1 million families who had received benefits in the years prior to welfare reform (Falk 2011).

7. B. Roberts, Povich, and Mather (2011–12).

8. See Pew Research Center (2011, 13).

9. NPR, Henry J. Kaiser Family Foundation, Harvard University Kennedy School of Government (2001).

10. Robinson (2010).

11. Brownstein (2012).

12. NPR, Henry J. Kaiser Family Foundation, Harvard University Kennedy School of Government (2001).

13. Quinnipiac University Polling Institute (2010). See also the Bloomberg Poll conducted by Selzer & Co. on July 9–12, 2010 (PollingReport.com. 2010).

14. Blank (2010).

15. "'Mothers' Pensions'" (1914); "Social Security Act" (1937); "Countywide Study Urged" (1956).

16. Marlantes (2012); Friedman (2012).

17. Falk (2013).

18. Hungerford and Thiess (2013).

19. Bradley (2011); DeParle and Gebeloff (2009); Haskins (2012, 2007); B. Miller and Swartz (2002).

20. For effects on children's achievement and health, see Baughman (2012); Chetty, Friedman, and Rockoff (2011); G. Dahl and Lochner (2012); Hoynes, Miller, and Simon (2012); Michelmore (2013). For effects on parents' health, see Evans and Garthwaite (2013).

21. Arkes et al. (1994); Hodge and Mason (1995); Zelizer ([1994] 1997, 1979, 1989, 1996).

22. Quadagno (1996).

23. See Garfinkel and McLanahan (1986).

24. See also Sykes et al. (forthcoming). This raises the possibility that the EITC may create positive policy feedback loops in which the incorporative effects of the policy lead to positive externalities, such as greater civic engagement and political participation (for background information on policy feedback loops, see Bruch, Ferree, and Soss 2010). Future research should explore such potential effects.

25. H&R Block has trademarked the phrase "I've got people" (US Patent and Trademark Office 2007) and applied for, but never received, trademark status for the phrase used in its ad slogan "You've got people" (US Patent and Trademark Office 2008). The company's website continues to display this phrase at www.hrblock.com/company/blocknet/hrblock_employees.html (accessed March 7, 2014).

26. Although not widely discussed, higher-income households stand to gain more in dollar value from the tax system because many low-income households may see their tax liability reduced to zero, meaning that additional tax deductions and nonrefundable credits bring no additional benefits (for further discussion, see Center on Budget and Policy Priorities (2013b).

27. Mendenhall et al. (2012); Shaefer, Song, and Williams Shanks (2013).

28. Morin and Taylor (2009).

29. Pugh (2009).

30. Lamont (2000); D. Miller (1998); Zelizer (2004); Zukin (2004).

31. See also Sykes (2011).

32. Ziliak, Hardy, and Bollinger (2011).

33. Ziliak, Hardy, and Bollinger (2011, 749). For men with a high school degree in 1973, the chance of being unemployed at both points in time was 2 percent;

by 2008, this was nearly six times as large at almost 12 percent. The situation is different for women because of variation in their labor force entrance and participation patterns; for women with less than a high school degree, the chance of not being employed at both points in time was nearly 43 percent, while in 2008 this stood at just over 50 percent (comparable figures for women with a high school degree show this group actually experienced less volatility over time: chances of not working stood at 35 percent in 1973 versus 26 percent in 2008).

34. Hacker and Jacobs (2008).

35. Hacker and Jacobs (2008); Conger and Elder (1994); McLoyd (1998).

36. Leigh (2010).

37. Pew Research Center (2009).

38. Taylor et al. (2011, 1).

39. Taylor et al. (2011, 1).

40. Arnold (2012).

41. See Forrester (1994, 394).

42. Sugrue (2009); Gyourko (2008).

43. Arkes et al. (1994); Epley and Gneezy (2007); Epley, Mak, and Idson (2006); Hodge and Mason (1995); D. Johnson, Parker, and Souleles (2004); Kahneman and Tversky (1979); Thaler (1980); Thaler and Johnson (1990).

44. See Arkes et al. (1994); Epley and Gneezy (2007); Epley, Mak, and Idson (2006); Hodge and Mason (1995); Zelizer ([1994] 1997, 211 n. 104).

45. D. Johnson, Parker, and Souleles (2004).

46. See also DeParle (2004).

47. Research has shown that one of the reasons people seem to think about and spend windfall income differently from regular income is that it is unexpected (Arkes et al. 1994; Epley and Gneezy 2007). In this way, the experience our respondents describe of being unsure from year to year how much they will get in their tax refund checks until their tax preparer tells them probably adds to the windfall effect of the EITC.

48. Rhine et al. (2005).

49. Holt (2011).

50. Ben-Shalom, Moffitt, and Scholz (2012).

51. Shaefer and Edin (forthcoming).

52. Sherman (2009).

53. Shaefer and Edin (2012).

54. Kwon and Meyer (2011); Loprest (2003).

55. McGranahan and Schazenbach (2013).

56. Averett and Wang (2012); Baker (2008); Chetty, Friedman, and Rockoff (2011); Cowan and Tefft (2012); Evans and Garthwaite (2013); Hoynes, Miller, and Simon (2012); Manoli and Turner (2014); Michelmore (2013). However, there are some indications that the EITC may discourage less educated, single

mothers from enrolling in college, presumably because of the increased payoff of employment (Celik 2011).

57. On the basis of our research, there are some issues to which future studies in this arena should attend. First, many of the studies do not specify during what time of year their survey information is collected; our research suggests we might expect the impact of the EITC's income boost on health to vary substantially—to be more influential during tax season and least important the following fall, the average time span by which families have spent down most of their refund money. If such variation is not observed, it would seem to indicate one of two possibilities: the EITC money entirely displaces money that would be spent in any event (meaning that money is then available to be spent at other times of year, thereby boosting income year-round) or that experiencing even a temporary income boost has long-lasting benefits.

Second, studies in this area often try to generalize their findings from the EITC to the question of how income more generally affects health. However, our findings (building on the work of economic psychologists and sociologists described above) indicate that the EITC can't be used as a stand-in for regular income. The sort of impact various sources of income have on health may be quite different from the tax refund's windfall, especially since this source of income doesn't carry stigma (i.e., a similar sum of money from welfare would probably not have the same effect on health). This is because the EITC generates both different expenditure patterns, which translate into material well-being, and different psychological reactions, which translate into greater social inclusion and reduced stress. Policy proposals and future research that draw on the lessons of these studies, with the aim of raising families' incomes in order to create better health and educational outcomes, must be cautious to attend to the meaning and delivery method attached to the money, since not every dollar may have the equivalent ability to improve material well-being or provide stress relief and social inclusion.

58. Barnes and Smith (2009); Evans and Garthwaite (2013).

59. Aizer, Stroud, and Buka (2009); Copper et al. (1996).

60. See, for example, Baumeister, Vohs, and Tice (2007); Mullainathan and Shafir (2013); Shah, Mullainathan, and Shafir (2012); Spears (2011).

61. Edin and Lein (1997, ch. 7).

62. Therefore, it is not surprising that previous research has found that adults manipulate their decision-making environment to make it easier to act in their own long-term financial interest. For example, credit card holders may opt to use a debit card instead when spending, since this puts a lower limit on their spending and limits their ability to rack up debts (Sprenger and Stavins 2008). And, as we also find here, taxpayers purposely elect to overwithhold because it serves a "forced savings" function (see also Barr and Dokko 2008).

63. Family Nutrition Programs (2013).

256   NOTES TO CHAPTER 6

64. In a study of farmers' cognitive capacity in India before and after harvest, Mullainathan, Shafir, and two other colleagues found an increase in IQ of 10 points after harvest, when scarcity was relieved, "which in a common descriptive classification is the distance between 'average' and 'superior' intelligence," wrote Mullainathan in a *New York Times* op-ed (Mullainathan 2013).

65. Cattell (2001).

66. Bruch, Ferree, and Soss (2010); Mettler (2002); Mettler and Soss (2004).

67. Marshall (1950).

68. Harris and Sammartino (2011).

69. Isaacs, Sawhill, and Haskins (2009). See also Hacker and Jacobs (2008, 12). Other researchers have found similar evidence of growing income volatility (see, for example, Dynan, Elmendorf, and Sichel 2012); Moffitt and Gottschalk 2012. For notable exceptions, see Congressional Budget Office (2008); M. Dahl, DeLeire, and Schwabish (2011); and Winship (2011).

70. Beller and Hout (2006); Isaacs, Sawhill, and Haskins (2009).

71. Jäntti et al. (2006).

72. S. Martin (2004); McLanahan (2004).

73. Osborne, Manning, and Smock (2007).

74. Blank (2009).

75. Hacker and Jacobs (2008).

76. This is a particularly important feature of this new system because, as Esping-Andersen (1990) has argued, one of the primary purposes of a welfare regime is to offer decommodification. This process of making citizens less dependent on the market for their survival is exactly the opposite of the intentions of the new welfare regime instituted in the United States over the last fifteen years, which, in essence, aims to maximize people's dependence on the market by tying their benefits to their market work.

77. Shaw (2009).

78. We would like to thank our "brain trust" for their assistance in developing these policy recommendations. All the best ideas are theirs, and any mistakes are ours. Thank you to Maria Cancian, J. Michael Collins, Dan Meyer, Andrew Reschovsky, John Karl Scholz, and Timothy Smeeding.

79. To draw this conclusion, we compare the distribution of earnings among EITC recipients (Eissa and Hoynes 2011) to the federal poverty threshold for that year (US Department of Health and Human Services 2010). Against a poverty threshold for a family of two of $12,490, 62.3 percent of EITC recipients had earnings of $12,500 or more, while 47.5 percent of recipients had earnings of $15,000 or more against a poverty threshold for a family of three of $15,670. Given that most EITC families are headed by a single parent and are approximately evenly divided between those with one versus two or more children (Eissa and Hoynes 2011), comparing recipients' earnings against the poverty threshold

for families of two or three people gives us a rough estimate of how many recipient families are at or above the poverty line on the basis of earnings alone.

80. Primarily, the income limit for married parents has been raised (now reaching $47,162 for married couples with two children for tax year 2012), and an additional layer of benefits has been added for families with three or more children (offering a maximum benefit of $5,891 in 2012).

81. In addition, thought could be given to ways to combine the EITC and CTC into a more seamless benefit package for low-income families with children.

82. This would go in the opposite direction from current policy moves, which have seen states cut back on their EITC programs (as in Michigan and Wisconsin) (Schott and Finch 2010).

83. A. Nichols, Sorensen, and Lippold (2012); Sorensen (2010); Wheaton and Sorensen (2009).

84. Marr, Huang, and Frentz (2014).

85. This lay in stark contrast with a companion project we carried out in cooperation with another research team in Illinois, where families expressed a good deal of concern about health insurance access.

86. While the ACA may bring some new costs to those who are not currently insured (as they either buy insurance or pay the tax for not doing so), the subsidies and assistance available should ease the acquisition of insurance coverage for lower-income families; the peace of mind that insurance coverage brings also cannot be quantified.

87. See also Sternberg Greene (2013).

88. Orszag (2009).

89. Thank you to Maria Cancian for developing this idea with us.

90. We would suggest that the deferred EITC be made the default option, with tax filers needing to "opt out" of the deferred option in order to receive the lump sum. Previous research has demonstrated that people are more likely to follow whatever option is made into the default (see, for example, Gale, Iwry, and Orszag 2005).

91. Tax filers could be offered a selection from among their deferred EITC options by adding questions to the existing EITC tax schedule. The tax filer could select from among four options, for example:

(1) Receiving 25 percent of the EITC immediately + 75 percent of the EITC in deferred payments over the next twelve months + a certain percentage of the EITC as a monthly bonus

(2) Receiving 50 percent of the EITC immediately + 50 percent in deferred payments + a monthly bonus

(3) Receiving 75 percent of the EITC immediately + 25 percent in deferred payments + a monthly bonus

(4) Receiving 100 percent of the EITC immediately + no monthly bonus

The form would allow the filer or tax preparer to calculate how much these various options would work out to. For instance, if the monthly bonus was set at 20 percent of the deferred EITC and someone were eligible for $2,000 through the EITC, her options would be:

(1) Receiving $500 now + $1,500 in deferred payments + $300 in monthly bonuses = $2,300 total

(2) Receiving $1,000 now + $1,000 in deferred payments + $200 in monthly bonuses = $2,200 total

(3) Receiving $1,500 now + $500 in deferred payments + $100 in monthly bonuses = $2,100 total

(4) Receiving $2,000 now = $2,000 total

92. The Working Tax Credit in the United Kingdom is akin to the EITC insofar as it provides a benefit to employed parents; however, it is distributed regularly throughout the year, rather than once a year as a lump sum. Evidence indicates that this benefit, in combination with related reforms intended to boost the financial situation of low-income parents, led to increased expenditures among low-income families in categories such as food, children's clothing, and durable goods (Gregg, Waldfogel, and Washbrook 2006). This suggests that the lump sum payment of the EITC may not be essential to the program's success in terms of boosting families' current financial situations. It is an empirical question, however, whether disbursing the payment in smaller increments at more regular intervals takes away from the aspirational element of the current EITC, which motivates future orientation and related behaviors. The deferred EITC option could hopefully retain this aspirational feature, as claimants could make an annual decision about saving or spending the money, allowing planning for and dreaming about the future.

93. See, for example, Bax et al. (2005); Gorham et al. (2002); Grinstein-Weiss et al. (2011).

94. See also Sykes et al. (forthcoming).

95. In fact, Celik (2011) found that increased EITC benefits were associated with a decreased likelihood of college enrollment among single mothers with a high school education; the speculation is that the increased payoff from working, due to the incentives from the EITC, leads parents to choose employment over education.

96. Reynolds et al. (2011).

97. White House (2011).

98. Although over 80 percent of community college students say they aspire to get at least a bachelor's degree, within five years of their first entry to a community college only 20 percent have earned a certificate or AA degree, only 21 percent have transferred to a four-year school, and only 6 percent have earned a bachelor's degree (see US Department of Education 2011, tables 1-A and 2-A).

99. White House (2011).

100. White House (2011).

101. Newman (2007). The American Opportunity Tax Credit is currently refundable (up to $1,000); however, like the EITC expansions that were part of the ARRA passed in response to the Great Recession, it is set to expire in 2017.

102. Pavetti and Schott (2011).

APPENDIX A: INTRODUCTION TO BOSTON AND THE RESEARCH PROJECT

1. Casaburi and Sumner (1976); *East Boston* (1976); Sammarco (1997); Sumner (1858).

2. In other regions of the country, other for-profit tax preparers like Jackson Hewitt take the place of H&R Block stores. In the Boston area, however, H&R Block is by far the dominant force in the for-profit tax preparation market.

3. Rhine et al. (2005).

4. This is the income limit for a single parent head of household with two minor children for the 2006 tax year—the year in question during our data collection in 2007. The upper limit for a married couple is $2,000 higher.

5. The survey was similar to the one used by Smeeding and his collaborators (Smeeding, Phillips, and O'Connor 2000) but was designed in collaboration with the Boston Mayor's Office EITC Campaign, which administers an annual survey of this kind in all Boston nonprofit tax preparation sites. We do not have a precise response rate for these surveys because people may have declined to participate because they did not want to or because they had not received the EITC and therefore knew they were ineligible. The few who told us they had received the credit but couldn't take the survey often provided explanations such as their being double-parked, running late, or having a taxi waiting for them. Of the 332 people surveyed, only 9 declined to provide contact information so they could potentially be included in the in-depth interview portion of the study.

6. American Fact Finder (2010a).

7. Our racial groups are based on respondents' self-reported racial identification.

8. Our sample includes only legal immigrants. Therefore, the financial management behaviors and attitudes of undocumented immigrants are not represented here.

Bibliography

Aizer, Anna, Laura Stroud, and Stephen Buka. 2009. "Maternal Stress and Child Well-Being: Evidence from Siblings." Unpublished manuscript, Brown University.

Albelda, Randy. 2001. "Welfare-to-Work, Farewell to Families? US Welfare Reform and Work/Family Debates." *Feminist Economics* 7 (1): 119–35.

Albelda, Randy, and Jennifer Shea. 2007. *Bridging the Gaps between Earnings and Basic Needs in Massachusetts: Executive Summary and Final Report.* Boston: Center for Economic and Policy Research, University of Massachusetts. http://scholarworks.umb.edu/csp_pubs/37.

American Fact Finder. 2010a. "Community Facts: Boston City, Massachusetts." Accessed September 1, 2013. http://factfinder2.census.gov/faces/nav/jsf/pages /community_facts.xhtml.

———. 2010b. "Profile of General Population and Housing Characteristics: 2010." Accessed September 1, 2013. http://factfinder2.census.gov/faces /tableservices/jsf/pages/productview.xhtml?pid=DEC_10_DP_DPDP1.

"America's Most Expensive Cities." 2009. *Forbes Magazine*, October 7.

Anderson, Steven G. 2001. "Welfare Recipient Views about Caseworker Performance: Lessons for Developing TANF Case Management Practices." *Families in Society: The Journal of Contemporary Human Services* 82 (2): 165–74.

Appelbaum, Lauren D. 2001. "The Influence of Perceived Deservingness on Policy Decisions Regarding Aid to the Poor." *Political Psychology* 22 (3): 419–42.

Arkes, Hal R., Cynthia A. Joyner, Mark V. Pezzo, Jane Gradwohl Nash, Karen Siegel-Jacobs, and Eric Stone. 1994. "The Psychology of Windfall Gains." *Organizational Behavior and Human Decision Processes* 59:331–47.

Arnold, Chris. 2012. "After the Housing Bust, Revisiting Homeownership." National Public Radio, June 4.

Asen, Robert. 2002. *Visions of Poverty: Welfare Policy and Political Imagination.* East Lansing: Michigan State University Press.

Averett, Susan L., and Yang Wang. 2012. "The Effects of Earned Income Tax Credit Payment Expansion on Maternal Smoking." *Health Economics* 22 (11): 1344–59.

Baker, Kevin. 2008. "Do Cash Transfer Programs Improve Infant Health: Evidence from the 1993 Expansion of the Earned Income Tax Credit." Mimeo, University of Notre Dame.

Bane, Mary Jo, and David Ellwood. 1994. *Welfare Realities: From Rhetoric to Reform.* Cambridge, MA: Harvard University Press.

Barnes, Michael G., and Trenton G. Smith. 2009. "Tobacco Use as Response to Economic Insecurity: Evidence from the National Longitudinal Survey of Youth." *B.E. Journal of Economic Analysis and Policy* 9 (1): article 47.

Barr, Michael S., and Jane K. Dokko. 2008. "Paying to Save: Tax Withholding and Asset Allocation among Low- and Moderate-Income Taxpayers." Working paper, Finance and Economics Discussion Series 2008–11, Divisions of Research and Statistics and Monetary Affairs, Federal Reserve Board, Washington, DC.

Batchelder, Lily L., Fred T. Goldberg Jr., and Peter R. Orszag. 2006. "Efficiency and Tax Incentives: The Case for Refundable Tax Credits." *Stanford Law Review* 59 (23): 23–76.

Baughman, Reagan A. 2012. "The Effect of State EITC Expansion on Children's Health." Carsey Institute, University of New Hampshire, Issue Brief 48. Spring. www.carseyinstitute.unh.edu/publications/IB-Baughman-EITC-Child-Health.pdf.

Baumeister, Roy F., Kathleen D. Vohs, and Dianne M. Tice. 2007. "The Strength Model of Self-Control." *Current Directions in Psychological Science* 16 (6): 351–55.

Bax, Elizabeth, Laronda Blessing, Anu Gurung, Sarah Harger, Will Lambe, and Justin Wheeler. 2005. *Administering the Individual Development Account: A Report for the North Carolina Department of Labor.* Raleigh: North Carolina Department of Labor.

Beller, Emily, and Michael Hout. 2006. "Intergenerational Social Mobility: The United States in Comparative Perspective." *Future of Children* 16 (2): 19–36.

Benefits.Gov. 2013. "Washington Special Supplemental Nutrition Program for Women, Infants, and Children (WIC)." Accessed February 2. www.benefits.gov/benefits/benefit-details/2031.

Ben-Shalom, Yonatan, Robert Moffitt, and John Karl Scholz. 2012. "An Assessment of the Effectiveness of Antipoverty Programs in the United States." In *The Oxford Handbook of the Economics of Poverty*, edited by Philip N. Jefferson, 709–49. New York: Oxford University Press.

Berger, Lawrence M., J. Michael Collins, and Laura Cuesta. 2013. "Household Debt and Adult Depressive Symptoms." Working paper. http://ssrn.com /abstract=2200927 or http://dx.doi.org/10.2139/ssrn.2200927.

Bernstein, Jared. 2002. "Two Cheers for the EITC." *American Prospect*, November 30.

Berry, Christopher. 2005. "To Bank or Not to Bank? A Survey of Low-Income Households." In *Building Assets, Building Credit: Creating Wealth in Low-Income Communities*, edited by Nicolas P. Retsinas and Eric S. Belsky, 47–70. Washington, DC: Brookings Institution.

Berube, Alan, Anne Kim, Benjamin Forman, and Megan Burns. 2002. *The Price of Paying Taxes: How Tax Preparation and Refund Loan Fees Erode the Benefits of the EITC*. Washington, DC: Center on Urban and Metropolitan Policy, Brookings Institution.

Bitler, Marianne, Hilary Hoynes, and Elira Kuka. 2013. "Do In-Work Tax Credits Serve as a Safety Net?" NBER Working Paper 19785, National Bureau of Economic Research.

Blank, Rebecca M. 2009. "Economic Change and the Structure of Opportunity for Less-Skilled Workers." *Focus* 26 (2): 14–20.

———. 2010. "The New American Model of Work-Conditioned Public Support." In *United in Diversity? Comparing Social Models in Europe and America*, edited by Jens Alber and Neil Gilbert, 176–98. New York: Oxford University Press.

Boston Housing Authority. 2009. *Admissions and Continued Occupancy Policy for the Public Housing Programs*. Boston. www.bostonhousing.org/pdfs /OCC2009ACOP.pdf.

———. 2010. *Leased Housing Division Administrative Plan for Section 8 Programs*. Boston. www.bostonhousing.org/pdfs/LHS2010AdminPlan.pdf.

———. 2011. "Welcome to the Boston Housing Authority." Accessed January 6, 2014. www.bostonhousing.org/.

Boston Landmarks Commission. 1994. *Exploring Boston's Neighborhoods: East Boston*. Boston.

Boulding, Kenneth E. 1967. "The Boundaries of Social Policy." *Social Work* 12 (1): 3–11.

Bradley, Katherine. 2011. "Picking Up Where '96 Welfare Reform Left Off." *National Review Online*, March 17.

Brookings Institution. 2010. "Earned Income Tax Credit (EITC) Interactive." www.brookings.edu/projects/EITC.aspx.

Brown, Tim. 2013. "It Pays to Not Work: Welfare Recipients Now Receiving More Money Than Private Sector Jobs." *Freedom Outpost*, August 22.

Brownstein, Ronald. 2012. "Poll: Americans Split on Concern for Very Poor." *National Journal*, February 13.

Bruch, Sarah K., Myra Max Ferree, and Joe Soss. 2010. "From Policy to Polity: Democracy, Paternalism and the Incorporation of Disadvantaged Citizens." *American Sociological Review* 75 (2): 205–26.

Bureau of Labor Statistics. 2012. "Occupational Outlook Handbook: Drafters." Washington, DC: Office of Occupational Statistics and Employment Projections, Bureau of Labor Statistics. Last modified June 26. www.bls.gov/ooh /architecture-and-engineering/drafters.htm.

Campbell, Andrea. 2003. *How Policies Make Citizens: Senior Political Activism and the American Welfare State*. Princeton, NJ: Princeton University Press.

Carasso, Adam, and Signe-Mary McKernan. 2007. *The Balance Sheets of Low-Income Households: What We Know about Their Assets and Liabilities*. Poor Finances: Assets and Low-Income Households Series. Washington, DC: Urban Institute.

Carasso, Adam, and Eugene C. Steuerle. 2005. "The Hefty Penalty on Marriage Facing Many Households with Children." *Future of Children* 15 (2): 157–75.

Casaburi, Victor F., and William H. Sumner. 1976. *A Colonial History of East Boston*. Self-published.

Caskey, John P. 1997. *Lower Income Americans, Higher Cost Financial Services*. Madison: Filene Research Institute, University of Wisconsin-Madison.

Castner, Laura, and James Mabli. 2010. *Low-Income Household Spending Patterns and Measures of Poverty*. Washington, DC: Mathematica Policy Research.

Cattell, Vicky. 2001. "Poor People, Poor Places, and Poor Health: The Mediating Role of Social Networks and Social Capital." *Social Science and Medicine* 52 (10): 1501–16.

Celik, Sule. 2011. "The Impact of the Earned Income Tax Credit on the Educational Investments of Single Mothers: Evidence from State EITCs." Unpublished manuscript, University of Houston.

Center on Budget and Policy Priorities. 2013a. "National TANF Caseload Fact Sheet." www.cbpp.org/files/11-19-13tanf/US.pdf.

———. 2013b. "Policy Basics: Tax Exemptions, Deductions, and Credits." Last modified April 16. www.cbpp.org/cms/index.cfm?fa=view&id=3763.

Cherlin, Andrew J. 2009. *The Marriage-Go-Round: The State of Marriage and the Family in America Today*. New York: Alfred A. Knopf.

Chetty, Raj, John N. Friedman, and Jonah Rockoff. 2011. "New Evidence on the Long-Term Impacts of Tax Credits." IRS Statistics of Income White Paper Series. www.irs.gov/pub/irs-soi/11rpchettyfriedmanrockoff.pdf.

Child Care Aware. 2012. *Parents and the High Cost of Child Care: 2012 Report*. Arlington, VA: Child Care Aware of America.

Clinton, William J. 1991. "The New Covenant: Responsibility and Rebuilding the American Community." Remarks to students at Georgetown University, October 23. www.dlc.org/ndol_ci4c81.html?kaid=127&subid=173&contentid=2783.

———. 1992. "Address Accepting the Presidential Nomination at the Democratic National Convention in New York." Transcript, American Presidency Project. Accessed January 29, 2014. www.presidency.ucsb.edu/ws/?pid=25958.

Cohen, Rebecca, and Keith Wardrip. 2011. *Should I Stay or Should I Go? Exploring the Effects of Housing Instability and Mobility on Children*. Washington, DC: National Housing Conference and Center for Housing Policy, MacArthur Foundation.

Cohen, Richard. 1995. "A Baby and a Welfare Check." *Washington Post*, March 24.

Conger, Rand D., and Glen H. Elder Jr. 1994. *Families in Troubled Times*. New York: Walter de Gruyter.

Congressional Budget Office. 2008. *Recent Trends in the Variability of Individual Earnings and Household Income*. Washington, DC: Congress of the United States.

Copper, Rachel L., Robert L. Goldenberg, Anita Das, Nancy Elder, Melissa Swain, Gwendolyn Norman, Risa Ramsey, Peggy Cotroneo, Beth A. Collins, Francee Johnson, Phyllis Jones, and Arlene Meier. 1996. "The Preterm Prediction Study: Maternal Stress Is Associated with Spontaneous Preterm Birth at Less Than Thirty-Five Weeks' Gestation." *American Journal of Obstetrics and Gynecology* 175 (5): 1286–92.

"Countywide Study Urged of Social Welfare Needs." 1956. *St. Petersburg Times*, December 13.

Cowan, Benjamin, and Nathan Tefft. 2012. "Education, Maternal Smoking, and the Earned Income Tax Credit." *B.E. Journal of Economic Analysis and Policy* 12 (1): article 45.

Crouse, Gil, Susan Hauan, and Annette Waters Rogers. 2008. *Indicators of Welfare Dependence: Annual Report to Congress, 2008*. Washington, DC: Office of Human Services Policy. http://aspe.hhs.gov/hsp/indicators08/index.shtml.

Dahl, Gordon B., and Lance Lochner. 2012. "The Impact of Family Income on Child Achievement: Evidence from the Earned Income Tax Credit." *American Economic Review* 102 (5): 1927–56.

Dahl, Molly, Thomas DeLeire, and Jonathan A. Schwabish. 2011. "Estimates of Year-to-Year Volatility in Earnings and in Household Incomes from Administrative, Survey, and Matched Data." *Journal of Human Resources* 46 (4): 750–74.

Dahl, Molly, and Kevin Perese. 2013. *The Distribution of Federal Spending and Taxes in 2006*. Washington, DC: Congressional Budget Office, Congress of the United States.

DeParle, Jason. 2004. *American Dream: Three Women, Ten Kids, and a Nation's Drive to End Welfare.* New York: Penguin.

DeParle, Jason, and Robert Gebeloff. 2009. "Food Stamp Use Soars, and Stigma Fades." *New York Times,* November 28.

Dickert-Conlin, Stacy, and Scott Houser. 2002. "EITC and Marriage." *National Tax Journal* 55 (1): 25–40.

Dorn, Stan. 2008. *Health Coverage Tax Credits: A Small Program Offering Large Policy Lessons.* Washington, DC: Urban Institute.

Dowd, Tim, and John B. Horowitz. 2011. "Income Mobility and the Earned Income Tax Credit: Short-Term Safety Net or Long-Term Income Support." *Public Finance Review* 39 (5): 619–52.

Draut, Tamara, and Javier Silva. 2003. *Borrowing to Make Ends Meet: The Growth of Credit Card Debt in the '90s.* New York: Demos.

———. 2004. *Generation Broke: The Growth of Debt among Young Americans Borrowing to Make Ends Meet.* Briefing Paper #2. New York: Demos.

Dynan, Karen, Douglas Elmendorf, and Daniel Sichel. 2012. "The Evolution of Household Income Volatility." *B.E. Journal of Economic Analysis and Policy* 12 (2): article 3.

East Boston. 1976. Boston 200 Neighborhood History Series. Boston: Boston 200 Corporation.

Edin, Kathryn. 1993. *There's a Lot of Month Left at the End of the Money.* New York: Garland Press.

———. 2000. "What Do Low-Income Single Mothers Say about Marriage?" *Social Problems* 47 (1): 112–33.

Edin, Kathryn, and Maria Kefalas. 2005. *Promises I Can Keep: How Poor Women Put Motherhood before Marriage.* Berkeley: University of California Press.

Edin, Kathryn, and Rebecca Joyce Kissane. 2010. "Poverty and the American Family: A Decade in Review." *Journal of Marriage and Family* 72 (3): 460–79.

Edin, Kathryn, and Laura Lein. 1997. *Making Ends Meet: How Single Mothers Survive Welfare and Low-Wage Work.* New York: Russell Sage Foundation.

Eissa, Nada, and Hilary W. Hoynes. 2004. "Taxes and the Labor Market Participation of Married Couples: The Earned Income Tax Credit." *Journal of Public Economics* 88:1931–58.

———. 2006. "Behavioral Responses to Taxes: Lessons from the EITC and Labor Supply." *Tax Policy and the Economy* 20:73–110.

———. 2011. "Redistribution and Tax Expenditures: The Earned Income Tax Credit." *National Tax Journal* 64 (2): 689–729.

Eissa, Nada, and Jeffrey B. Liebman. 1996. "Labor Supply Response to the Earned Income Tax Credit." *Quarterly Journal of Economics* 111 (2): 605–37.

Ellis, Blake. 2013. "Buyer Beware: Retail Cards Have Costly Trap." *CNN Money*, November 26.

Ellwood, David. 2000. "The Impact of the Earned Income Tax Credit and Social Policy Reforms on Work, Marriage and Living Arrangements." *National Tax Journal* 53 (4): 1063–105.

———. 2001. "The Impact of the Earned Income Tax Credit and Social Policy Reforms on Work, Marriage, and Living Arrangements." In *Making Work Pay: The Earned Income Tax Credit and Its Impact on America's Families*, edited by Bruce D. Meyer and Douglas Holtz-Eakin, 116–65. New York: Russell Sage Foundation.

Eowyn. 2013. "Why Americans Don't Work: Welfare Pays Better Than Minimum Wage." *Daily Sheeple*, October 27.

Epley, Nicholas, and Ayelet Gneezy. 2007. "The Framing of Financial Windfalls and Implications for Public Policy." *Journal of Socio-Economics* 36:36–47.

Epley, Nicholas, Dennis Mak, and Lorraine Chen Idson. 2006. "Bonus of Rebate? The Impact of Income Framing on Spending and Saving." *Journal of Behavioral Decision Making* 19 (3): 213–27.

Esping-Andersen, Gosta. 1990. *The Three Worlds of Welfare Capitalism*. Princeton, NJ: Princeton University Press.

Evans, William N., and Craig L. Garthwaite. 2013. "Giving Mom a Break: The Impact of Higher EITC Payments on Maternal Health." NBER Working Paper 16296, National Bureau of Economic Research, Inc.

Falk, Gene. 2011. *The Temporary Assistance for Needy Families Block Grant: Issues for the 112th Congress*. Congressional Research Report for Congress. Washington, DC: Congressional Research Service.

———. 2013. *The Temporary Assistance for Needy Families (TANF) Block Grant: Responses to Frequently Asked Questions*. Report Prepared for Members and Committees of Congress. Washington, DC: Congressional Research Service.

Family Nutrition Programs. 2013. *SNAP Food Security In-Depth Interview Study: Final Report*. Nutrition Assistance Program Report Series. Washington, DC: Office of Research and Analysis, US Department of Agriculture.

Feeding America. 2011. "Food Banks: Hunger's New Staple. Preliminary Findings." http://feedingamerica.org/press-room/in-the-news/the-new-normal.aspx.

FinAid. 2012. "Student Loans." Accessed June 12, 2013. www.finaid.org/loans/.

Finch, Ife, and Liz Schott. 2011. *TANF Benefits Fell Further in 2011 and Are Worth Much Less Than in 1996 in Most States*. Washington, DC: Center on Budget and Policy Priorities.

Fischer, Claude S. 2011. *Made In America: A Social History of American Culture and Character*. Chicago: University of Chicago Press.

Food and Nutrition Service. 2011. *Benefit Redemption Patterns in the Supplemental Nutrition Assistance Program*. Nutrition Assistance Report Series Final Report. Washington, DC: US Department of Agriculture.

————. 2013. "FY 2006 Allotments and Deduction Information." Last modified November 15. www.fns.usda.gov/snap/government/updates/FY06_Allot_Deduct.htm.

Forrester, Julia Patterson. 1994. "Mortgaging the American Dream: A Critical Evaluation of the Federal Government's Promotion of Home Equity Financing." *Tulane Law Review* 69:373–456.

Friedman, Emily. 2012. "Romney Comments on Working Moms, Ann Says Women Aren't Special Interest, Just Special." ABC News, April 13.

Gale, William G., J. Mark Iwry, and Peter R. Orszag. 2005. "The Automatic 401(k): A Simple Way to Strengthen Retirement Saving." *Tax Notes*, March 7: 1207–14.

Gans, Herbert. 1995. *The War against the Poor: The Underclass and Antipoverty Policy*. New York: Basic Books.

Garfinkel, Irwin, and Sara S. McLanahan. 1986. *Single Mothers and Their Children: A New American Dilemma*. Washington DC: Urban Institute Press.

Gilens, Martin. 1999. *Why Americans Hate Welfare: Race, Media, and the Politics of Antipoverty Policy*. Chicago: University of Chicago Press.

Gorham, Lucy S., Roberto G. Quercia, William M. Rohe, and Jonathan R. Toppen. 2002. *Low-Income Families Building Assets: Individual Development Account Programs—Lessons and Best Practices*. Chapel Hill: University of North Carolina, Center for Urban and Regional Studies.

Government Accountability Office. 2010. *Health Coverage Tax Credit: Participation and Administrative Costs*. GAO-10-521R. Washington, DC: GAO.

Grabowski, Lorie J. Schabo. 2006. "'It Still Don't Make You Feel Like You're Doin' It': Welfare Reform and Perceived Economic Self-Efficacy." *Journal of Poverty* 10 (3): 69–91.

Green, Joshua. 2000. "A Conversation with David Ellwood." *American Prospect*, November 28.

Greenstone, Michael, and Adam Looney. 2011. "Trends: Reduced Earnings for Men in America." *Milken Institute Review*, July: 8–16.

Gregg, Paul, Jane Waldfogel, and Elizabeth Washbrook. 2006. "Family Expenditures Post–Welfare Reform in the UK: Are Low-Income Families Starting to Catch Up?" *Labour Economics* 13 (6): 721–46.

Grinstein-Weiss, Michal, Michael Sherraden, William Gale, William M. Rohe, Mark Schreiner, and Clinton Key. 2011. "Ten-Year Impacts of Individual Development Accounts on Homeownership." Center for Social Development Working Paper 11–07, George Warren Brown School of Social Work, Washington University, St. Louis.

Grogger, Jeffrey. 2003. "The Effects of Time Limits, the EITC, and Other Policy Changes on Welfare Use, Work, and Income among Female-Headed Families." *Review of Economics and Statistics* 85 (2): 394–408.

Gross, Tal, Matthew J. Notowidigdo, and Jialan Wang. 2012. "Liquidity Constraints and Consumer Bankruptcy: Evidence from Tax Rebates." NBER Working Paper 17807, National Bureau of Economic Research, Inc.

Gyourko, Joseph. 2008. "Full Interview: Joseph Gyourko." Federal Reserve Bank of Richmond. www.richmondfed.org/publications/research/region_focus/2008/fall/full_interview.cfm.

Hacker, Jacob S., and Elisabeth Jacobs. 2008. *The Rising Instability of American Family Incomes, 1969–2004: Evidence from the Panel Study of Income Dynamics.* EPI Briefing Paper 213. Washington, DC: Economic Policy Institute.

Hall, Crystal C., Jiaying Zhao, and Eldar Shafir. 2014. "Self-Affirmation among the Poor: Cognitive and Behavioral Implications." *Psychological Science* 25:619–25.

Harknett, Kristen. 2006. "The Relationship between Private Safety Nets and Economic Outcomes among Single Mothers." *Journal of Marriage and Family* 68 (1): 172–91.

Harris, Edward, and Frank Sammartino. 2011. *Trends in Household Income Concentration Between 1979 and 2007.* Washington, DC: Congressional Budget Office, Congress of the United States.

Haskins, Ron. 2007. "The Rise of the Bottom Fifth." *Washington Post,* May 29.

———. 2012. "Testimony before the Subcommittee on Nutrition and Horticulture, U.S. House of Representatives." May 8.

Hays, Sharon. 2003. *Flat Broke with Children: Women in the Age of Welfare Reform.* New York: Oxford University Press.

Heflin, Colleen M., and Mary Pattillo. 2002. "Kin Effects on Black-White Account and Home Ownership." *Sociological Inquiry* 72 (2): 220–39.

Henly, Julia R., Sandra K. Danziger, and Shira Offer. 2005. "The Contribution of Social Support to the Material Well-Being of Low-Income Families." *Journal of Marriage and Family* 67 (1): 122–40.

Hennrikus, Kathleen. 2006. "His Political Career." *Boston Globe,* June 7.

Himmelstein, David U., Elizabeth Warren, Deborah Thorne, and Steffie Woolhandler. 2005. "Illness and Injury as Contributors to Bankruptcy." *Health Affairs,* February: 63–73.

Hodge, Sharon K., and Charlotte H. Mason. 1995. "Work versus Windfall: An Exploration of Saving on Subsequent Purchase." *Marketing Letters* 6 (2): 91–100.

Holt, Steve. 2006. *The Earned Income Tax Credit at Age 30: What We Know.* Washington, DC: Metropolitan Policy Program, Brookings Institution.

———. 2011. *Ten Years of the EITC Movement: Making Work Pay Then and Now.* Washington, DC: Metropolitan Policy Program, Brookings Institution.

Hotz, V. Joseph, and John Karl Scholz. 2003. "The Earned Income Tax Credit." In *Means-Tested Transfer Programs in the United States*, edited by Robert A. Moffitt, 141–98. Chicago: University of Chicago Press.

Hoynes, Hilary W., Douglas L. Miller, and David Simon. 2012. "Income, the Earned Income Tax Credit, and Infant Health." NBER Working Paper 18206, National Bureau of Economic Research, Inc.

Hungerford, Thomas L., and Rebecca Thiess. 2013. *The Earned Income Tax Credit and the Child Tax Credit: History, Purpose, Goals, and Effectiveness*. Issue Brief #370. Washington, DC: Economic Policy Institute.

Internal Revenue Service. 2005. "A Qualifying Child." Accessed February 25, 2014. www.irs.gov/uac/A-"Qualifying-Child".

———. 2011. *Internal Revenue Service Data Book, 2011*. Publication No. 55B. Washington, DC.

———. 2013. "ARRA and the Earned Income Tax Credit." Last modified May 31. www.irs.gov/uac/ARRA-and-the-Earned-Income-Tax-Credit.

———. 2014a. "EITC, Earned Income Tax Credit, Questions and Answers." Last modified January 6. www.irs.gov/Individuals/EITC,-Earned-Income-Tax-Credit,-Questions-and-Answers.

———. 2014b. "2012 EITC Income Limits, Maximum Credit Amounts, and Tax Law Updates." Last modified January 3. www.irs.gov/Individuals/2012-EITC-Income-Limits,-Maximum-Credit—Amounts-and-Tax-Law-Updates.

Isaacs, Julia B., Isabel V. Sawhill, and Rob Haskins. 2009. *Getting Ahead or Losing Ground: Economic Mobility in America*. Washington, DC: Pew Economic Mobility Project and Brookings Institution.

Jäntti, Markus, Bernt Bratsberg, Knut Røed, Oddbjørn Raaum, Robin Naylor, Eva Österbacka, Anders Björklund, and Tor Eriksson. 2006. "American Exceptionalism in a New Light: A Comparison of Intergenerational Earnings Mobility in the Nordic Countries, the United Kingdom, and the United States." IZA Discussion Paper 1938, Institute for the Study of Labor. http://ftp.iza.org/dp1938.pdf.

Jayakody, Rukmalie, Linda M. Chatters, and Robert Joseph Taylor. 1993. "Family Support to Single and Married African American Mothers: The Provision of Financial, Emotional, and Child Care Assistance." *Journal of Marriage and Family* 55 (2): 261–76.

Jencks, Christopher. 1992. *Rethinking Social Policy: Race, Poverty, and the Underclass*. Cambridge, MA: Harvard University Press.

Johnson, Allie. 2013. "Refund Anticipation Loans Live On in New Disguises." *Fox Business*, February 12.

Johnson, David S., Jonathan A. Parker, and Nicholas S. Souleles. 2004. "Household Expenditure and the Income Tax Rebates of 2001." NBER Working Paper 10784, National Bureau of Economic Research, Inc.

Jones, Jeffrey M. 2007. "Public: Family of Four Needs to Earn Average of $52,000 to Get By." Gallup, February 9. www.gallup.com/poll/26467 /public-family-four-needs-earn-average-52000-get.aspx.

Kahneman, Daniel, and Amos Tversky. 1979. "Prospect Theory: An Analysis of Decision under Risk." *Econometrica* 47 (2): 263–92.

Katz, Michael B. 1993. "The Urban 'Underclass' As a Metaphor of Social Transformation." In *The "Underclass" Debate: Views from History,* edited by Michael B. Katz, 3–26. Princeton, NJ: Princeton University Press.

Kiviat, Barbara. 2013. "Borrowing History: The Spread of Bad Credit." Unpublished manuscript.

Kushel, Margot B., Reena Gupta, Lauren Gee, and Jennifer S. Haas. 2006. "Housing Instability and Food Insecurity as Barriers to Health Care among Low-Income Americans." *Journal of General Internal Medicine* 21 (1): 71–77.

Kwon, Hyeok Chang, and Daniel R. Meyer. 2011. "How Do Economic Downturns Affect Welfare Leavers? A Comparison of Two Cohorts." *Children and Youth Services Review* 33 (5): 588–97.

Lamont, Michèle. 2000. *The Dignity of Working Men.* New York: Russell Sage Foundation; Cambridge, MA: Harvard University Press.

Lampman, Robert J. 1969. "Nixon's Family Assistance Plan." Institute for Research on Poverty Discussion Paper 57–69, University of Wisconsin, Madison.

Lawless, Jennifer L., and Richard L. Fox. 2001. "Political Participation of the Urban Poor." *Social Problems* 48 (3): 362–85.

Lee, Yean-Ju, and Isik A. Aytac. 1998. "Intergenerational Financial Support among Whites, African Americans, and Latinos." *Journal of Marriage and Family* 60 (2): 426–41.

Leftin, Joshua, Esa Eslami, and Mark Strayer. 2011. *Trends in Supplemental Nutrition Assistance Program Participation Rates: Fiscal Years 2002–2009.* Report submitted by Mathematica Policy Research to the US Department of Agriculture, Food, and Nutrition Service. Washington, DC: USDA Office of Research and Analysis.

Leigh, Andrew. 2010. "Who Benefits from the Earned Income Tax Credit? Incidence among Recipients, Coworkers and Firms." *B.E. Journal of Economic Analysis and Policy* 10 (1): article 45.

London, Andrew S., Ellen K. Scott, Kathryn Edin, and Vicki Hunter. 2004. "Welfare Reform, Work-Family Tradeoffs, and Child Well-Being." *Family Relations* 53 (2): 148–58.

Loprest, Pamela. 2003. "Fewer Welfare Leavers Employed in Weak Economy." Snapshots of America's Families No. 5. Washington, DC: Urban Institute.

Manoli, Dayanand S., and Nicholas Turner. 2014. "Cash-on-Hand and College Enrollment: Evidence from Population Tax Data and Policy

Nonlinearities." NBER Working Paper 19836, National Bureau of Economic Research, Inc.

Marlantes, Liz. 2012. "Mitt Romney's Flip-Flop on Stay-at-Home Moms: Will It Matter?" *Christian Science Monitor,* April 16.

Marr, Chuck, and Chye-Ching Huang. 2013. *Earned Income Tax Credit Promotes Work, Encourages Children's Success at School, Research Finds.* Washington, DC: Center on Budget and Policy Priorities.

Marr, Chuck, Chye-Ching Huang, and Nathaniel Frentz. 2014. *Strengthening the EITC for Childless Workers Would Promote Work and Reduce Poverty.* Washington, DC: Center on Budget and Policy Priorities.

Marshall, Thomas Humphrey. 1950. *Citizenship and Social Class and Other Essays.* Cambridge: Cambridge University Press.

Martin, Nathalie. 2005. "Poverty, Culture and the Bankruptcy Code: Narratives from the Money Law Clinic." *Clinical Law Review* 12:203–41.

Martin, Steven P. 2004. "Growing Evidence of a Divorce Divide? Education and Marital Dissolution Rates in the U.S. since the 1970s." Russell Sage Foundation Working Paper Series.

Massachusetts Asset Development Commission. 2009. *Asset Development: Removing Barriers, Building Futures.* Boston: Massachusetts Asset Development Commission.

Massachusetts Executive Office of Health and Human Services. 2014. "Health Care and Insurance." Accessed March 7. www.mass.gov/eohhs/insurance/.

Massachusetts Executive Office of Labor and Workforce Development. 2013. "Unemployment Insurance: Benefits FAQ." Accessed February 2, 2014. www.mass.gov/lwd/unemployment-insur/resources/questions-and-answers/claimants/benefits-faq.html.

McGranahan, Leslie, and Diane W. Schazenbach. 2013. "The Earned Income Tax Credit and Food Consumption Patterns." Federal Reserve Bank of Chicago Working Paper 2013–14.

McLanahan, Sara. 2004. "Diverging Destinies: How Children Are Faring under the Second Demographic Transition." *Demography* 41 (4): 607–27.

McLoyd, Vonnie C. 1998. "Socioeconomic Disadvantage and Child Development." *American Psychologist* 53 (2): 185–204.

Mead, Lawrence M. 1999. "The Decline of Welfare in Wisconsin." *Journal of Public Administration Research and Theory* 9 (4): 597–622.

Mendenhall, Ruby, Kathryn Edin, Susan Crowley, Jennifer Sykes, Laura Tach, Katrin Kriz, and Jeffrey R. Kling. 2012. "The Role of Earned Income Tax Credit in the Budgets of Low-Income Families." *Social Service Review* 86:367–400.

Mettler, Suzanne. 2002. "Bringing the State Back in to Civic Engagement: Policy Feedback Effects of the G.I. Bill for World War II Veterans." *American Political Science Review* 96 (2): 351–65.

———. 2005. *Soldiers to Citizens: The G.I. Bill and the Making of the Greatest Generation.* New York: Oxford University Press.

Mettler, Suzanne, and Joe Soss. 2004. "The Consequences of Public Policy for Democratic Citizenship: Bridging Policy Studies and Mass Politics." *Perspectives on Politics* 2 (1): 55–73.

Mettler, Suzanne, and Jeffrey Stonecash. 2008. "Government Program Usage and Political Voice." *Social Science Quarterly* 89 (2): 273–93.

Meyer, Bruce D. 2007. "The U.S. Earned Income Tax Credit, Its Effects, and Possible Reforms." Harris School Working Paper 07–20, University of Chicago.

Meyer, Bruce D., and Dan T. Rosenbaum. 2001. "Welfare, the Earned Income Tax Credit, and the Labor Supply of Single Mothers." *Quarterly Journal of Economics* 116 (3): 1063–1114.

Meyer, Bruce D., and James X. Sullivan. 2003. "Measuring the Well-Being of the Poor Using Income and Consumption." *Journal of Human Resources* 38:1180–1220.

———. 2007. "Further Results on Measuring the Well-Being of the Poor Using Income and Consumption." NBER Working Paper 13413, National Bureau of Economic Research, Inc.

———. 2009. "Five Decades of Consumption and Income Poverty." MFI Working Paper Series, No. 2010–003, Milton Friedman Institute for Research in Economics, University of Chicago.

Michalopoulos, Charles, Kathryn Edin, Barbara Fink, Mirella Landriscina, Denise Polit, Judy Polyne, Lashawn Richburg-Hayes, David Seith, and Nandita Verma. 2003. *Welfare Reform in Philadelphia: Implementation, Effects, and Experiences of Poor Families and Neighborhoods.* New York: MDRC.

Michelmore, Katherine. 2013. "The Effect of Income on Educational Attainment: Evidence from State Earned Income Tax Credit Expansions." Working paper. www.human.cornell.edu/pam/academics/phd/upload/Michelmore_Draft_November_2013.pdf.

Miller, Brian, and Rebecca Swartz. 2002. *Welfare Reform and Housing.* Policy Brief 16. Washington, DC: Center of Budget and Policy Priorities, Brookings Institution.

Miller, Daniel. 1998. *A Theory of Shopping.* Ithaca, NY: Cornell University Press.

Mink, Gwendolyn. 1998. *Welfare's End.* Ithaca, NY: Cornell University Press.

Moffitt, Robert, and Peter Gottschalk. 2012. "Trends in the Transitory Variance of Male Earnings: Methods and Evidence." *Journal of Human Resources* 47 (1): 204–36.

Morin, Rich, and Paul Taylor. 2009. "Luxury or Necessity? The Public Makes a U-Turn." Pew Research Center Social and Demographic Trends, April 23.

www.pewsocialtrends.org/2009/04/23/luxury-or-necessity-the-public-makes-a-u-turn/.

"'Mothers' Pensions Keep Children Better,' He Says." 1914. *Milwaukee Journal Sentinel*, October 11.

Mullainathan, Sendhil. 2013. "The Mental Strain of Making Do with Less." *New York Times*, September 21.

Mullainathan, Sendhil, and Eldar Shafir. 2013. *Scarcity: Why Having Too Little Means So Much*. New York: Times Books.

Murray, Charles. 1984. *Losing Ground: American Social Policy, 1950–1980*. New York: Basic Books.

National Center for Children in Poverty. 2010. "Measuring Poverty." Accessed September 1, 2013. www.nccp.org/topics/measuringpoverty.html.

Newman, Katherine S. 2007. "Up and Out-When the Working Poor Are Poor No More." In *Ending Poverty in America: How to Restore the American Dream*, edited by John Edwards, Marion Crain, and Arne L. Kalleberg. New York: New Press.

Newman, Katherine S., and Rourke O'Brien. 2011. *Taxing the Poor: Doing Damage to the Truly Disadvantaged*. Berkeley: University of California Press.

Nichols, Austin, Elaine Sorensen, and Kye Lippold. 2012. *The New York Noncustodial Parent EITC: Its Impact on Child Support Payments and Employment*. Washington, DC: Urban Institute.

Nichols, Nathaniel C. 1994. "The Poor Need Not Apply: Moralistic Barriers to Bankruptcy's Fresh Start." *Rutgers Law Journal* 25:329–57.

NPR, Henry J. Kaiser Family Foundation, and Harvard University Kennedy School of Government. 2001. "Poverty in America." NPR/Kaiser/Kennedy School Poll. \www.npr.org/programs/specials/poll/poverty/staticresults.html.

Office of Family Assistance, Administration for Children and Families, US Department of Health and Human Services. 1996–2010. "Data and Reports, Caseload Data." www.acf.hhs.gov/programs/ofa/programs/tanf/data-reports.

———. 2010. "TANF Caseload Data 2007." Last modified April 1. www.acf.hhs.gov/programs/ofa/resource/caseload2007.

Office of Policy, Office of Research, Evaluation, and Statistics. 2007. *Fast Facts and Figures about Social Security, 2007*. Washington, DC: Social Security Administration.

Office of the Inspector General, Social Security Administration. 2013. "Is Social Security Disability the 'New Welfare'?" Beyond the Numbers, July 17. http://oig.ssa.gov/newsroom/blog/july17-post.

Orszag, Peter. 2009. Press briefing, February 26, Office of the Press Secretary, White House. www.whitehouse.gov/the_press_office/Press-Briefing-by-OMB-Director-Peter-Orszag-and-CEA-Chair-Christina-Romer.

Osborne, Cynthia, Wendy D. Manning, and Pamela J. Smock. 2007. "Married and Cohabitating Parents' Relationship Stability: A Focus on Race and Ethnicity." *Journal of Marriage and Family* 69 (5): 1345–66.

Parish, William L., Lingxin Hao, and Dennis P. Hogan. 1991. "Family Support Networks, Welfare, and Work among Young Mothers." *Journal of Marriage and Family* 53 (1): 203–15.

Pattillo-McCoy, Mary. 1999. *Black Picket Fences: Privilege and Peril among the Black Middle Class.* Chicago: University of Chicago Press.

Pavetti, LaDonna, and Liz Schott. 2011. *TANF's Inadequate Response to Recession Highlights Weakness of Block-Grant Structure: Proponents Wrong to See It as Model for Medicaid, SNAP, or Other Low-Income Programs.* Washington, DC: Center on Budget and Policy Priorities.

Perez, William. 2013. "Tax Preparation Prices and Feeds: What's a Reasonable Price to Pay for Preparing Tax Returns?" Accessed February 10. http://taxes .about.com/od/findataxpreparer/a/prices.htm.

Pew Research Center. 2009. "Even as Housing Values Sink, There's Comfort in Homeownership." Pew Research Center Social and Demographic Trends, February 19. www.pewsocialtrends.org/2009/02/19/even-as-housing-values-sink-theres-comfort-in-homeownership/.

———. 2011. *The American-Western European Values Gap.* Washington, DC: Pew Research Center Global Attitudes Project.

Phillips, Katherin R. 2001. *Who Knows about the Earned Income Tax Credit?* New Federalism National Survey of America's Families, Series B, No. B-27. Washington, DC: Program to Assess Changing Social Policies, Urban Institute.

Plueger, Dean. 2009. *Earned Income Tax Credit: Participation Rate for Tax Year 2005.* Internal Revenue Service Research Bulletin: Proceedings of the 2009 IRS Research Conference.

PollingReport.com. 2010. "Bloomberg Poll Conducted by Selzer & Co., July 9–12, 2010: Budget, Taxes, Economic Policy." Accessed October 9, 2013. www.pollingreport.com/budget.htm.

Powers, Martine. 2013. "Silver Line Route Mapped Out for Chelsea, East Boston." *Boston Globe,* May 5.

Pugh, Allison J. 2009. *Longing and Belonging: Parents, Children, and Consumer Culture.* Berkeley: University of California Press.

Quadagno, Jill. 1996. *The Color of Welfare: How Racism Undermined the War on Poverty.* New York: Oxford University Press.

Quinnipiac University Polling Institute. 2010. "American Voters Want Jobs over Deficit Reduction 2-1, Quinnipiac University National Poll Finds; Most Say Recovery Has Not Begun." Accessed October 9, 2013. www.quinnipiac .edu/institutes-and-centers/polling-institute/national/release-detail? ReleaseID=1479.

Raab, Barbara. 2013. "Has Disability Become a 'De Facto Welfare Program'?" *In Plain Sight: Poverty in America*, March 28.

Rank, Mark R. 1994. "A View from the Inside Out: Recipients' Perceptions of Welfare." *Journal of Sociology and Social Welfare* 21 (2): 27–47.

Rector, Robert. 2012. "How Poor Is 'Poor'?" *National Review*, September 13.

Reynolds, Arthur J., Judy A. Temple, Suh-Ruu Ou, Irma A. Arteaga, and Barry A. B. White. 2011. "School-Based Early Childhood Education and Age-28 Well-Being: Effects by Timing, Dosage, and Subgroups." *Science Express* 333 (6040): 360–64.

Rhine, Sherrie L. W., Sabrina Su, Yazmin Osaki, and Steven Y. Lee. 2005. "Householder Response to the Earned Income Tax Credit: Path of Sustenance or Road to Asset Building." Working Paper, Office of Regional and Community Affairs, Federal Reserve Bank of New York and Community Food Resource Center.

Rice, Douglas, and Barbara Sard. 2009. *Decade of Neglect Has Weakened Federal Low-Income Housing Programs*. Washington, DC: Center on Budget and Policy Priorities.

Roberts, Brandon, Deborah Povich, and Mark Mather. 2011–12. *Overlooked and Underpaid: Number of Low-Income Working Families Increases to 10.2 Million*. Policy Brief, Working Poor Families Project. www.workingpoor families.org/pdfs/Overlooked_Dec2011.pdf.

Roberts, Dorothy E. 2004. "Welfare Reform and Economic Freedom: Low-Income Mothers' Decisions about Work at Home and in the Market." *Santa Clara Law Review* 44 (4): 1029–63.

Robinson, Michael J. 2010. "Static America: Myths about Political Change in the U.S." Special Report to the Pew Research Center. www.pewresearch.org /files/old-assets/pdf/1743-static-america.pdf.

Romich, Jennifer L., and Thomas S. Weisner. 2001. "How Families View and Use Lump-Sum Payments from the Earned Income Tax Credit." In *For Better and for Worse: Welfare Reform and the Well-Being of Children and Families*, edited by Greg J. Duncan and P. Lindsay Chase-Lansdale, 201–21. New York: Russell Sage Press.

Rosenbaum, James E., Regina Deil-Amen, and Ann E. Person. 2009. *After Admission: From College Access to College Success*. New York: Russell Sage Foundation.

Rothstein, Jesse. 2008. "The Unintended Consequences of Encouraging Work: Tax Incidence and the EITC." CEPS Working Paper No. 165, Center for Economic Policy Studies. www.princeton.edu/ceps/workingpapers/165rothstein .pdf.

Sack, Kevin. 1992. "The 1992 Campaign: Issues; The New, Volatile Politics of Welfare." *New York Times*, March 15.

Sammarco, Anthony M. 1997. *East Boston*. Charleston, SC: Arcadia Publishing.

Sarkisian, Natalia, and Naomi Gerstel. 2004. "Kin Support among Blacks and Whites: Race and Family Organization." *American Sociological Review* 69:812–37.

Schott, Liz, and Ife Finch. 2010. *TANF Benefits Are Low and Have Not Kept Pace with Inflation: Benefits Are Not Enough to Meet Families' Basic Needs.* Washington, DC: Center on Budget and Policy Priorities.

Scott, Ellen K., Kathryn Edin, Andrew S. London, and Rebecca Joyce Kissane. 2004. "Unstable Work, Unstable Income: Implications for Family Well-Being in the Era of Time-Limited Welfare." *Journal of Poverty* 8 (1): 61–88.

Scott, Ellen K., Kathryn Edin, Andrew S. London, and Joan Maya Mazelis. 2001. "My Children Come First: Welfare-Reliant Women's Post-TANF Views of Work-Family Tradeoffs and Marriage." In *For Better and for Worse: Welfare Reform and the Well-Being of Children and Families*, edited by Greg J. Duncan and P. Lindsay Chase-Lansdale, 132–53. New York: Russell Sage Press.

Seccombe, Karen, Delores James, and Kimberly Battle Walters. 1998. "'They Think You Ain't Much of Nothing': The Social Construction of the Welfare Mother." *Journal of Marriage and Family* 60 (4): 849–65.

Semega, Jessica. 2009. *Median Household Income for States: 2007 and 2008 American Community Surveys.* Washington, DC: Department of Commerce, Economics, and Statistics Administration, US Census Bureau.

Shaefer, H. Luke, and Kathryn Edin. 2012. "Extreme Poverty in the United States: 1996 to 2011." National Poverty Center Policy Brief #28.

———. Forthcoming. "The Rise of Extreme Poverty in the U.S." *Pathways.*

Shaefer, H. Luke, Xiaoqing Song, and Trina R. Williams Shanks. 2013. "Do Single Mothers in the United States Use the Earned Income Tax Credit to Reduce Unsecured Debt?" *Review of Economics of the Household* 11 (4): 659–80.

Shah, Anuj K., Sendhil Mullainathan, and Eldar Shafir. 2012. "Some Consequences of Having Too Little." *Science* 338 (6107): 682–85.

Shaw, Greg M. 2009. "Changes in Public Opinion and the American Welfare State." *Political Science Quarterly* 124 (4): 627–53.

Shefrin, Hersh M., and Richard H. Thaler. 1988. "The Behavioral Life-Cycle Hypothesis." *Economic Inquiry* 26 (4): 609–43.

Sherman, Arloc. 2009. *Safety Net Effective at Fighting Poverty but Has Weakened for the Very Poorest.* Washington, DC: Center on Budget and Policy Priorities.

Sherraden, Michael. 1991. *Assets and the Poor: A New American Welfare Policy.* New York: M. E. Sharpe.

Smeeding, Timothy M., Katherin Ross Phillips, and Michael O'Connor. 2000. "The EITC: Expectation, Knowledge, Use, and Economic and Social Mobility." *National Tax Journal* 53 (4): 1187–210.

"Social Security Act When Children Need a Friend." 1937. *Sarasota Herald-Tribune,* July 29.

Social Security Administration. 2014a. *Benefits for Children with Disabilities.* SSA Publication No. 05–10026.

———. 2014b. "Disability Planner: Benefits for your Children." Accessed March 7. www.ssa.gov/dibplan/dfamily4.htm.

Sorensen, Elaine. 2010. *New York Noncustodial Parent EITC: Implementation and First-Year Findings.* Washington, DC: Urban Institute.

Soss, Joe. 2000. *Unwanted Claims: The Politics of Participation in the U.S. Welfare System.* Ann Arbor: University of Michigan Press.

Spears, Dean. 2011. "Economic Decision-Making in Poverty Depletes Behavioral Control." *B.E. Journal of Economic Analysis and Policy* 11 (1): article 72.

Sprenger, Charles, and Joanna Stavins. 2008. "Credit Card Debt and Payment Use." Federal Reserve Bank of Boston, Working Paper 08–2. http://papers.ssrn.com/sol3/papers.cfm?abstract_id=2088904.

Stack, Carol B. 1974. *All Our Kin: Strategies for Survival in a Black Community.* New York: Harper and Row.

Sternberg Greene, Sara. 2013. "The Broken Safety Net: A Study of Earned Income Tax Credit Recipients and a Proposal for Repair." *New York University Law Review* 88 (2): 515–88.

Sternberg Greene, Sara, Melody Boyd, and Kathryn Edin. 2010. "In and Out of Financial Crisis: The Role of Kin Networks." Paper presented at the Eastern Sociological Society, Boston.

Sugrue, Thomas J. 2009. "The New American Dream: Renting." *Wall Street Journal,* August 14.

Sullivan, Brian. 2013. "HUD Reports Continued Increase in 'Worst Case Needs' in 2011." US Department of Housing and Urban Development Press Release 13–028, February 22.

Sumner, William H. 1858. *A History of East Boston; With Bibliographical Sketches of Its Early Proprietors.* Boston: J. E. Tilton.

Swartz, Teresa Toguchi. 2009. "Intergenerational Family Relations in Adulthood: Patterns, Variations, and Implications in the Contemporary United States." *Annual Review of Sociology* 35:191–212.

Sykes, Jennifer. 2011. "Paychecks and Parenting: Taxes, Symbolic Spending, and Child Expenditures among Low-Income Working Parents." PhD diss., Harvard University.

Sykes, Jennifer, Kathryn Edin, Katrin Kriz, and Sarah Halpern-Meekin. Forthcoming. "Dignity and Dreams: What the Earned Income Tax Credit Means to Low-Income Working Families." *American Sociological Review.*

Tach, Laura, and Sarah Halpern-Meekin. 2014. "The Earned Income Tax Credit: Tax Refund Expectations and Behavioral Responses." *Journal of Policy Analysis and Management* 33 (2): 413–39.

Tach, Laura, and Sara Sternberg Greene. 2014. "'Robbing Peter to Pay Paul': Economic and Cultural Explanations for How Lower-Income Families Manage Debt." *Social Problems* 61 (1): 1–21.

Tax Policy Center. 2014. "Earned Income Tax Credit Parameters, 1975–2014." Accessed January 29. www.taxpolicycenter.org/taxfacts/Content/PDF/historical_eitc_parameters.pdf.

Taylor, Paul, Kim Parker, Rakesh Kochhar, Wendy Wang, Gabriel Velasco, and Daniel Dockterman. 2011. *Five Years after the Bubble Burst: Home Sweet Home. Still.* Washington, DC: Social and Demographic Trends, Pew Research Center.

Teitler, Julien O., Nancy E. Reichman, Lenna Nepomnyaschy, and Irwin Garfinkel. 2006. "Effects of Welfare Participation on Marriage." Center for Research on Child Wellbeing, Working Paper 2005–24. http://crcw.princeton.edu/workingpapers/WP05–24–FF.pdf.

Thaler, Richard H. 1980. "Toward a Positive Theory of Consumer Choice." *Journal of Economic Behavior and Organization* 1 (1): 39–60.

Thaler, Richard H., and Eric J. Johnson. 1990. "Gambling with the House Money and Trying to Break Even: The Effects of Prior Outcomes on Risky Choice." *Management Science* 36 (6): 643–60.

Thorne, Deborah, and Leon Anderson. 2006. "Managing the Stigma of Personal Bankruptcy." *Sociological Focus* 39 (2): 77–97.

Toner, Robin. 1995. "Senators Gain on Welfare Bill but Delay Vote." *New York Times*, September 15.

———. 2002. "Sort of Deserving: Helping the Poor in the Post-welfare Era." *New York Times*, March 3.

Traub, Amy. 2013. *Discredited: How Employer Credit Checks Keep Qualified Workers Out of a Job.* New York: Demos.

US Bureau of Labor Statistics. 2007. "Unemployment Rates for Metropolitan Areas, 2007." US Department of Labor. www.bls.gov/lau/lamtrk07.htm.

———. 2010. "Unemployment Rates for Metropolitan Areas, 2010." US Department of Labor. www.bls.gov/lau/lamtrk10.htm.

US Census Bureau. 2011. "The Research Supplemental Poverty Measure: 2010." Brookings/Census Bureau Meeting on Improved Poverty Measurement. Last modified November 7. www.census.gov/newsroom/releases/pdf/2011–11–07_spm1_slides.pdf.

US Department of Education. 2011. "Community College Student Outcomes: 1994–2009." Web Tables, NCES 2012–253. Institute of Education Sciences, National Center for Education Statistics, US Department of Education.

US Department of Health and Human Services. 2010. "The 2004 HHS Poverty Guidelines: One Version of the (U.S.) Federal Poverty Measure." Last modified January 29. http://aspe.hhs.gov/poverty/04poverty.shtml.

US Department of Housing and Urban Development. 2009. "Final FY 2009 Fair Market Rent Documentation System." Last modified April 13. www

.huduser.org/datasets/fmr/fmrs/fy2009_code/2009summary.odn?inputnam
e=METRO14460MM1120*Boston-Cambridge-Quincy,%20MA-NH%20
HUD%20Metro%20FMR%20Area&data=2009&fmrtype=Final.

———. 2013a. "Housing Choice Vouchers Fact Sheet." Accessed February 2.
http://portal.hud.gov/hudportal/HUD?src=/topics/housing_choice_voucher_
program_section_8.

———. 2013b. "HUD'S Public Housing Program." Accessed February 2. http://
portal.hud.gov/hudportal/HUD?src=/topics/rental_assistance/phprog.

———. 2014. "FY 2013 Fair Market Rent Documentation System." Accessed
January 7. www.huduser.org/portal/datasets/fmr/fmrs/FY2013_
code/2013summary.odn?INPUTNAME=METRO14460MM1120*Bos
ton-Cambridge-Quincy,+MA-NH+HUD+Metro+FMR+Area&data=2013&ye
ar=2013&fmrtype=%24fmrtype%24&incpath=C:%5CHUDUSER%5Cwww
Main%5Cdatasets%5Cfmr%5Cfmrs%5CFY2013_Code&selection_type=hmf
a&path=C:%5Chuduser%5Cwwwdata%5Cdatabase.

US Department of Treasury. 2009. *The Risk of Losing Health Insurance over a
Decade: New Findings from Longitudinal Data.* Washington, DC: US
Department of Treasury.

US Patent and Trademark Office. 2007. "Trademark Status and Document
Retrieval." Department of Commerce. Last modified April 15, 2008. http://
tarr.uspto.gov/servlet/tarr?regser=serial&entry=78974176.

———. 2008. "Trademark Status and Document Retrieval." Department of
Commerce. Last modified February 8, 2010. http://tarr.uspto.gov/servlet/tar
r?regser=serial&entry=77468486.

Verba, Sidney, Kay Lehman Schlozman, and Henry Brady. 1995. *Voice and
Equality: Civic Voluntarism in American Democracy.* Cambridge, MA:
Harvard University Press.

Warren, Elizabeth. 2003. "Financial Collapse and Class Status: Who Goes
Bankrupt?" *Osgoode Hall Law Journal* 41 (1): 115–46.

Warren, Elizabeth, and Amelia Warren Tyagi. 2003. *The Two-Income Trap: Why
Middle-Class Mothers and Fathers Are Going Broke.* New York: Basic Books.

Welfare Recipient: "I Get to Sit Home . . . I Get to Smoke Weed . . ." 2013. Video
clip. Uploaded by *Daily Sheeple.* Last modified November 20. www.youtube.
com/watch?v=a_r_v9cYBPY.+++

Welsh, Kristy. 2011. "Is Unpaid Credit Card Debt Still Valid after Seven Years?"
Credit InfoCenter, April 22. www.creditinfocenter.com/wordpress/2011
/04/22/is-unpaid-credit-card-debt-still-valid-after-seven-years/.

Wetzstein, Cheryl. 1995. "Virginia in Top 3 for Welfare Reform; Massachusetts,
Wisconsin Also Leaders." *Washington Times,* March 13.

Wheaton, Laura, and Elaine Sorensen. 2009. *Extending the EITC to Noncustodial Parents: Potential Impacts and Design Considerations.* Washington,
DC: Urban Institute.

White House. 2011. *The White House Summit on Community Colleges: Summit Report.* Washington, DC: White House. www.whitehouse.gov/sites/default/files/uploads/community_college_summit_report.pdf.

White, Michelle J. 1998. "Why Don't More Households File for Bankruptcy?" *Journal of Law, Economics, and Organization* 14 (2): 205–31.

Wiley, Chip. n.d. "Tax Season Is Here." *Dealer Marketing Magazine.* Accessed April 3, 2014. www.dealermarketing.com/bizdev/f-and-i-solutions/1823-tax-season-is-here.

Wilson, Jeff A., Tom Beers, Amy Ibbotson, Mike Nestor, Mark Hutchens, Carol Hatch, and Mark Everett. 2007. "Impact of Taxpayer Representation on the Outcome of Earned Income Credit Audits." In *The IRS Research Bulletin: Proceedings of the 2007 IRS Research Conference,* Publication 1500, 91–114. Washington, DC: Internal Revenue Service.

Wilson, William Julius. 1987. *The Truly Disadvantaged: The Inner City, the Underclass, and Public Policy.* Chicago: University of Chicago Press.

———. 1996. *When Work Disappears: The World of the New Urban Poor.* New York: Alfred A. Knopf.

Winship, Scott. 2011. "Economic Instability Trends and Levels across Household Surveys." National Poverty Center Working Paper 11–13. www.npc.umich.edu/publications/working_papers/?publication_id=209&.

Yen, Hope. 2011. "New Formula Finds More Americans in Poverty." *Boston Globe,* January 6.

Zelizer, Viviana A. 1979. *Morals and Markets: The Development of Life Insurance in the United States.* New Brunswick, NJ: Transaction Publishers.

———. 1989. "The Social Meaning of Money: 'Special Monies.'" *American Journal of Sociology* 95 (2): 342–77.

———. (1994) 1997. *The Social Meaning of Money: Pin Money, Paychecks, Poor Relief, and Other Currencies.* Princeton, NJ: Princeton University Press.

———. 1996. "Payments and Social Ties." *Sociological Forum* 11 (3): 481–95.

———. 2004. *The Purchase of Intimacy.* Princeton, NJ: Princeton University Press.

Ziliak, James P., Bradley Hardy, and Christopher Bollinger. 2011. "Earnings Volatility in America: Evidence from Matched CPS." *Labour Economics* 18 (6): 742–54.

Zukin, Sharon. 2004. *Point of Purchase: How Shopping Changed American Culture.* New York: Routledge.

Index

ABCD. *See* Action for Boston Community Development

Abraham, Spencer, 117

Action for Boston Community Development (ABCD), 82, 217

ADC. *See* Aid to Dependent Children

Advance Holiday Loan, 80. *See also* H&R Block

AFDC. *See* Aid to Families with Dependent Children

Affordable Care Act, 158, 208, 237n33

Aid to Dependent Children (ADC), 189

Aid to Families with Dependent Children (AFDC), 6, 38, 101, 108–10, 112, 153, 193, 203, 206, 228, 238n6, 245nn7,9, 246n25

American dream, 13, 34, 42, 69, 132, 134, 180, 196–97, 215

American Opportunity Credit, 214, 259n101

American Recovery and Reinvestment Act (ARRA), 84, 259n101

American welfare state, 8, 22, 194. *See also* welfare

APAC. *See* East Boston Area Planning Action Council

ARRA. *See* American Recovery and Reinvestment Act

asset building, 19, 95–96, 149, 150–51, 200, 211, 213, 249n12

Bane, Mary Jo, 101, 117, 123

Boston Housing Authority, 27, 37, 42, 81, 128, 154, 160, 172

British Poor Laws, 8, 112

Brookings Institution, 109

Bureau of Labor Statistics, 32, 40, 183. *See also* Consumer Expenditure Survey

Carter, Jimmy, 8

Census Bureau, 24, 238n1, 239n24

Center for Budget and Policy Priorities, 111, 199

checking account, 130–31, 138–39, 143, 146–48, 152, 155, 165, 230. *See also* informal savings; retirement savings; savings account

child care: centers, 33, 82; expenses, 9, 24, 28, 33, 41, 44–45, 53, 57, 159, 172; subsidies, 123; vouchers, 120, 153, 155, 159, 189–90. *See also* Head Start

Children's Health Insurance Program (CHIP), 122, 190, 237n33

child support: enforced, 112, 250n9; as financial relief, 34–36, 66, 71, 206; in government and state programs, 103, 108; in household budgets, 54, 60, 86, 95, 146, 155, 163–64, 172, 187, 190, 208; and taxes, 72, 75, 91, 243n25

child tax credit (CTC), 36, 62, 74, 90, 108, 126, 189, 207, 257n81. *See also* earned income tax credit (EITC)
CHIP. *See* Children's Health Insurance Program
Clinton, Bill, 3, 5, 8, 10, 26, 102–4, 109, 117, 123, 194, 207
commitment mechanism, 71, 211
Consumer Expenditure Survey, 40, 240n37. *See also* Bureau of Labor Statistics
Creedon, Michael C., 117
CTC. *See* child tax credit
current consumption, 63–64, 75, 96, 174–75, 193, 197, 201, 242n11
Current Population Survey, 195

debt, 21; banking charges and, 165–66; bankruptcy and, 179–80, 250n5; counseling and assistance, 179–80; credit and, 18, 29, 30, 148, 152, 158–64, 209, 251n11; cycle of, 19; and depression, 251n16; deferred EITC and, 212; to IRS, 72; educational, 167–69, 251n15; juggling, 156, 173–74; medical, 166–67, 250n5; paying off, 41, 46, 64, 171–73, 174–78; paying off with tax refund, 18, 19, 63, 66, 92–94, 96, 178, 193, 197; personal loans, 169–70; reasons for, 170–71; types of, 159; unexpected, 28, 95; and upward mobility, 96, 126, 180–81

earned income tax credit (EITC), 2, 4–7, 19–22, 55; Advance EITC vs. deferred, 209–13; benefits, 95, 98–99, 130, 190, 200–204, 239n31, 258n95; in case studies, 11, 13, 15, 19, 24–25, 34, 36, 186, 220–21, 236n24, 237n30, 256n79; disincentives, 84, 86, 235n8; and health, 255n57; household uses of, 43, 57, 178, 184, 255n57; perceptions of, 73–76, 114, 122–25, 127, 181, 192, 197; in policy and welfare reform, 100, 102–5, 189, 207–8, 245n7; and taxes, 60, 62–71, 73–76, 78, 198, 241n6, 242n8, 243n21, 254n56, 257n91, 258n92; wages, 48, 195, 244n33, 245nn4,6. *See also* child tax credit (CTC); forced saving; tax credit
Earned Income Tax Credit Coalition, 82
East Boston Area Planning Action Council (APAC), 217–21
EBT. *See* Electronic Benefit Transfer
Edin, Kathryn, and Laura Lein, 8–10, 21, 44, 67, 120, 122, 126, 202–3

EITC. *See* earned income tax credit
Electronic Benefit Transfer (EBT), 122
Ellwood, David, 5, 10, 16, 100–104, 107, 112, 117, 123, 245n4
Emerald Card, 77, 80, 210. *See also* H&R Block
European Union, 23

Family Assistance Plan, 4. *See also* Nixon, Richard
Family Support Act, 108
food stamps, 6, 25, 37, 49–50, 101, 110, 115, 121, 228. *See also* safety net; welfare
forced saving, 15, 70–71, 149, 211–12, 243n20, 255n62. *See also* earned income tax credit (EITC)
Ford, Gerald, 8
future-oriented behavior, 17, 203

Gallup, 24
Gilens, Martin, 113
government handout, 9, 15, 19, 51, 66–67, 73, 100, 103, 115, 118, 192, 204
Great Recession, 22, 33, 109–11, 113, 133, 182–83, 185, 187–88, 194–96, 199–200, 206, 252n6, 259n259

H&R Block: advertising, 77–79, 253n25; in case studies, 29, 60, 73, 251n15; offices in Boston neighborhoods, 10, 20, 76–77, 219–20, 259n2; and Refund Anticipation Loan, 79–82; and tax-filing services, 2, 5, 17, 74, 193. *See also* Advance Holiday Loan; Emerald Card; Refund Anticipation Checks
Head Start, 11–12, 26–28, 32, 82, 87, 92, 123–24, 168, 184, 205, 221, 245n7. *See also* child care
Health and Human Services, 103–5
Heritage Foundation, 23, 117
housing choice voucher (Section 8), 27, 37, 122, 127–28, 238nn11,16, 252n20. *See also* public housing

IDA. *See* Individual Development Account
immigrants, 2–3, 13, 33, 79, 166, 177, 218–19, 222, 259n8
Individual Development Account (IDA), 98, 150, 211–12
informal savings, 131, 139–40, 143, 231. *See also* checking account; retirement savings; savings account
Internal Revenue Service (IRS): administration of EITC, 62, 125, 204, 210, 241n1,

243n24, 244n38; and intermediaries, 78–79, 83, 243n25; and tax filing process, 34, 69, 90–92, 193; and tax refunds, 72, 74–75, 81, 86, 128–29, 191

Johnson, Lyndon, 8

Kennedy, John F., 8
kinship support, 36

Lein, Laura, 9–10, 21, 44, 67, 120, 122, 126, 202–3
Lifetime Learning Credit, 214
Long, Russell, 4
lower-income families, 11, 15–16, 31–34; and kinship support, 51, 91, 243n20; spending patterns and credit, 40–42, 56, 130–131, 148–49, 157, 180, 209; and taxes, 77–82, 192, 247n33; views of welfare, 120, 123–4
Low Income Heating Assistance Program, 82, 133–34

Marshall, T. H., 8, 112, 205
Massachusetts Asset Development Commission, 130, 248n6
MassHealth, 13, 37–38, 44, 115, 122, 158, 166–67, 184, 186, 237n33. *See also* Medicaid
Medicaid, 6, 17, 21, 25, 101, 158, 166, 187, 190, 208. *See also* MassHealth; safety net; welfare
mental accounting, 31, 176, 197
mortgage, 41–42, 125, 132–35, 137, 144, 150, 159, 175, 193, 196, 209, 248n6, 251n12
Mullainathan, Sendhil, 20, 201–2, 256n64
Murray, Charles, 88, 100

National Bureau of Economic Research, 110
National Center for Children in Poverty, 24
National Welfare Rights Organization (NWRO), 191
1935 Social Security Act, 189
1996 welfare reform, 7–9, 25, 100, 103–5, 108–10, 113, 115, 117, 120, 122–23, 182, 188, 190, 192, 198–99, 236n15, 245n6. *See also* welfare
Nixon, Richard, 4, 8, 102. *See also* Family Assistance Plan
NWRO. *See* National Welfare Rights Organization

Obama, Barack, 3, 207, 246n23, 251n12
Office of Family Assistance, 109
Overseers of the Public Welfare, 10, 112

Personal Responsibility and Work Opportunity Reconciliation Act (PRWORA), 105, 110, 246n25
Poor Laws. *See* British Poor Laws
poverty line, 23, 37–38, 40, 50, 57, 188, 198–200, 214, 238n8; and EITC, 11, 62, 207, 245n4; and income, 14, 239n26, 256–57n79
poverty threshold. *See* poverty line
prowork policy, 4, 67, 102, 235n8
PRWORA. *See* Personal Responsibility and Work Opportunity Reconciliation Act
public housing, 37, 78, 81, 148, 160, 174, 239n31. *See also* housing choice voucher

RAL. *See* Refund Anticipation Loan
Reagan, Ronald, 4, 8, 108
Rector, Robert, 23, 117
Reed, Bruce, 103, 105
Refund Anticipation Checks, 81, 243n22. *See also* H&R Block
Refund Anticipation Loan (RAL), 74, 79–80, 98
Republicans: tax credits and, 5; welfare and, 246n23
retirement savings, 18, 130–31, 140–41, 143, 165. *See also* checking account; informal savings; savings account
Romney, Mitt, 189
Roosevelt, Franklin Delano, 3
Roosevelt, Theodore, 3
Ryan, Paul, 3

safety net: exclusion from, 21–22, 94, 171, 196, 198–99; government programs as, 36–37, 39, 55, 111, 184; personal credit card as, 28–29, 208–9; personal savings as, 46, 144, 211; work-based vs. need-based, 6–7, 10–11, 17, 26, 105–8, 152, 187–88, 190, 205–6, 214–15. *See also* food stamps; Medicare; welfare
savings account: balances, 138–39, 249n11; in case studies, 18, 87, 95–96, 134, 185, 187; goals and strategies, 129–31, 143, 145, 147–51, 193, 212; and tax refunds, 98, 149. *See also* checking account; informal savings; retirement savings
SCHIP. *See* State Child Health Insurance Program
Second Bill of Rights, 3
Section 8. *See* housing choice voucher
Shafir, Eldar, 20, 201–2, 256n64

single mother(s): in case studies, 42, 49, 53, 68, 76, 78, 90, 105, 116, 120–21, 134, 136, 138, 142, 145–46, 149–50, 159, 162–63, 186; and EITC, 6, 13, 62, 88–90, 178, 244n33, 258n95; as welfare recipients, 9–10, 44, 104–5, 189, 191

SNAP. *See* Supplemental Nutrition Assistance Program

social security, 2, 4–5, 38, 124–25, 131, 160, 189, 192, 211; disability insurance, 38, 125, 160; number, 2, 5

Special Supplemental Nutrition Program for Women, Infants, and Children (WIC), 37–39, 111, 122–24, 205, 245n7, 246–47n26

Stack, Carol, 51

State Child Health Insurance Program (SCHIP), 166

Supplemental Nutrition Assistance Program (SNAP): in case studies, 42–43, 48–49, 55, 68, 121–22, 129, 155, 160, 184–87; vs. EITC, 17, 22, 62, 66, 239n28, 243n21; eligibility, 37, 86, 190, 205, 240n45; and other government programs, 6, 25, 35–39, 110–11, 124, 171, 245–46n26; restrictions on use, 15; scarcity under, 20–21, 42–43, 48–49, 203

Supplemental Security Income (SSI), 35–36, 38–39, 43, 95, 125, 228

Supreme Court, 152, 157

TAFDC. *See* Transitional Aid to Families with Dependent Children

TANF. *See* Temporary Assistance for Needy Families

tax credit: average sum, 36; disbursement of, 64, 130, 193; factors affecting, 62, 67, 74, 87–88, 204, 247n1; perceptions of, 65–66, 204; refundable, 4, 62, 72, 108, 114, 195, 204, 209, 211, 213–14, 217, 219; use of, 164, 198; vs. welfare, 192, 199. *See also* child tax credit (CTC); earned income tax credit (EITC)

tax refund: anticipation of, 18, 28, 55–56, 94, 197, 214, 254n47, 255n57; calculating and garnishing, 48, 62, 72, 75, 85, 88, 243n21, 251n15; in case studies, 50, 69, 128–29, 199; and EITC, 17; and financial goals, 149–51, 191, 196, 204; and H&R Block,

79–80; spending, 15–16, 20, 30, 43, 61, 70, 92–93, 105–6, 126, 133, 135, 140, 142, 145–46, 168, 170, 178, 184–85, 187, 193, 197–98, 201–3, 222–23

Temporary Assistance for Needy Families (TANF), 6, 35, 187, 189, 252n1; benefits of, 25–26, 238n8; in case studies, 107–12; vs. EITC, 22, 62, 66, 192, 215; negative views of, 108–12, 171, 203, 206. *See also* Transitional Aid to Families with Dependent Children (TAFDC)

Third World poverty, 21, 199

Transitional Aid to Families with Dependent Children (TAFDC), 108, 117, 250n9. *See also* Temporary Assistance for Needy Families (TANF)

TurboTax, 75

unemployment insurance, 22, 28, 35–36, 38–39, 57, 87, 124, 134, 211, 240n44

unionization, 4

VITA. *See* Volunteer Income Tax Assistance

Volunteer Income Tax Assistance (VITA), 82–83

W-2 forms, 2, 5, 73

welfare: benefits, 50, 88, 108, 114, 122, 190, 193, 246n24; check, 9, 21, 67, 162, 204; office, 8, 10, 76, 83, 112, 119, 192–93, 205; program, 6, 17, 66, 88, 112, 189, 204; reform, 6, 103–4, 108–9, 246n24; rolls, 6–7, 9, 26, 104, 106, 108, 110–11, 119, 125, 182, 190–91, 235n10, 252n6; state, 17; system, 7–8, 10, 17, 21, 25, 55, 100, 105, 107–8, 116–17, 119, 171, 191, 206, 214, 236n20. *See also* American welfare state; food stamps; Medicare; 1996 Welfare Reform; safety net

WIC. *See* Special Supplemental Nutrition Program for Women, Infants, and Children

work-based safety net. *See* safety net

workers: semiskilled, 94, 182, 252n1; skilled, 214–15; unskilled, 4, 94, 182, 208, 252n1

Working Tax Credit (U.K.), 258n92

World Bank, 21

Zelizer, Viviana, 65, 191–92, 249n15